in wonder with
OSHO

BODHISATTVA
SWAMI ANAND ARUN

With gratitude to the Osho Tapoban Book Seller group
who graciously contributed for the publication of this book.

Copyright © 2017 by Swami Anand Arun

First edition : June 2017

Published by:
Osho Tapoban Publication
Nagarjuna Hills, Kathmandu, Nepal
sales.tapoban@gmail.com, www.tapoban.com
+977 01 5112012/13 +977 9851124801

Editing by
Ma Dyan Sampada

Assistance to the Bodhisattva:
Swami Anand Suvam,
Ma Bodhi Mudita, Swami Aatmo Neerav

Design & artwork by Swami Dhyan Yatri

Cover design by Swami Aatmo Neerav

Photography: Ma Bodhi Chhaya, Swami Anand Arhat

Artwork © Swami Dhyan Yatri

ISBN: 978-9937-686-39-6

PRICE: ₹ 390.00 / Nrs 590.00

ओशो की सजल स्मृतियों को समर्पित

TO THOSE BEAUTIFUL MEMORIES OF HIS
THAT STILL BRING TEARS IN THESE EYES...

FOREWORD

The book you hold in your hands is a love story, a love story that has a beginning but no end.

This story begins in the spring of 1969 when I first met Osho, the beloved of my heart. It covers the days I spent with him between March 1969 and May 1981. Its upcoming sequel will cover the days between June 1981 and today.

For the last twenty seven years I was pregnant with the idea of this book but since it was not taking shape I was in an almost three decade long labour pain. Today when you hold this book in your hands, it gives me immense joy inexpressible in words. I would like to thank Swami Dhyan Yatri, Ma Bodhi Mudita, Swami Anand Suvam, Swami Atmo Neerav, Swami Anand Arhat, Swami Anand Saurav and Ma Dhyan Sampada for their dedicated effort at manifesting this book.

From my very childhood a kind of restlessness and search plagued my soul. It was the same search that took me to different gurus and ashrams. But only when I met Osho, I felt assured that there is a goal to this quest. Osho personified everything I was searching for. Only when I met him did my restless soul find its calm. Most likely I won't have to take a human form again and drift in this mirage-like world.

There is no doubt that he *punya* of my past lives led me to Osho, but my fear and unawareness kept me anchored to misery, which I had mistaken to be my destiny and my home. Back then it was hard to believe that such unbound joy awaited to unfold in my life. Krishnamurti couldn't have been more right when he says the fear of freedom itself prevents us from taking the jump into it. In October 1974 I finally mustered enough courage to take the jump and took *sannyas*. This jump proved to be an opening into the portal of boundless sky of freedom not only for me, but for thousands of seekers, who are walking along with me today.

Meeting a real enlightened master is the most fortunate moment in the life of a seeker. But even after meeting a master, we continue to cling to our miserable past. Our investment in our miseries is so huge that we don't want to let go of them. Only a few daredevils can become disciples and risk to efface ego and ignorance, which are at the source of all our misery and suffering. Liberation is not difficult; it is our very nature. The real difficulty is to find enough courage to walk out of the hell we have created for ourselves and the people around us. And this courage can only flower in the presence of an enlightened master.

Nanak had a penetrating insight and he said,

"Nanak dukhiya sab sansaar"

(Except for a few godward souls, Nanak sees that the whole world is suffering without an exception.)

Kabir said,

"Raja Dukhi, Praja Dukhi,
Jogi ka Dukh Duna.
Kahat Kabir Suno bhai Sadho,
ekau Ghar na Suna.

("The king is suffering,
The subjects are suffering,
The yogi is suffering twice as much,
Says Kabir, listen o seeker,
Not a single house is spared as such.")

The first realization of Buddha was,

"This life is suffering."

All those who are born in this part of the world have heard these types of couplets since childhood but hearing is not enough. Despite hearing it countless times, we still fail to grasp the true meaning of such visionary verses. By Osho's grace, today I am not only seeing this truth but also living it and understanding it. Just as Osho has said repeatedly, right vision is enough to transform.

When we see things as they are, in their real nature, one doesn't need to do anything else. Seeing the truth is becoming the truth.

This universe is infinite. Billions of suns are being orbited by billions of planets and yet in this vast expanse of existence we are yet to come across a planet where life has manifested in as eclectic and as lively forms; Where there are forests, rivers, lakes and mountains; Where there is poetry, love, music and meditation. Up to now, in spite of great search, the scientists haven't found another planet where life has reached to such a crescendo. However we are also in that period of time when our prejudices, blind nationalism and fanaticism are also at their peaks. If not checked in time, our madness can turn this planet into a lifeless desert.

This earth is endlessly beautiful, but human stupidity is as endless. We are on the brink of a global suicide. Unless the human psyche goes through an extensive revolution and there is a great shift in the human consciousness, we cannot prevent the destruction that we are heading towards, that too at an alarming speed. Osho is the harbinger of this revolution, the revolution of giving birth to the new human consciousness. The more people read and listen to Osho, the more readily they can divert from this death centric approach towards a life of greater creativity, celebration, love and gratitude and this book is just one such flower of gratitude.

I am grateful to my master for giving me this realization that 'this very body is the Buddha and this very Earth, the lotus paradise'. We do not have to seek for a paradise after death but to create one here by our own understanding, creativity and awareness. Dedicated disciples of Osho have created few such oases in this dying world. I bow down to my master for making me an instrument in creating such oases around the world. Our

Himalayan paradise, Osho Tapoban, is one such oasis where I spend the majority of my time. I invite all sincere seekers to come and experience this buddhafield for themselves.

What you hold in your hands is a love story for which I have risked my all. It is a poem of my life long affair with my beloved. It is the memoir of my romance with the man who not only dreamt but materialized paradise on earth. If these stories sound otherworldly to you, they *are* otherworldly!

Bodhisattva Swami Anand Arun
26 June, 2017
Osho Tapoban

CONTENTS

CONTENTS

CONTENTS

CONTENTS

PART I

The beginning of an endless continuum

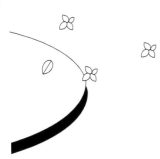

The Prophet, the Poet and the Prophecy

Osho, also known as Acharya Shree Rajneesh and Bhagwan Shree Rajneesh in different periods of hislife, is too beautiful to be expressed in words. And yet when I write about him, I do so because the lives of such people give hope and assurance to us that divinity, after all, is not just wishful thinking, but very much a reality we can all realize. It was miraculous that such a fragile flower had bloomed among us.

In 1969, Haribansha Rai Bachchan, the noted Indian romantic poet and the recipient of the Padma Bhushan award and also the father of famous Indian Actor Amitabh Bachchan, was attending one of the literary congregations at Delhi where Acharya Rajneesh had also been invited to speak.

Earlier the same year, Bachchan had met Osho and had

been mesmerized by the totality and immensity of his personality. As he reminisces in his autobiography *In the Afternoon of Life,* "I saw him to be a well-built man in his late thirties. His eyes were wide and piercing. His appearance gave the sense of a highly individual personality, and I found that he talked openly and with a transparent, mirror-like clarity."

Bachchan, who was already a literary star in India, listened to Osho's rebellious and fiery words in awe. As the discourse continued, the poet was absolutely enflamed by the fire that was Osho. When it was Bachchan's turn to speak, he moved close to Osho, held his hand passionately, and declared over the microphone, "Rajneesh, I am not a mystic like you. I am just a poet. I cannot make prophecies about the future. But I can tell this much, you are too beautiful to be true. In fact, you are so beautiful that this world will not tolerate you. I am afraid you will be killed."

Strangely enough, the poet had made a prophetic declaration.

Osho replied immediately, "I don't wish to die on a hospital bed, either. I know the price of speaking the truth in this hypocritical society. If I am murdered, my death will only prove this.

If Socrates, Jesus and Gandhi were not murdered, their message would not have reached so many people. I am making use of my lifetime, and if necessary, I will also make use of death."

The Beginning of a Love Affair

The fateful evening of the 29th of March 1969 stands out vividly in my memory. That evening I had the *darshan* of my guru, Acharya Rajneesh, for the first time. The cool breeze rolled in waves from the banks of the Ganga. The air was spiced with the fragrance of flowers and fruits. Just when I thought the evening couldn't get any more beautiful, there walked in Acharya Rajneesh, serene and otherworldly, in a white *lungi* and white shawl. My heart skipped a beat. I had never seen a mortal so beautiful, so sublime, so god-like.

Back then, I was doing my engineering course at Patna University. In my spare time, I frequented Sinha Library (in the city) which had a collection of rare books on spirituality. Engineering didn't intrigue me at all. If the truth be told, I was doing the course basically because of my parents' insistence. My real interest lay in spirituality. On the slightest pretext, I would abandon my classes and visit different religious gurus and their ashrams.

One afternoon, after spending a rather fruitful time in Sinha Library, I was walking out of the hall when I noticed a poster for yet another religious talk in town. The poster announced that someone named Acharya Rajneesh was giving a discourse in the library garden that very evening. That was the first time I had heard the name Acharya Rajneesh.

My fascination with meditation and gurus had survived the test of time. Since childhood, I exhibited a great deal of interest in meditation, yoga and naturopathy, which often troubled my parents. They tried their best to discourage me from pursuing spirituality, chastising me every now and then for what they thought was a deplorable hobby for a young student. But I stood determined and continued my pursuit.

By then I had travelled to most of the ashrams of North India and met most of the popular gurus of that time. Among them were Anandmurti, Maharshi Mahesh Yogi, Anukul Chand Thakur, Swami Shivananda of Rishikesh, Madhavrao Golwalker of the Rastrya Soyamsewak Sangh, and *sannyasins* of the Ramakrishna Ashram and a few other gurus who were not very popular. They all were special in their own ways and I did learn something from each of these gurus, but I was not completely satisfied by them and I was still waiting for my own guru.

The Sarvodaya Movement, based on the philosophy of Gandhi and Vinowa Bhave, had taken India by storm. Jayaprakash Narayanan had also recently left politics and joined the Sarvodaya Movement. I had met Jayaprakashin Musahari, Bihar, and found in him a deep quest for truth and a heart that was open to the woes of the masses. This greatly inspired me, also, to do something to uplift society.

I was in a state of great turmoil and confusion when I first met Acharya Rajneesh. I was searching for the balance between Krishna's devotion and celebration, Buddha's peace and meditation, Swami Vivekananda's fiery grace, and Gandhi's truth and non-violence. I felt betrayed by time. I used to think that had I been born in their time and become their disciple, I wouldn't have been as lost.

Naturally, when I saw the poster I decided to give it a try. I was so excited that I was one of the earliest to arrive at the garden, and took my seat in the first row. Right at six o'clock, Acharya Rajneesh walked in. He had a very graceful way with his body. His hands had the beauty and precision of a classical dancer... Now he folds his hands in namaste, now he holds the seam of his *lungi* gently and now he strokes his beard...I turned around in my seat and watched him walk towards me. His long black beard and hair danced to the rhythm of the evening breeze, his radiant face, blanched with the rays of the moon, emanated grace. I looked at him in disbelief. I couldn't believe a human body could be so beautiful. My heart was filled with the loftiest sentiments. He looked like a luminous being who had just descended from the land of the *rishis*.

Acharya Rajneesh sat down on the podium and closed his eyes. I was still struck by his beauty and couldn't take my eyes off him. A woman started singing a verse by Kabir in a very melodious voice. I learnt later that Acharya loved the songs of Kabir and Meera and in those days, their songs usually preceded his discourses. Her voice filled the campus with calm. The evening was still, except for the cool breeze off the Ganga. Beauty reigned everywhere.

"My beloved ones...." Acharya began his discourse.

My heart started to beat in violent spasms and tears rolled down my cheeks unchecked. A long-forgotten chamber of my heart had opened, some long-lost beloved was remembered. Acharya continued the discourse in his deep, hypnotic voice, and I kept sinking into the core of my being. My handkerchief was already drenched in tears, and yet the sea that my heart had become was in no hurry to calm down. My tears alarmed a friend of mine who had accompanied me to the discourse.

"What's happening to you? Why are you crying so much?" He kept asking me. If only I knew why.

Every single word Acharya uttered shook my being. He was strongly denouncing celibacy, Gandhism, and religious leaders. At that time, I was fascinated by all three and was trying to lead the very life Acharya was denouncing. His discourse went against my education and my conditioning. My rational mind was rejecting his ideas, but deep down the truth in his words had already won me over. Somebody from the audience asked, "Gandhi was a saint and he always travelled in the third-class compartment of trains, but why do you, a *sadhu,* only travel first class?"

Acharya answered, "Gandhi used to say that he travelled third class because there was no fourth class on Indian trains, but I say that I travel first class because there is no air-conditioned carriage on Indian trains yet. The day they put air-conditioned carriages on Indian trains, I will stop using first class. Unlike Gandhi, I do not consider poverty divine. For me poverty is a disease sprung out of stupidity and an unscientific outlook on life. Today, due to the proper use of science and technology, the whole of Europe and America are travelling in air-conditioned carriages, so what great sins have we committed that we Indians always have to travel in third class while all the trains in the world have become air-conditioned?"

Acharya's logic was unparalleled. Even those who did not like his philosophy were stupefied by his analytical ability. He was destroying my borrowed beliefs and conditioning with his sharp logic. My mind was resisting with all its might and yet my heart had already recognized that the master I had always prayed for was sitting in front of me; graceful like a *rishi*, adroit like a warrior.

Acharya ended his talk with these words, "I am grateful that you listened to me with such patience and love. There is no reason to believe what I have said. Doubt my words, think about them, meditate on them. Accept only that which feels right to you. In the end, I pay my respects to the divine residing within all of you. Please accept my *pranam*."

As soon as Acharya finished his discourse, a crowd surrounded him. People were frantically trying to hug him, touch his feet or wherever they could manage to touch. The crowd was impenetrable. I stood frozen in my place. Then slowly I walked towards the book stall instead. They were registering the names of annual subscribers for the Hindi magazine called *Yukrand,* which propagated Acharya's philosophy. The annual subscription cost twelve rupees and the half-yearly cost six rupees. I only had three rupees in my pocket, so I asked them if I could make a quarterly subscription. They didn't have provision for quarterly subscriptions, so I came up with an idea. But all the copies had already been sold out.

"Take three rupees and give me a yearly subscription. I will send you the remaining nine rupees in a money order," I said rather hesitantly.

9

The volunteer trusted me and handed me a bill that read, "Yearly subscription with nine rupees owing." With that he gave me the first issue of Yukrand as they had run out of the recent issue.

That was the most important and intelligent, and valuable investment of my life. It not only transformed my life, but also became a catalyst for the transformation of thousands of lives all around the world.

After some time, it was announced that Acharya would give a discourse on Mahavir at Rabindra Bhawan in a programme organized by the Jain community, and then he would return to Jabalpur on an express train that same night.

Mesmerized, I decided to follow Acharya to Rabindra Bhawan. Acharya left in an Ambassador car. I didn't have a single paisa left in my pocket, so I covered the distance of four kilometres by running after the car. Since Acharya's car was slowed down by the evening traffic, I reached Rabindra Bhawan just in time for his discourse, although rather exhausted.

In those days, Acharya's discourses used to be fiery, and he attacked all kinds of blind religious faiths and superstitions. During that particular discourse about Mahavir, he was saying how the Jains did not understand a word said by Mahavir and were only blind devotees. I could feel the tension brewing in the room, as all the organizers were Jains. Acharya's talk stunned the audience as much as it disturbed the organizers. Honestly speaking, I was worried if Acharya's words were going to provoke a furore among the Jains who sat dignified in the first few rows of the audience. Despite the thick smoke of tension that filled the hall, the organizers exhibited no outward agitation on their faces. Since Acharya was from a Jain family, the organizers had not expected such criticism from a saint who they thought was one of their own.

Acharya's talk ended. It was announced that he would go directly to the railway station from the hall. I had a great desire to go to the station, but I had neither money nor remaining strength to run the distance. Instead, I slowly walked the seven-kilometre distance to my hostel, submerged in indescribable bliss.

acharya rajneesh

kamala nehru nagar : jabalapur (m.p.). phone : 2957

प्रिय भगवान,

पत्र/ के जवाब में था/ नौकर के लिए छुटकारा नहीं मिलता है/
अक्टूबर २२, २४, २०, २१ इनका से वह व्याख्यान निश्चित है/
वहां आपको भी आकाश है/
बंगलीभागा में दूसरी किसी पार्टी आना लगती है/
रोल मिलाते पर/
सरकार व्याख्यान विस्तार की विस्तृत जानकारी मिलत चले पर के भिजा लगेगी.
श्री पुष्कर भरद्वाज,
जीवन जागृति केन्द्र,
जबलपुर,
हरदा (गुजरात)

■ *English translation of Osho's letter in Hindi from page no. 12*

Beloved Arun,

Love. I was travelling so I only just received your letter.
There is a meditation camp in Dwarika on October 28, 29, 30, 31.
It will be good if you can come there.
Meditation can become your path for transformation.
We shall talk more when we meet.
The information regarding the Dwarika camp can be found by writing on the following address:
Shree Pushkar Gokani,
Jeevan Jagriti Kendra,
Jawahar Road,
Dwarika (Gujrat)

Osho

The First
Experience of Satori

T he love affair between a disciple and a master
is the highest expression of love. A master is a
cool moon, where all the heat of passion has
purified and become a soothing, tranquil wave of compassion.
The Hindus call *sannyasins "dweej"*, the twice born. They say
that our biological birth is simply an opportunity to allow our
consciousness to flower. If one really wants to reach the lofty
peaks of consciousness, one must be reborn as a disciple or a
seeker. Therefore, a master is a womb. His love becomes our flesh
and bones, his love becomes the bridge to the unknown.

Therefore, when a disciple meets his master for the first
time, there is a great explosion of love. The fire that had erupted
in my heart after meeting Acharyashree for the first time was
still very bright when I went to attend my first meditation

camp with him in Dwaraka in October 1969. I had already been corresponding regularly with him. In one of his letters, he had invited me to join the camp there, and so it was that the love affair which began in Sinha Library in Patna was destined to blossom in Dwaraka, the eternal buddhafield of Lord Krishna. I was probably the only non-Gujarati participant in the camp.

For a retreat that was held in one of the most beautiful places on Earth, Acharyashree had chosen a rather strange topic – Death. The discourses from that camp have been compiled in *And Here and Now (Main Mrityu Sikhatahun)*. Through his words and silence, Acharyashree took us on an extraordinary pilgrimage - he made us aware of the silence of our own hearts to show there was no need to search for any temple outside. When one's mind is silent and one's heart open, one becomes the abode of the divine.

"The temples which have been created out of fear and greed are not the temples of God. The prayers which have been composed out of the fear of death are not prayers to God, either. Only one who is filled with the joy of life reaches the temple of God. God's kingdom is filled with joy and beauty, and the bells of God's temple ring only for those who are free from all kinds of fears, for those who have become fearless." - Osho

The eternal, blue waters of the Arabian Sea stretched as far as the eyes could see. All the noise of the world merged into the sea and formed a deep resounding silence. In this silence, Acharyashree revealed the deepest secrets of life and death.

"Birth and death are simply stations where vehicles are changed, -where the old vehicles are left behind, where tired horses are abandoned and fresh ones are acquired. But both these acts

take place in our state of unconsciousness. And one whose birth and death happens in this unconscious state cannot live a conscious life -he functions in an almost half-conscious state, in an almost half-awakened state of life.

What I wish to say is that it is essential to see death, to understand it, to recognize it. But this is possible only when we die; one can only see it while dying. Then what is the way now? And if one sees death only while dying, then there is no way to understand it -because at the time of death one will be unconscious.

Yes, there is a way now. We can go through an experiment of entering into death of our own free will. And may I say that meditation, or samadhi, *is nothing else but that. The experience of entering death voluntarily is meditation,* samadhi.*"- Osho*

Meditation cannot be explained with words or in formulae. It is a knack. If a disciple is receptive, like a hollow valley, the master can pour himself into this womb of receptivity. I had been reading about meditation for a long time. I had already visited so many masters, so many ashrams, and yet my quest remained unfulfilled. But for the first time in my life, Acharyashree not only addressed my quest, but also gave me the direct taste of meditation. We were not simply listening to a religious discourse. Acharyashree shared the taste of his silence with us. What would have taken a meditator years of disciplined pursuit was given to us in the span of a few days. Acharyashree gave discourses in the morning in a school ground, and on the silent Arabian Sea beaches at night. I loved his discourses, but what nourished me the most were the afternoon silent sitting sessions.

Acharyashree emphasized again and again that words were not a good medium for expression. Words could be interpreted according to the intelligence of the listener. That is why the teachings of the buddhas are interpreted in so many different ways. The truth can only be communicated through silence. The profound experiences of life are too enormous to be contained in words.

During these silent sitting sessions, Acharyashree thwarted the basic instinct of our minds to analyse everything with thoughts and words. Every afternoon between four and five o'clock, we all gathered for the session. Acharyashree used to arrive at four sharp. We had been instructed to shower and wear loose and comfortable, clean clothes.

He would sit down on a chair and go deeply into deep meditation. We would sit in a circle around him on the floor, and a strong current of energy would radiate from him and penetrate us. The quest, which began even before we learnt to speak and analyse, cannot be contained in words. I understood this profound truth as Acharyashree untangled the confusion in our minds without uttering a single word. His presence was like a magnetic field. As we sat silently with him, attuned to his rhythm, a certain harmony permeated us as well. Just as the real treasure of the ocean is hidden deeply within the womb of the waters where no superficial navigator can reach, so are the treasures of our beings also buried much deeper than words or thoughts can penetrate.

Acharyashree was transforming us from within. He spoke to us in the language that can only be understood by hearts. Meditation was easy and effortless in his presence. We had been instructed that if we felt he was calling us, we could go and touch his feet and sit with him for a short time before returning to our place. For seekers who had a deep longing for his energy, this was the best experience of their life. These sessions were so overwhelming that many people burst into tears or fell into a trance.

One the first evening of the camp, I went into a deep trance. When I woke up it was already late into the night. I was alone in the dark hall. Everything had turned cold and dim. I did not have any sense of time or space. I was immersed in silent bliss. I went back to my room, but I couldn't eat anything that night. When I went to sleep, I was still floating high on that mysterious energy. Much later I understood - it was an experience of *satori*, which filled me with deep contentment, bliss and a sense of centering.

The Fragrance
of Samadhi

I wanted to have a *darshan* with Acharyashree but I did not have enough courage to ask for a private meeting. On the last day of the camp, I casually asked one of the organizers if we could have a personal meeting with him. The person informed me that every day, between two and three in the afternoon, Acharyashree gave a personal *darshan* to the camp participants at his residence.

"But it is not possible anymore because he is leaving tomorrow after the morning discourse," he informed me.

I was shocked because I had come to Dwaraka camp specifically to meet Acharyashree and ask him questions that were troubling me on my spiritual journey. Nevertheless, I asked the address of the place where he was staying. It was at the Indian Navy Guest-house, which was a few kilometres away from the camp venue. I couldn't sleep well that night because I kept thinking of him and the questions I was going to ask. So the next morning, before sunrise, I started walking towards the guest-house. The air from the sea was crisp and salty. I walked along the empty streets, thinking only of Acharyashree. When I reached the main gate, I found that the guard was blissfully asleep. I slipped noiselessly into the compound. It was a nice bungalow with a well-maintained garden on the shore of the Arabian Sea. I did not know the exact room where Acharyashree was staying, but intuitively walked towards the large suite that overlooked the seemingly endless body of the Arabian Sea. I turned the knob; the room hadn't been locked from inside. I walked in silently. The room was empty, except for a bed, a reclining chair and a few of his belongings. I immediately realized it was his room. I could hear the sound of water running from a tap. Acharyashree was probably having a shower. As I was to learn later, he had a deep love affair with water. He often took long, leisurely showers.

The room was filled with a dense, sweet fragrance. I felt intoxicated. Since there was nobody around, I just sat down on the floor near the bathroom door, absolutely drunk on the aroma and mysterious energy. I came to realize that this fragrance was unique to Acharayashree. Some people who wanted to defame him spread the rumour that he used hypnotic perfumes. But he was allergic to odours, and never used any perfume at all. It was the fragrance of his *samadhi*. Just as ripened fruit has its own aroma, ripened consciousness also emits a fragrance.

His clothes, and all the places where he has lived still carry this fragrance. It is difficult to define it but it has the sublime aroma of sandalwood, camphor, eucalyptus and saffron fused together. Later on, *sannyasins* in Pune tried to create a perfume similar to his fragrance by mixing the ingredients mentioned above. It wasn't exactly the fragrance of his body, but it was very similar and had a sweet, beautiful aroma. They had rightly named it 'Ecstasy.' Ma Neelam had given me a small bottle of the perfume, which is one of the best gifts I have received in my life. It kept me enchanted for months.

Osho has said that when passion becomes compassion, the body becomes purified and sometimes emits a sweet fragrance. In fact, it is said that Gautam Buddha used to have a very strong perfume around him as well. That is why Buddha's room was called *Gandhakuti*, the house of fragrance.

I have also sensed a unique fragrance around Dalai Lama each time I have met him. Aurobindo's room in Pondicherry Ashram, Krishnamurti's room in Ojai, Swami Yogananda's room at Encinitas, and Shivapuri Baba's *samadhi* at Dhruvas*thali* Ashram, Kathmandu also have a mystical fragrance.

Dilip Kumar Roy, the guru of Indira Devi, has cited a similar phenomenon in his autobiography, *The Pilgrims of the Stars.* Every time Indira Devi went into a trance, she emitted a strong fragrance of sandalwood from her body, especially from her hands. When she touched any disciple while in that state, they would come back with the lingering aroma of her fragrance.

Just as when one moves deeply into meditation, and emits a certain fragrance, so too can meditation be induced by the use of fragrance. In many traditions, people have experimented using incense and other exotic fragrances. That is why camphor, sandalwood, *lobhans* and other fragrances were used in temples and mosques, and during *puja* and worships - just to create a similar milieu.

The East has spent thousands of years researching to

understand the science behind this phenomenon. Fragrance and light are food for the astral being. That is why in all religions there are rituals of burning candles and incense in addition to mantra chanting while invoking higher souls.

Mysteriously, a few years ago I had a divine inspiration to start the evening celebration of light, music and fragrance at Tapoban. It came about unexpectedly. There was a strong transcendental presence that inspired me to initiate this celebration, and now it has become one of the most powerful and popular meditations at Tapoban. People from all religious backgrounds, be they Christians, Jews, Muslims, Hindus, Buddhists or Sikhs, have reported that they experienced a strong and elevating energy during the celebration. After the celebration, we listen to an Osho discourse on the Bhagavad Gita, Upanishads or Vigyan Bhairav Tantra which deepens our ecstasy and transports us to *rishilokas*. Listening to Osho has always been a delight, but when we listen to him meditatively, after showering, during the group evening celebration, the words penetrate deeply into our hearts and leave a lasting impact. I have been listening to his lectures for the last forty-seven years on a daily basis, but listening to him after the evening celebration casts an unforgettable impression. Everybody in the ashram waits for the evening celebration and it has become the most popular session at Tapoban.

But for people who have been against me and the work I am doing around the world, this has become a new excuse to criticize me. They accuse me of having become traditional and ritualistic. But there are certain practices which have evolved over years of research, and through intuitive understanding of energy phenomenon. Some of these are: touching the feet of the master, the wearing of maroon robes such as those used by Mahayana

Buddhists for thousands of years, the growing of beards by yogis and *sannyasins*, vegetarianism, which is practiced in most of the Eastern religions, and initiation and use of the *mala*. Sufi dancing, Vipassana and Zazen are also well-known techniques. Above all, the relationship between the master and disciple has a long history as a most powerful device. Meditation itself is an ancient practice.

For meditators, these practices and techniques are not just milestones in the history of spirituality, but they are as significant devices today as they ever were.

It saddens me to see that despite Osho's clear instruction regarding the significance of his pictures, the *mala* and the master-disciple relationship (which he emphasized) as devices to connect with his energy, many *sannyasins* are against these devices simply in an attempt to prove themselves modern and non-traditional. Management at our main ashram in Pune has played the main role in spreading this misconception among people. And people follow it blindly without any understanding and without questioning. The managers have totally destroyed the sanctity of *sannyas* celebration, which is at the heart of the Osho movement. Ironically, some of the group leaders, who are against wearing the *mala*, continue to give the Osho *mala* during the initiation of new *sannyasins*. Shouldn't someone ask that if the *mala* has to be dropped, why give it in the first place?

The beauty of Osho's teaching is that he took the best practices from all religious traditions and made them palatable for the modern mind. He also criticized many traditions and those who practice them, but he spoke from a higher plane, and with a specific purpose.

It is good not to carry the unnecessary burden of the past,

and instead to become spontaneous and intuitive in the present. But at the same time, it is also not good to label things as bad simply because they are traditional. The key to spontaneity is to respond to each moment with an open and unprejudiced mind. Any prejudice, whether traditional or modern, steals openness, and confines us within the cocoon of a certain belief-system to which we adapt. Osho's work, on the other hand, is multi-dimensional. He has revived the techniques of Sufism, Hasidism, Hinduism, Buddhism, Tantra, Yoga, and the Gurdjieffian school of meditation, to name just a few, and incorporated the modern-day wisdom of psychotherapists like Reich, Janov, Jung, Adler and Fromm to give a wholisticholistic package to seekers from all backgrounds.

No technique in itself is good or bad. One should always take into consideration the person who is practising it. Analogous to this is the pine tree. It thrives in cold climate - you cannot plant a mango tree in the same climate and expect it to grow well. There are so many different techniques in the world. Certain sects of Hindu Brahmins consider it sacrilegious to consume alcohol. Christians, on the other hand, drink wine to celebrate Christ. These behavioural differences do not affect the final attainment of enlightenment. To criticize one religion and favour another, or to disregard one technique to exalt another, simply shows that one is still 'a fanatic' deep down. The problem is not as much about the techniques as it is with the fanatical state of mind.

At Tapoban, we are trying to create a space that celebrates diversity - people from all walks of life, and from as many religious traditions. Each individual is celebrated regardless of religious background or traditional belief. And all these different people have brought a unique flavour to Tapoban. We use Sufi techniques,

Buddhist techniques, therapies and techniques from different schools of Hinduism like Yoga, Tantra, and Bhakti, so that we create a powerful transformative space for everyone who visits the place.

I am trying to put all my effort into creating a space as Osho envisioned:

"The new commune is going to be of a totally new kind of religiousness, spirituality. Nobody is going to be a Hindu or a Mohammedan or a Christian or a Jaina, but everybody is going to be religious – just religious. To me, religion needs no adjectives.

And the moment a religion becomes attached to an adjective, it is no longer religion – it becomes politics. Bayazid is not Mohammedan. Mohammed himself is not Mohammedan, cannot be. Christ is not Christian and Buddha is not Buddhist. They are simply religious. They have a certain flavour, a certain silence, a certain grace, surrounding them. They are windows to the beyond. Through them you can see the beyond, through them God goes on singing a thousand and one songs.

The new commune is not going to be of any religion. It will be religious. But the religion will not be unearthly, it will be very down to earth; hence it will be creative, it will explore all possibilities of being creative. All kinds of creativity will be supported, nourished. The real religious man has to contribute to the world. He has to make it a little more beautiful than he found it when he came into the world. He has to make it a little more joyous. He has to make it a little more perfumed. He has to make it a little more harmonious. That is going to be his contribution."

The Revolution
Begins

Slowly the sun rose from the horizon, spilling a translucent orange blanket over the sea. Acharyashree opened the bathroom door and walked out. A fresh rush of the familiar fragrance flooded the room. He was wrapped in a plain white *lungi* and had a towel over his shoulder. I had been struck by Acharyashree's grace and beauty since the time I first saw him. Now, standing only a few feet away from him, I was physically affected by it. His beautiful, well-proportioned body, long black beard and bright, mysterious eyes left an otherworldly and unforgettable impression on me.

Acharyashree wasn't angry to find an uninvited guest in his room. Instead he smiled at me and asked me lovingly, "Who are you?"

"I have come from Kathmandu. I am a student of engineering

and I am the one who corresponds with you from Patna", I said nervously, and touched his feet. He gazed at me unwaveringly for a while and then chuckled, "I see. I remember everything."

I knew he had remembered more than just my letters, but just how much more I couldn't say. It felt as though he had looked into my past lives, the complexities of my present and charted my future. I was ready to bare the deepest secrets of my heart with no fear, but in great trust and love I had not known until I met him that day.

Acharyashree sat on the chair and I sat on the marble floor. He told me to sit on his bed instead. I felt uncomfortable sitting on his bed. But Acharyashree was insistent. "I am telling you to sit on the bed. The marble floor is cold." he said firmly. I obeyed. I then started talking about all my problems and queries. At times I couldn't talk coherently, but he listened very patiently and compassionately.

I started narrating to him the story of how I had first seen him in Patna, about the discourse, about how he had given me the dawn of a new hope and fuelled my drive for truth all over again - how his words touched me deeply.

I was so moved by his presence that I could barely keep my narration linear. I told him about my search, how it had taken me to many different gurus but how these wanderings had been futile and how that quest in my heart had remained, burning and as unsatisfied as ever. I told him how I had started to read his work regularly since the meeting. If the truth be told, there wasn't a single day that would go by without me reading his words for at least a few hours.

He asked me about my family; I told him a little.

Acharyashree told me Nepal had great spiritual potential.

Just as the entire terrain of Tibet vibrated with the teachings of Buddha, Nepal has the same potential to imbibe Acharyashree's message. Padmasambhav single-handedly spread the teachings of Buddha in Tibet, Sanghamitra and Mahendra revived Buddhism in Sri Lanka, and in the same way, Nepal, too, has been waiting for a dedicated seeker who would establish Acharyashree's (Osho's) vision in the beautiful kingdom of the Himalayas.

"If you are ready," he had told me, "Nepal is ready for me."

He then reminded me lovingly of the stories of Bodhidharma, Padmasambhav,and Sanghamitra and Mahendra. These stories sounded like wonderful fables, but that's all. Myth lends a unique aura to history, and the mind is ready to accept the surreal without questioning much. But here Acharyashree was talking as though these fables were waiting to be repeated in Nepal, and was that to be via me? I didn't doubt his vision; I doubted my own ability. What he was saying was too grand to be true. And surreal, of course.

As though reading my mind, he said, "When a disciple is ready to surrender, he transcends his personal boundary and limitation, and the entire universe starts functioning through him."

Acharyashree asked me what I enjoyed the most. I replied immediately – "travelling!" In fact, after passing my I. Sc., I had appeared for the aviation entrance exam as well. But my parents freaked out when they learnt of this, and locked me in my room the day I was to appear for the interview. My dream of becoming a pilot was therefore terminated. Even when I was doing my engineering course, I had made up my mind to practice either with the Indian Railway or an airline, so I could at least get free tickets to travel all around the world. I had read *Athato Ghumakkad Jigyasa* by

Rahul Sankrityayan, which had further fueled my longing to travel.

Acharyashree chuckled, and said, "Pilots don't get to see the world, they just get to see the airports. You just make yourself worthy. When you are ready, I will make you travel around the world with my message. In every corner of the world there will be people who will receive you with great love. But you will have to make yourself worthy of that love, first."

He not only fulfilled his promise, but as is his way, fulfilled it extravagantly. These days, for six months a year, I travel all around the world sharing Osho's love and vision. If I were to accept all the invitations, I could travel all year round. But owing responsibility to my communes in Nepal, I have curtailed my travel plans to six months a year. The truth is, the wanderlust in me is so utterly satiated that I am looking forward to the years of solitude and quietude. But as it appears, Osho is hell-bent on annihilating the last seed of the travelling desire in me. So, despite my ageing body, Osho is still taking me around the world. Of course, as always, he was right about everything. Everywhere I've been, I have been received as though I had been a part of the family, with such great love and warmth. I can see now why Osho laughed when I had said I wanted to be a pilot. Osho has given me a thousand-fold more than what I could have dreamt for myself. His grace exceeds even the wildest of my fantasies.

I was thrilled to be in such close proximity of Acharyashree. He asked me a few questions and I answered them in detail. Hearing of my obsession with self-control, celibacy and my past religious journey, Acharyashree said in jest, "You have read the traditional religious books a little more than was necessary. And you have been spoiled by this literature, it seems."

Then he advised me to read his book, *From Sex to*

Superconsciousness. The book had recently been released and had become an instant sensation. As our conversation continued, he said, "I have started getting invitations from abroad as well. I will probably go to Nairobi in March."

"Don't go!" I heard myself say impulsively.

"Why?" Acharyashree was clearly bemused by my sudden outburst.

"Because once you start travelling, foreigners will not lose a moment in recognizing your worth. And it will be impossible for simple folks like us to meet you", I said.

"See, this young man talks sense," Acharyashree pointed at me while talking to the others in the room. "This is exactly what is going to happen."

Encouraged by his words, I said, "Please don't go anywhere else in March. Please come to Kathmandu instead."

He looked at me intently and said, "Will you be able to organize it?"

I was so overcome with love for him I overestimated my own strength. I told him, "My parents have a certain political background and they can help us organize something."

He said, "Okay but I don't prefer staying in a hotel, so I will stay at your place."

In those days, we used to live in a small rented flat in Putalisadak, Kathmandu. It was a three-story house. The ground floor served as my father's office, and we used to live on the first floor. When I decided to invite Acharyashree to Nepal, I suddenly realised we only had one common bathroom in the entire flat. I was aware how particular he was about his privacy, so I told him wrote to let him know it would be best for him to stay at the Hotel Paras at Newroad, the only rated hotel in Kathmandu then. Also, apart from the bathroom situation, the guest room at our flat was furnished, rather too congested for his taste. And of course, our house was always visited by politicians, thanks to my parents' political affiliations. So in I insisted that he stay at the hotel. He replied, "I am coming for you, and will stay in your house."

When I mentioned the bathroom, he only said, "That's not a problem, I'll manage. Don't worry. I don't need comfort, I need love. And the tears in your eyes are proof enough I will be happier at your place."

I told him Nepal was not yet ready for a camp, but we could definitely organize public discourses and personal meetings.

He smiled with that mysterious glint in his eyes, and said, "You don't know the potential of Nepal yet. If you are ready, Nepal is up for a great spiritual revolution."

When I walked out of his room that day, the revolution had already begun.

In the Eye
of the Storm

It was an early January morning in 1970. The entire railway station was still asleep under a blanket of thick mist. A few tea vendors were ready to set up their stalls. Some were rubbing their frozen hands together in a desperate attempt to warm themselves. Winter had unleashed her force mercilessly, yet the thought that soon I would see Acharyashree kept me warm from the inside.

Acharyashree was arriving by Toofan Express at 6:00 am. I, along with my friend, Atma Vijay Gupta, (Dr. Ramchandra Prasad, who was then the head of the English Department at Patna University, and who later become the Vice Chancellor there), his daughter and a university student leader (whose name was also incidentally Toofan) had arrived at the station to receive him. We had invited Acharyashree for satsang and public discourse in Patna for four days.

Toofan, which means cyclone in Urdu, was an apt name for the train that brought Acharyashree to Patna. I felt an unusual calmness in my being, the calmness that precedes a cyclone. None of us were certain of the exact position of the platform where his carriage would stop, so we dispersed ourselves to five different places. Call it my good fortune, Acharyashree walked out right where I was standing.

Wrapped only in a white *lungi* and shawl, he walked out gracefully. A few beads of water rolled down his freshly washed hair onto his body. The presence of Acharyashree brought a freshness to the entire ambience of the place, which only a moment ago had seemed so dull and lethargic. It seemed incredible to me that even at such an early hour, he had already had a shower and was ready for action. In those days in the first-class compartments, they had provisions for short, cold showers. I touched his feet and held his hand as he climbed down onto the platform.

"Arun, but I thought you had your examinations; how come you are here?" Acharyashree asked.

I was surprised he knew about it because I didn't remember writing it in the letters. I only remembered later that I had casually mentioned to him, five months ago when I had met him in Dwaraka, that I had my exams in January. His memory was razor-sharp. Over the years, I realised he had an uncanny ability to remember things. He never forgot something he had heard or seen or read.

"How could I remain at the hostel when you are here?"

He smiled. I went on board to fetch his luggage. He was here just for four days, but he had three suitcases and two bags. Acharyashree scanned the luggage and said, "But where is my bullworker? Did you not find it with the rest of the luggage?"

I had seen a bullworker, but I couldn't put the image of him and a bullworker together. I had thought it probably belonged to some other passenger in the train, and left it there intentionally. But as I would learn later, he was very particular about his health, and exercised regularly in those days. His body had the grace and beauty of a yogi. Two of his suitcases contained a pillow each. Two other suitcases contained his *lungis* and shawls, and the rest of it was for books. Acharyashree read three to five books on average per day. Whenever we watched him read a book, it was as though he was casually flipping through it, but then immediately afterwards he could give the most profound analysis of anything he had read, as though he had been reading the text for years. Tesla and Swami Vivekananda also had a similar gift. Swami Vivekananda attributed this gift to his spiritual life, and to celibacy in particular.

There are over one hundred thousand books in Acharyashree's (Osho's) personal library at Pune Ashram, and they contain his underlines and notes. People often asked him why he consumed the books voraciously despite being enlightened. Weren't all his questions answered?

His reply had touched me very much. He said, "My hunger for knowledge has been utterly sated. But if I am to help the people, I need to speak to them in the language they understand, to trace the history of their thought process and the surroundings that shape their thoughts. Therefore, if I am to help them, I have to be one among them. It is a torture for me to read all this nonsense. Once you know yourself, there is nothing worth knowing. But I want to reach out to as many people as possible, and I must be more informed than they are if I have to convince them to listen to me."

Osho is undoubtedly one of the most well-read people in

human history. His discourses reflect the depth and breadth of his understanding with unmatched grace and intelligence. After his enlightenment, he saw that intellectuals can only be impressed by one's ability to reason.

And he is not just widely read; he also left a rare legacy of over seven hundred books which are related to the total transformation of human consciousness, and have been translated, and published in all the major languages. His books are among the best-selling spiritual books, but the world is yet to evaluate and acknowledge his enormous contribution to humanity.

The clear influence of Osho can be seen in the discourses of all the spiritual leaders of today. Most of them read Osho's work regularly, and their talks are full of anecdotes and examples from Osho literature. In spite of this, most of them are too miserly to give him due credit, or even to mention his name.

After we put the entire luggage in the car, there was only enough space left for Acharyashree, Dr. Ramchandra and his daughter. Acharyashree had travelled all night, so we had assumed he would like to rest in the afternoon. We had designed the schedule accordingly. Since there wasn't any space left in the car, we had to hire another rickshaw to return to our university. So we said to Acharyashree, "Please rest for a while and we will see you there whenever you are ready."

"I am ready," he replied. "I must discuss the programme. Just follow us in the rickshaw." Acharyashree astonished us with his vigour. In those days he was in his *Rajas* phase. Being with him was like being in the eye of a storm. It was difficult to keep up with his pace. It was as though he could stretch time at will. A day would seem like a lifetime. Later, he spoke about this phase in his Bhagavad Gita discourse series:

"When this second phase - that of Rajas - began, I kept on travelling throughout the country. As much as I travelled in those ten to fifteen years, no one would travel even in two or three lives. As much as I spoke during those ten to fifteen years would ordinarily require ten to fifteen lives. From morning until night I was on the move, travelling everywhere. With or without any reason, I was creating controversies and making criticisms - because the more controversies, the quicker the transition through the second phase of activity. I therefore began to criticize Gandhiji, I began to criticize socialism.

Neither did I have any relationship with these subjects, nor was there any attachment to politics. I had no interest whatsoever in these. But when the entire population of the country was absorbed in these tensions, and I had to pass by this same population, there seemed, even if just for fun, a necessity to create controversies. Therefore, during this transition of my second phase of activity, I engineered a number of controversies and enjoyed them.

If these controversies had been created due to tension-filled actions motivated by desire, it would have brought me unhappiness. But as all this was just for the necessity to develop the rajas guna, *just for its expression, there was fun and interest in it."*

For the first thirty-two years of his life, Osho lived his *Tamasik* phase in totality. During that time he lived as inactively as Lao Tzu or Raman Maharshi. His parents were mystified as to how he could even sustain himself with such an inactive life devoid of ambition.

But this energy transmuted into *Rajas* in the beginning of 1960. During this phase, the brilliance of his enlightenment expressed itself in an astounding explosion of activity, rebellion and originality. This phase lasted until 1970. He travelled extensively around India and gave his provocative discourses, shaking the whole nation from its foundations. It was during this period that his controversial books, *From Sex to Superconsciousness, Beware of Socialism, Revolution in Education, Gandhism; an Analysis* and *The Burning Questions of India* were published. Due to his truthful and uncompromising delivery, he became notorious as a controversial and rebellious figure.

Those four days with him in Patna were the expression of the same explosive energy. They were no less than four lives, each day deserving a separate book of its own.

We reached Dr. Prasad's house, where Acharyashree was to stay for the next four days. He told us he would have just a glass of fruit juice and have his brunch at eleven, then he started discussing the programme.

Acharyashree preferred his room to be as empty as possible, so, except for a bed, we had emptied the room and laid a carpet on the floor. This less than two hundred square foot room was his bedroom and also the living room where he received people in the afternoon. We showed him the tentative outline of the schedule. We had planned for his discourse to be followed by a Question and Answer session, and then meditation, all in the morning, and a similar schedule for the evenings. Acharyashree looked at our schedule and frowned, "What am I doing the entire day?" We told him we had arranged for the meetings with journalists and writers in the afternoon. He was clearly disappointed with the answer. He asked us to insert a few meetings and public talks in between. We tried to convince him that it was difficult to restructure the programme at such short notice, but he wouldn't take no for an answer. He said we could organize a talk programme in our college or at the local Rotary or Lions clubs, or at the Medical

Association, Teacher Associations, Chamber of Commerce... basically wherever we could manage to organize it. We organizers were very disappointed because we wanted to spend more time with him and didn't want to waste time arranging new meetings.

Acharyashree turned to me and asked, "Arun, did you make proper advertisement of the programme?" I told him we had printed several pamphlets and stuck them around the city.

"I want to knock at every door. I don't want anyone to tell me that they hadn't heard about the programme. So Arun, you just take a loudspeaker and go around the town and make announcements."

I couldn't believe he just said that. When Acharyashree arrived that morning and we showed him the schedule, we had thought the ordeal was over. If only we knew, actually, the ordeal had just begun.

Rather reluctantly, Toofan and I hired a rickshaw, took a loudspeaker and went through the dusty streets of Patna announcing, *"Attention! Attention!! Attention!!! This evening Acharyashree Rajneesh, celebrated author of the book 'From Sex to Superconsciousness', is giving a lecture at Sinha Library."*

Not many people had heard of Acharyashree then so we added, *"Acharyashree's revolutionary analysis of religion is bound to stun you. Come together with your family for the discourse. Join the discourse every day from 7:00-9:00 in the morning and 6:00-8:00 in the evening."*

Toofan was a student leader and had a natural flair for these sorts of things. I sat half-heartedly in the rickshaw as the dust and the stench made me feverish. I could barely muster up the energy to make the announcement, but Toofan seemed to enjoy the ride endlessly. I told Toofan he was a much better speaker than I was, and persuaded him to take care of the affair single-handedly. He was only too happy to oblige. So I took early leave, and went back to Acharyashree.

When I reached Dr. Prasad's house, Acharyashree saw me arrive, and just as I was at the threshold, he asked me, "Where is Mathura Prasad Mishra? Get him here."

Mathura Prasad was the Member of Parliament, and in those days he was far more famous than Acharyashree in Bihar. I knew that Mathura Prasad used to reside in Rajendranagar, too, not too far away from Dr. Prasad's home. I rushed to fetch him. When I reached his residence, he was having an informal sort of meeting with his party cadres. He was a very popular Congress leader at the time. I told him I had come on behalf of Acharyashree to extend his invitation to see him. Mathura Prasad responded with great enthusiasm. He was a connoisseur of tea. Nothing pleased him more than a cup of well-brewed tea. Since he was very particular about his tea, he often used to prepare it himself. That day too he had prepared tea himself. He served me a cup, and excused himself for a quick shave. A little later, he accompanied me to Dr. Prasad's house.

Mathura Prasad was a man of unusual devotion and integrity. After taking *sannyas,* he became Swami Anand Maitreya, and became an intrinsic part of Osho's work. Later, he had been given a small storeroom in Lao Tzu House in Pune. In those days, Pune Ashram had only two buildings: Lao Tzu House and Krishna House. Lao Tzu House used to be a residence of a former Maharaja. It had four large bedrooms, a well-maintained lawn and spacious verandas. Apart from Acharyashree, the others staying at Lao Tzu House were Vivek, Laxmi, Mukta and her two daughters. Although Anand Maitreya had served as a Member of Parliament for twenty years, he was one of the quietest and most humble residents at Pune Ashram, and remained so until he left his body on the 17th of July 1987. For years, he had lived in that small storeroom about 100 square feet in Lao Tzu House, and he left his body in that same room. As the ashram became more affluent, Laxmi had offered Maitreya Swami to move into a more spacious room in Krishna House. But small though it was, he loved that room, as it was close to the room of Acharyashree.

In the early days, Maitreya Swami's association with Acharyashree created a scandal. Later, it even sparked a new rumour in Patna. Maitreya Swami, Rajendra Prasad, Toofan and I came from the same Bhumihar Brahmin ancestry, the so-called upper class Brahmin clan. Patna was rife with racial politics, and when the four of us, all Bhumihar Brahmins, were seen actively professing our love and dedication to Acharyashree, the communists spread the rumour that Acharyashree was an elitist Hindu leader. When I recounted this to Acharyashree later, he was surprised and asked, "So people in Patna don't even know that I come from a Jain family?"

I triumphantly ushered Mathura Prasad to Acharyashree's room. I was hopeful that after this I would get to spend some time with him, but as I entered the room, he asked me to go around and find a place and audience for the afternoon talk. I told him flatly that it wasn't possible to organize talk programmes at such short notice. He was in no mood to listen to me.

His visit had coincided with Saraswati Puja, the spring festival celebrated throughout India and Nepal to appease Saraswati, the goddess of knowledge and arts. On that day, the larger-than-life earthen statues of the goddess are worshipped in every nook and cranny of the country. We found one such

41

congregation, with a ready-made stage and a sound system. At such a short notice, there was no way we could hope to design a stage of our own, so we pleaded with the organizer to give us the stage for a religious discourse for one hour. These were simple folks. They wanted to know who the orator was. I showed them Acharyashree's picture. The organizer looked at the picture closely, and asked again, "A Hindu saint?"

"Yes, a Hindu."

They obviously saw no harm in letting him do his talk for a little while; none of them knew anything about him.

Acharyashree climbed gracefully up onto the dais. The audience consisted of very ordinary people - street vendors, rickshaw pullers and a few religious enthusiasts, who I could see weren't prepared for Acharyashree at all. Perhaps the only people who could understand a little bit of what he was saying were we, the organizers.

Acharyashree sat down on the elevated wooden podium and looked around. He was clearly dismayed by the quality of the stage and audience. We could see that he was disappointed with the arrangement, but the show had to go on!

"Such is the humour of time!" Acharyashree began his discourse in Hindi, pointing towards the huge clay statue of the goddess Saraswati beneath which he was placed. "I have always been a staunch opponent of idol-worshipping, and here I am, seated underneath a larger-than-life statue of the goddess, who seems to have long left this country."

The opening lines of his discourse shocked the audience, most of whom had gathered to hear the glorification of the goddess and about the significance of the day, and they became even more confused as the discourse progressed.

"We worship Saraswati, the goddess of knowledge, in each corner of this country, and yet she chooses to reside in Oxford, Cambridge and Harvard. Indians have even started going to the West to do their higher studies on Indian culture, Hinduism and Oriental mysticism. We worship Laxmi, the goddess of wealth, with such zeal, but it seems she has left this country for the cleaner and quieter atmosphere of the West, which has embraced science and technology to enhance the quality of life. Instead of creating wealth, eradicating poverty, and addressing the question of development, we are content to install the statues of gods and goddesses by beating drums, screaming *bhajans*, dancing fanatically on the streets and burning firecrackers just to add more pollution to the already polluted cities of India."

The puja organizers had started throwing alarming glances at us. The tension was visible. The audience was at a loss. But I was absolutely revelling in the discourse, and wanted it to go on. Yet I knew it was about time we had to get Acharyashree safely out of the place. It was almost always the case, Acharyashree hit where it hurt the most. Audiences were always left bewildered and enraged by his discourses. The greatest challenge for us as organizers in those days was to get him safely back to the car.

"Why is your goddess angry with you all?" he was asking. Even amidst their anger and confusion, the audience were curious to find out why. Silence fell on the place. "It is because you have neglected science and technology, and resorted to trying to appease the lifeless statues of gods and goddesses instead."

He couldn't be any truer, because during that time we didn't even have a recorder to record this discourse. A foreign student in my hostel had a tape recorder. I had asked him to record Acharyashree's discourse but he had let me down at the last minute. This important discourse by Acharyashree during his five day visit to Patna couldn't be recorded. In this city where the goddess of affluence was worshiped on every corner, we couldn't even find a tape recorder.

The evening event, however, went better than expected. The lawn of the Sinha Library was packed with people of high intellect. They were all mesmerized by Acharyashree's beautiful oration and his unique analysis. But more than that, they were touched deeply by the twenty-minute mindfulness meditation he conducted at the end of the session. In this meditation, he gave them the taste of no-mind, which was effortless in his presence.

He began his discourse by saying, "Firstly, neither do I have an association nor an organization. I speak as an individual. I speak only that which I feel is right. It is not necessary for you to agree with my thinking. You will probably think most of what I say is wrong because I talk against all the conditionings that humanity has gathered to date. All philosophers, reformers and politicians want to provide humanity with a certain way of life, a set of morals and a religion. I only see slavery and bondage in it. I don't want to give you a way of life, rather I want humanity to be free of all conditionings.

"Humanity has created law in order to enslave itself. Law means that you live according to the rules of society. Character means something else. It means that it is not the society that decides, but the individual. If we analyse in detail, then we will find that the majority of our moral conduct is sex centred. When we say that a man is characterless, we immediately think that he is having multiple sexual relations. We will not think that he cheats, skips taxes, lies or is corrupt. For us, all these things carry no value. For us, sex is the primary thing to decide one's character.

A society that bases its morality on sex is perverted. It makes those who are forced to live with one partner feel that all other human beings are immoral. Actually, sex is a beautiful private affair between two people. Morality should be concerned with lying, tax evasion, hypocrisy, not fulfilling one's social duties, and violence and cruelty. As sex is an intrinsic biological need, to fulfil this need people will bypass all social norms and morality. This is why many socially recognized people have two faces. This is how the big web of hypocrisy begins. If you want to break this hypocrisy, then we should base our morality not on idealistic but realistic grounds."

The famed Indian poetess and Member of Parliament, Amrita Preetam, said, "While all religions make people fearful, Rajneesh's whole philosophy is to make humanity free from fear."

Acharyashree's words were novel and fiery, and it was impossible to remain indifferent after listening to them. Once the session was over, the crowd responded in a frenzy, and wanted to hug him, touch his feet, ask for his autograph, and basically mob him from all sides. We were still high from meditation, but it was time again to get him safely to the car.

The Making
of History

Without really being aware, I was in the middle of the making of history. Acharyashree's presence was enough to unleash the fountains of love in the hearts turned barren by years of mechanical living. It was magical, almost unbelievable, how people were transformed in his presence. But at the same time, it was equally unimaginable how the general public, who had never met him or heard him, had ungrounded bias and prejudice against him.

On the third day, we had scheduled for his talk programme to be in my college at Patna University. Even though I had arranged for that talk with great enthusiasm, I sank deeper into despair as the day approached. We had two factions among the students in our university - the Socialist Students Federation and the Hindu

Nationalist Students Council (Janasanghis), and both groups were against Acharyashree. The socialists were angry with him because of his book *Beware of Socialism,* and thought him an advocate of capitalism, funded by the Americans. His recent tussle with the Shankaracharya of Puri in the World Religion Conference, and his unorthodox views on religion, made him equally unpopular among Hindus who thought that he was influenced by communism, and called him an agent of the Russians.

I have seen the intellect of many intellectuals falter during Osho's life. His large commune in America, where labour itself was the wealth, and where money was not used at all, was similar to the commune envisioned by Karl Marx. Thus in America he was regarded as an agent of the KGB, while socialists thought him a spokesperson for capitalism. Those who did not want to think even that much said that he advocated promiscuity, and labelled him *Sex Guru.* But Osho's teaching was so radical and futuristic that it will take humanity a good many years before it can truly understand his message.

Osho has said, *"Karl Marx is basically a jealous Jew rationalizing his jealousy into beautiful jargon. The remedy that he proposes is fallacious. Firstly, if you distribute the wealth of those who are rich to the poor, what will be the result? The poor will not become rich, the rich will only become poor: you will be distributing poverty. Yes, people will not feel jealous anymore because they will all be equally poor. I am against poverty, hence I am against communism. I want people to be equally rich, not equally poor.*

But for that a totally different approach is needed. It is not a question of distribution of wealth -- because there is not much wealth to distribute. How many people are there who are rich? -- two percent in India.

47

Now, the wealth of two percent distributed to ninety-eight percent poor people is just like a spoonful of sugar thrown into the ocean to make it sweet. You are simply losing one spoonful of sugar unnecessarily. At least it could have given one man one cup of tea -even that is gone. Not that others are gaining anything, but they will all enjoy the idea: "Now nobody is drinking tea, we are all equal." Otherwise this man was drinking tea and everybody was jealous.

The people who have created wealth have a certain talent for creating it. You should use their talent; you should make it an art to be taught to everybody. They are not to be punished because they have created wealth.

I am against communism because it is only a negative philosophy. I am all for commune-ism.

That should be the right word: commune-ism.

A commune is respectful of every individual's uniqueness, respectful of every individual's talent, and tries to help his talent grow, help him grow towards his potential.

I want communes all over the world, so that slowly nations can disappear, and there are only communes - living, small units of humanity, totally, joyously helping everybody to be himself.

Marx proposes the dictatorship of the proletariat, the dictatorship of the poor. That is stupid. They are poor, and if they are in power they will make everybody poor. What else can they do?

I propose the dictatorship of the enlightened ones. Nobody has proposed it up to now. And sometimes out of my crazy mind...This idea I have carried my whole –life - dictatorship of the enlightened ones, because if it is of enlightened ones it cannot be dictatorship. It is a contradiction in terms."

So, it was only natural that he was misunderstood by

my fellow students at the university. As we started making preparations for his talk, I was approached by both factions with threats of assault if Acharyashree were to say anything against communism or religion. I pleaded with Acharyashree over and over again not to speak on either topic, and he had reassured me, yet I was nervous as the day approached. The programme had been scheduled for three o'clock in the afternoon and we had to wrap it up in an hour, as the Saraswati Puja Visarjan team was to proceed at four. The Visarjan team had threatened to dismantle the sound system should we fail to adhere to this plan. In a way, as a junior student, I had expected these bullies to do their usual duties. But as the day progressed I felt as though fate had totally abandoned me. I called Acharyashree frantically several times to ensure he would arrive at the venue at three o'clock sharp. I didn't know at that stage how punctual he was. Acharyashree arrived at the university gate right at quarter to three. Although my principal had been kind enough to provide us with the venue at such short notice, he not only refused to receive Acharyashree, but would not even preside over the talk programme.

As it happened, I had asked the university to provide me with a wooden platform and a few tables, but at the last moment they turned down the request. I was so nervous that I couldn't put my thoughts together. I just ran to my hostel and asked a few friends to help me carry my bed to the stage. Quickly we put together my mattress and one of the clean bed sheets, and made the podium, and when Acharyashree came, he sat on that. Fate has its own way of asserting itself; had it not been for the discourtesy of my friends at the university, I wouldn't have slept for the next four years in the bed where a Buddha once sat.

We had placed a small pot of fresh flowers nearby, and lit

some incense. In those days, Acharyashree wasn't particularly allergic to scents. I had asked the principle of the college to give a welcome speech. He agreed rather reluctantly. Most of the students and all the professors had come to listen to Acharyashree, but the principle never arrived to deliver his speech as promised. I then asked other senior professors, but all felt uncomfortable accepting the sudden request, and no-one came forward. I looked at Mathura *jee* and Toofan, and they signaled that I should take the lead. It had already been five minutes since Acharyashree had sat on the podium. My feet went cold and my throat became parched. I didn't know how to handle the situation. Just then somebody came and pushed me on to the podium, and said, "They are all a bunch of cowards. You go to the stage and introduce him yourself."

Before I could gather myself, I saw I was facing a mass of thousands, who were looking at me with a mixture of mockery and curiosity. I started speaking, at first in a subdued voice, but very soon I heard myself speaking with such authority I surprised myself, if not others.

"Dear friends, it is our great fortune that Acharyashree is among us today. It is also a matter of great pride for our college. This is an historic day. We had heard about Krishna, Kabir, Nanak and other enlightened beings, but such is our fortune that we are seated with the person who has walked right out of history."

Someone screamed from the crowd, "What is this history you are talking about? Where is his name inscribed? Who is he anyway?"

"I can only tell you this much - he is a dangerous man." I had found a new calm and strength. "I too had gone to him to find out about him, who he is and what was his teaching. But when I returned, I had returned with a different set of questions – who am I, why am I in this world, what is the purpose of my being? Acharyashree is not here to sing a lullaby to us, to help us sink deeper into our slumber. He is here to shake us out of our dreams, no matter how dear they be to us. He comes from the pages of the history, where Buddha, Christ, Kabir and Nanak live. He comes from the pages of the history from where the unknown beckons. He is the destroyer of dreams, a *swapna banjak.*"

The campus was the same, the students were the same, and the professors were the same. And yet how different it all was! The air had a different fragrance, as if Acharyashree had infused some magic into it. I walked back to the audience, but I was levitating in thin air, almost floating. History was in the making. How fortunate were those who witnessed it unfold!

O Youths!
Are Ye All Dead?

"My beloved ones," Acharyashree began the discourse. "I have been told repeatedly by our organizers to speak on youth issues. But to whom do I speak? I see no youths in this country. Here, a child is born and becomes old without ever entering into youth. If we had any youth in this country, we wouldn't have to have waited for Edmund Hillary from New Zealand to climb the Himalaya. How long is it since we have romanced with nature? How long since we attended to the calls of adventure? No, I see no youth here. No-one dares to respond to the call of rebellion anymore. The fires in our hearts have been blown out. All that remains is a few dying embers, without any rebel who would dare to fan them into flames again."

A strange stillness had descended. No-one dared to move.

It felt sacrilegious even to breathe. The audience was transfixed. Just then, Acharyashree looked at them and said, "Why are many of you staying so far away when there is so much space in the front?" We had made seating arrangements such that the girls were in the front rows, separate from the boys. This was general practice. It was believed that the only way to preserve our sexual moral values was to keep boys and girls as separate as possible. When Acharyashree asked that question, it was as though the boys had been awoken from a spell; they all ran towards the girls, and seated themselves happily.

"Youth means rebellion," Acharyashree went on. "It means courage, it means being a daredevil again. But we don't have a tradition of rebellion in this country. It is not surprising that we had the tradition of child-marriage here. A child is born and before he enters his sixteenth year, he becomes a father. A father can never be a youth; he will always be an old man full of responsibilities, regardless of his age. Now we have postponed the marriageable age, but the psychology remains the same. This is why we don't have rebels in this country.

If we had youth in this country, then injustice wouldn't have been so rampant. Just this morning I read that around six hundred and forty litres of ghee was drained down the streets to appease a sun god. In a country where children die of malnutrition every day, can we afford to carry on with such inhumane rituals? Why didn't a single youth in this country stand up and say this was unacceptable?

It is no coincidence that the prisons and universities in this country are designed in the same style. They almost look the same from the outside, and unfortunately, aren't much different from each other either. The English were interested in producing clerks, not rebels. They wanted to mass-produce clerks, who would enter into this slavery without ever questioning its validity. I call that man a genius, who comes out of the university without destroying his intelligence. The university is a mechanism to destroy genius, spontaneity and rebellion. The organizer has told me over and over again to speak on youth issues, but it seems, despite his age, he himself isn't so youthful. Otherwise, what is the logic behind keeping boys and girls separate? I am against such repressive vision. This forceful deprivation creates a repressed, miserable creature, and gives birth to all kinds of sexual perversions."

He was pointing out to me. How clearly his words penetrated me. I could see the utter folly of it all. Acharyashree's words cut through my conditioning like a sharp razor.

"I want to provoke the youth in you," Acharyashree was saying. "This is my crime. I want to rekindle that dying fire inside you again."

Acharyashree had finished his discourse right on time. The campus was reverberating with the thunderous rounds of applause. The students stood up from their chairs and went on clapping. A lump had arisen in my throat. I went on clapping, and tears rolled down my cheeks. There were no communists and no Janasanghis. In their stead, I could see only flames of light, burning brightly, overlapping each other. It was overwhelming. We were all burning, alight, engulfed in flame. I looked at the man who had threatened to dismantle the sound system. He, too, was clapping. I had read of miracles; but that day I witnessed them with my own eyes.

As Acharyashree stepped down from the podium, students and professors alike rushed to hug him and get his autograph. There was such a frenzy that people were picking up littered papers on which to get his autograph. We had to wrestle with the crowd to get him safely to the car. When the crowd became out of control, I had to announce that Acharyashree was going to appear for a public discourse in the evening at Sinha Library. Those who wanted to get his autograph or to meet him could come and see him in the evening. Then the crowd slowly, reluctantly, dispersed.

When I came back to the campus, the students had left. There were piles of bricks and pebbles under many chairs. I knew the communists and Janasanghis had been earnest when they had threatened of physical assault earlier. But when they left the campus that day, they had not left just those stones, but the dead weight in their hearts, too. I took a deep breath. The earth wasn't under the spell of gravitation that day. We were all levitating. The sky was beckoning and the flames had leapt upwards. All the heaviness had combusted.

Alchemy of Grace

During Acharyashree's stay in Patna, a poor man in tattered and dirty clothes arrived at our place and said he wanted to meet Acharyashree. He went by the name of Dubey *jee*. I looked at his lowly appearance and told him he could only meet Acharyashree later. I tried to explain that Acharyashree would be available for the public discourse in the evening, but he was very stubborn and loud. I couldn't persuade him to wait, so reluctantly I took him to Acharyashree.

Now I can see that he had brought a special flavour to Acharyashree's Patna visit. But back then, he was the cause of much trouble and jealousy to all the organizers.

When I took him to Acharyashree, much to my surprise, Acharyashree was loving towards him. He listened patiently to him as he recounted his story.

"I have read some of your fiery articles and I am immensely moved by them," Dubey said. "I came to know about your visit through one of the newspaper advertisements. When I read that you would be visiting Patna, I was so thrilled and joyful that I could not contain myself, and I have arrived all the way from Benaras this morning. I feel so fortunate to have met you and I do not want to part with you even for a second. But I also don't know anyone in this town who may possibly give me shelter."

Acharyashree welcomed him heartily, and said to me, "Arun, he looks tired. Make arrangements for his bath, rest, food and a place to stay while I am here."

We were struggling financially to make proper arrangements for Acharyashree's presence. Now it fell upon us to take care of Dubey, too. But as it was Acharyashree's wish, we somehow had to manage to find a place where he could bathe, and provided him with clean clothes and a room where he could rest. Ramchandra Prasad was kind enough to lend him a *kurta* and *dhoti*, and provide a place for him to stay at his home. When Dubey reappeared after a rather long bath, in clean clothes, he looked like a different man, almost a gentleman. But of course, no bath could clean off his stubborn nature. Nothing much had changed there.

Dubey *jee* had the rare privilege of being with Acharyashree all the time. He ate with him, travelled with him in the car, and sat next to him when Acharyashree gave private talks in the mornings and evenings, while we were kept away from him, running around, announcing Acharyashree's programmes over the loudspeaker, sticking notices on the walls and arranging meetings. We all grew increasingly envious of his privilege.

But gradually, we started noticing a new radiance about

him. During those four days, he underwent a visible change. He looked graceful and relaxed, and radiated a different kind of light. I noticed later how the physical proximity to Acharyashree, even for a short time, effected a magical transformation in people, but we grew bitter, then, all the same. *We* wanted to be close to Acharyashree. The more I noticed Dubey's transformation, the more my envy increased. But along with the envy, a new understanding also began to dawn upon me.

When I was a child I had often heard the story of Lord Krishna and Sudama – they had been childhood friends. Later, Krishna went on to become the king of Dwaraka, while Sudama remained a poor villager. Sushila, Sudama's wife, was distressed by their miserable and poor life, so she urged Sudama to go and meet his king friend and ask for his help. Sudama tried to explain to her that they had been friends a long time ago, and Krishna might not even remember him now. But Sushila was persistent, and so he decided to visit Krishna. When he reached Dwaraka, he told the gatekeeper that he was a childhood friend of Krishna's, and had come to meet him. The gatekeeper looked the poor Brahmin up and down in disbelief, and then went in to inform the king. When Lord Krishna heard Sudama was there, he stood up from his golden throne and tears filled his eyes. The gatekeeper asked the lord if he was to send the visitor in. Krishna replied he himself would go to receive the guest, and at the gate he embraced Sudama with great love. He had Sudama sit on a high pedestal while he, Krishna, washed his feet with perfumed water. Sudama had carried a small pouch of beaten rice as a snack for his journey.

The story goes that when they were living in Gurukul with their master, as young students, Sudama was a very greedy person. Their *guruma* used to send snacks for two of them with Sudama, who would eat it all, on his own. Because of this greed and the bad karma he earned by stealing Krishna's food, he remained very poor.

Krishna knew of everything, so when Sudama arrived at the palace, Krishna insisted on eating some of his beaten rice. Sudama was ashamed to share his ordinary treat with Krishna, but Krishna insisted. So Sudama handed over the pouch, and watched Krishna eat the food in sheer joy. The story goes that the lord ate the whole lot to relieve Sudama of his bad karma, but Sudama could not understand this at first.

He was overwhelmed by Krishna's kindness, and couldn't bring himself to ask for any financial help. His heart was overcome by Krishna's love, and he realised that no treasure could be more valuable. After spending a few days with Krishna, he returned home. To his utter surprise, he found a beautiful bungalow in place of his miserable hut. Sushila walked out of the house, and said that while he was away, Laxmi, the goddess of wealth, had visited, and blessed them with wealth and prosperity. Sudama listened to the story with tears in his eyes, and then realised that Krishna had eaten his snack to relieve him of his bad karma, and that to be loved by the lord was the greatest blessing of all. No wealth could compare to it.

During those four days I came to understand the essence of the Krishna-Sudama story. Dubey had arrived as an ordinary man, full of questions and unhappiness. He didn't practice any arduous techniques, nor was he extraordinarily bright; he reached his inner wealth simply by the grace of, and his proximity to, Acharyashree.

The Blind Saint

On the third day of the Patna sojourn, Acharyashree had retired for an afternoon sleep. The sun was feeble, and, craving for its warmth, we were sitting on the balcony. It must have been around three in the afternoon. A young man stepped down from a rickshaw and yelled from the road, asking if Acharya Rajneesh was staying there. I stood up and nodded affirmatively. Again he shouted from the road, "My guru, who is head of the Kabirpanthi ashram in Samastipur, has come to meet Acharyashree. We are coming up to meet him."

In those days Acharyashree was at the peak of his Rajas phase. I was always a little worried that he would burn himself out. So now that he was having his sleep, I was determined not to let anyone disturb him. I told the young man that Acharyashree was giving a discourse at Sinha Library in the evening, and he could come with his guru to the library to meet him. The man was adamant. But I was also determined not to let anyone disturb Acharyashree, so I also insisted that he could meet Acharyashree in the evening only. Ironically, our argument disturbed Acharyashree, and he woke up. He called me into his room and asked why I had been shouting. I told him of the man on the road and his guru, whom I hadn't seen yet. Acharyashree told me to arrange the meeting.

The guru, whom they affectionately called Saheb *jee*, was a tiny man of rather dark complexion. His disciple walked him carefully to Acharyashree's room. Saheb *jee* suffered from congenital blindness. After seating himself, he spoke softly, "I am blind, Acharyashree, but I had the good fortune of listening to some of your discourses via my disciples, who read them out to me. The moment I heard your words I knew none but Kabir Sahib himself would have spoken such fiery truth. So I asked my disciples to bring me to you because I feel you are the reincarnation of Kabir Sahib."

Acharyashree was smiling. Sahib *jee*, who was visibly touched by Acharyashree's presence, became teary-eyed, and continued speaking in his soft, trembling voice, "Whatever you say is as dangerous as Kabir Sahib's words. You speak pure truth. Alas! It is dangerous to do so. When I heard your words I had thought you must be a very beautiful man and I was a little sorry that I was blind and couldn't see you to confirm this. But now that I am here please allow me to touch you so I can feel your beauty for myself." Acharyashree moved closer to him and took his hand lovingly. Sahib *jee* traced the outlines of his face for a long time and slowly ran them through his body down to his feet. He touched

Acharyashree so tenderly, the way a lover caresses the body of his beloved. His fingers moved slowly with admiration and his eyelids rested, gazing unwaveringly at the beauty he must have seen through his inner eyes.

"I am blind but we blind people have very sensitive fingers. I can tell with certainty that you are a very beautiful person," he managed to say, and he broke into a sob. We were all moved by what had transpired between Acharyashree and Sahib *jee*. Profound silence filled the room.

After a while, still full of tears, Sahib *jee* held Acharyashree's hand and said, "But I have a complaint. You speak from such a height. Your teachings are fiery and dazzling like sun. Sometimes it is difficult for an illiterate man like myself to understand them fully. Why don't you come down to our level and preach in simple language so even illiterate people like me can understand fully."

"I can come down to the valleys and speak to you in your language, the way the other saints speak," answered Acharyashree. "I will be very popular that way, but I will not be of any use then. I can speak in accordance with common man's language and understanding, which will be palatable to him. I want to bring a revolution in human consciousness, so I will always challenge your intelligence and understanding. I shall keep on calling and inviting you from the peak of consciousness because you all have wings that have been clipped because nobody reminds you of them. I can come down to where you are, but just think how glorious it would be if you could open your wings and come to my height rather than pulling me down to your level!"

The Fate of Lovers

Acharyashree had left. It felt as though the winter had become more ruthless in those four days without my knowledge. It was only when Acharyashree left town, I gradually became aware of what we call reality - the open gutter by the roads, the heaps of garbage, the bustling city-dwellers moving frantically around the town like a caravan of ants, the whiff of fried samosas and Indian curry that interspersed with the thick blanket of winter mist and pervaded every corner of the streets. During those four days, so much had changed inside me. A lifetime had gone by. Acharyashree's presence, his love and his blessings had dissolved into me like sugar into water. Each bone, each tissue, each cell of my body had undergone a subtle metamorphosis. His presence had ingrained itself into the deepest core of my being. I wasn't the same person.

But being with Acharyashree is a unique experience. Just as a piece of iron temporarily becomes a magnet in a magnetic field, in his presence we were all transported into a different space. The town was the same, the smells, the people, the colours, the trees, and yet in his presence they all acquired a deeper meaning. The trees appeared more alive, colours were more vivid and a new music was heard in the wind. Nature in its entirety seemed to revel in his presence, exposing the most intimate and beautiful part of herself.

I had gone to the railway station a few days after he had left Patna. A new sense of emptiness was gnawing at my heart. I was in my early twenties and had had a few experiences of romantic love. But I had never known the intensity with which the beloved's absence undoes the peace of one's heart until that day. Sufis have the tradition of addressing god as the beloved, and they sing and dance to her glory. Ordinarily, such sentiments are applied only to lovers. But the love affair with the master surpasses all other love affairs. Acharyashree had opened those chambers in my heart that I didn't know existed. And with him gone, his absence was asserting itself like the swollen Ganges during the monsoon.

I kept watching the passengers, the carriages, and the beggars on the platform listlessly. I wondered where so many people were going. What destiny awaited them on the platforms where they planned to alight? Just when I was caught up in my own web of solitary musings, I saw a glimpse of her again. She must have been in her early thirties. She had become an intrinsic piece of the mosaic that was the Patna Railway station. I had seen her numerous times in the same tattered clothes, with the same unkempt, matted hair, running frantically when any train arrived at the platform and inspecting each compartment with strangely animated eyes. This animation brought a new lightness to her steps, and dilated her pupils. She would pry into each compartment, scanning each passenger, and then disappointed, run to another compartment. Countless times I had watched her scanning the trains. Each compartment left her disappointed. By the time she managed to scan the entire train, she would be engulfed by such great disappointment that she would crouch by a pillar on the platform and start staring into space again. Tears would roll down her cheeks, unchecked; it was heart-breaking to watch her. There was a strange beauty in her face, the beauty of melancholia, of the defeated, of the one who had given up on life. It didn't arouse passion, but it demanded to be seen. On her face,the suffering had acquired its most penetrating expression. She must have come from a good family; her frail and dainty body bore a certain refinement of manners.

After having seen her many times, I had inquired among the local vendors about her. What I heard left me in a daze for days on end. She came from a well-to-do family from a suburb in Patna. When she was still a young girl of around twenty, she had eloped with a man who went to the same college as she did. He had promised to marry her, and she must have left her home behind in the great hope of spending the rest of her life with her beloved. They had arrived late in the evening in Patna. The man had taken her to a hotel, where they must have consummated their love. They spent a few days in the city enjoying their new-found freedom. One fine morning, he woke up early and told her he had to go back to his house to get some money. They had both come to the station, and he had left with the promise of coming back. She sat down on one of the benches waiting for him to return. A day passed, and then another day, and another and another. At least a decade had passed and the man had not arrived. Gradually, desolation got the better of her. She had been sexually abused by many. Someday, she would be seen in torn clothes, with blue marks on her flesh that mutely testified the cruelties of her predators. But despite it all, she continued watching for her beloved to return. She had lost her mind totally. I had never seen her beg, though; people would just take pity on her and leave some food by her side. When she was finished staring vacantly, she would pick up whatever was left around her and eat it listlessly in a mechanical attempt to preserve his promise; how could she die before he returned? And what if he returned to find her dead?

It sent shivers through me when I thought of how she had forgotten everything - her name, her home, her history, herself - and yet through that ocean of dementia, she retained the memory of that promise...the promise of the beloved...the promise of the meeting...the promise of togetherness...the promise that had betrayed, and betrayed so ruthlessly. My heart welled up with tears. I watched her crouching by the pillar. She sat motionless with the resignation of a defeated sniper. How cruel the man must have been to desert her like that. And how unfortunate! Just how unfortunate.

Just then, a train was seen on the distant horizon. The long locomotive came by slowly like a giant reptile, radiating heat, and making the platform a few degrees warmer. Something stirred inside her. She looked at the train and her pupils dilated again. One could see the rush of blood in the green veins on her forehead that suddenly swelled. She clutched her blouse with her right hand and stood up expectantly. That instant, her whole body lit up with a new hope.

How could destiny be so cruel? How could the train carry thousands of passengers every day, but not that man? Even before the train stopped, she jumped into the first compartment that was close to her. Through the bars of the window, I saw her hurrying through the compartments. The passengers who were alighting looked at this crazed creature with disdain. Children dodged her in panic and women perused her torn clothes that momentarily exposed her young, beautiful body, and they twisted their lips in disgust. I just kept watching her. She scurried through them like a rat. People reluctantly made a passageway for her so she wouldn't touch them. And she ran past them untouched, untouched by their disdainful stare, untouched by their rational minds, untouched by everything. Her faith in love was so virginal. Nothing else existed except that promise. That moment she appeared to me like a mythical character, a *Majnun*, whose story was yet to be written. The world would someday read her story and weep for her agony. But in those moments as she ran past them they dismissed her like a freak, unworthy of their attention, let alone sympathy.

This has always been the fate of lovers.

My eyes were teary again. A turbulent storm was brewing inside me. Acharyashree had made no such promise to me, and yet I was his. I knew, just as a river seeks to merge into the ocean, I would find no peace until I met him again. I had seen that mad woman many times but that day we were tied together by a strange fate. I felt the enormity of the absence that ate her heart. I felt her pain of separation. I realised when one sees the glimmer of love, how everything else in the world fades in comparison. Although it is convenient to prune the branches of love from a very early age so that none witnesses its glory, and therefore can settle down in the mundane world with dull complacency, what a meaningless life that would be! True, love will bring agony, love will bring separation,but it is only in that violent pang of melancholia that life reveals its most intimate secrets. During those four days, Acharyashree had shown me the otherworld, the ecstasy of falling in love, of rising in love, of evaporating in love. Now it seemed foolish to go back to that dull complacent life again. I had been touched by the fire of love. And just like that woman, and all the lovers of the past and present, I was destined to walk alone, misunderstood. Some would pity me, some would be enthralled by my story, some would dismiss it as obsession. But it takes a lover to understand the story of a lover. There might not be many left, but I will feel fortunate if just one of you will read this and see that glimmer.

PART II

Woodlands

Woodlands

In 1972 we were in an all-India tour, myself and a group of students in their final year in my college. Acharyashree had been known as Bhagwan from May 1971. Bhagwan had moved to Bombay and was residing in the first-floor flat at Woodlands Apartment in Peddar Road, Bombay. I went to meet him there with my friend Nitish Kumar, who is now the Chief Minister of Bihar. Nitish had attended Bhagwan's discourse given in 1970 at our university in Patna. Like almost everyone who attended the discourse, he had been fascinated by Bhagwan's teachings. I started sharing Bhagwan's books with him, and we would spend hours discussing them. At that time, he was devoted to George Fernandez, the famous socialist leader in India. Nitish used to say, "There are only two people worth meeting in Bombay – Acharya Rajneesh and George Fernandez."

We went together to meet Bhagwan at Woodlands

Apartment. Before he moved into Woodlands, I had the privilege of going into his bedroom directly without any appointment. But in 1972, during his Bombay stay, everything changed. Ma Yoga Laxmi had started taking care of his work as his secretary. The Neo-Sannyas movement had already begun, and the whole apartment was filled with a swarm of orange-clad *sannyasins*, each with a *mala*. When I went to Laxmi and asked her to grant me a personal meeting with Bhagwan, she replied, "You cannot have a personal meeting with him. He will be giving a public discourse on the Bhagavad Gita at Cross Maidan, Bombay, soon. You can go and meet him there."

This was my first experience of official restrictions around Bhagwan. Although this had disappointed me, I also experienced a strange, elevating energy in the apartment. I was not familiar with the term buddhafield. Much later I came to understand that Nitish and I had been overwhelmed by the energy of a buddhafield. Laxmi offered us tea. Admittedly, that still remains the best tea of my life. It was flavoured with a lemongrass infusion. While enjoying the cup of tea, I tried to explain to Laxmi that we were both students and couldn't afford to stay at a hotel to wait for the discourse. I told her I had organized several of Bhagwan's talk programmes and was very intimate with him.

Laxmi was absolutely unimpressed by my story. She replied, "Everybody who comes here tells me the same thing. Bhagwan cannot meet people all day. Allow him some space. Or do you intend for him to be constantly bombarded by visitors?"

I insisted that I had been associated with Bhagwan for a while now, and needed guidance regarding something rather serious. She told me I could meet Swami Yog Chinmaya instead, and join in Dynamic meditation at Chowpatty Beach every morning.

I was not interested in either, but she called Chinmaya and

arranged the meeting. It was our first meeting. Swami Chinmaya came and sat in front of me with his peculiar and serious face. He was behaving like a guru, and was trying to dominate Nitish and me with his long beard and hair, and orange clothes and his grave, guru-like mannerisms. But we were not there for his sermon. I kept asking Laxmi to arrange a *darshan* for me, and finally, after much insistence on my part, she gave me a piece of paper and asked me to write down my request. She went to Bhagwan and came back with the answer that if I wanted to meet him alone, I could come tomorrow morning, but if I wanted to bring my friend along, I should come in the evening.

This came as a huge shock to me. I had always had access to him without any appointment. I had expected that after reading my letter, Bhagwan would summon me immediately. Nitish was already frustrated by what he saw as unnecessary harassment, and refused to join me for the meeting. He decided to meet George Fernandez instead.

Not surprisingly, that evening decided the fate of both of us. While my whole life is dedicated for Osho, Nitish Kumar has today emerged as one of the most influential politicians of India. But at his heart, Nitish is still a yogi. In 2016, he had been invited to attend a national congregation of Nepali Congress. We hadn't met each other for forty odd years but I couldn't resist the temptation of finally seeing the beloved friend of mine, so I reach the airport unannounced. I wasn't even sure that he would recognize me after the gap of forty-odd years. But the moment he walked out of the craft and noticed me, he broke into a smile and screamed, "Arun!"

You can imagine my joy! He walked straight over and hugged me. The government of Nepal had arranged a regal suite at one of the most expensive and luxurious hotels in Kathmandu, but he refused to stay there, and said he would be happier to spend time at our ashram. The security personnel objected. They said the ashram is in a jungle and it is not advisable to stay there for security reasons. He replied, "I don't have enemies in Nepal, only friends. And even if I am assassinated, could there be a better place to die than in an ashram!"

I was overwhelmed by his reply. Forty years had passed by, but I felt the same intimacy I shared with him on that evening we had gone to meet Osho.

So the next evening I went with another friend of mine, who wasn't really interested in Bhagwan's teaching. I should have known better than to drag someone as uninterested as him there, but I didn't dare go alone. We were called, and we went into his bedroom. I was meeting Bhagwan after two years. There were books everywhere. The room had that peculiar, sweet fragrance of his. Bhagwan put aside the book he was reading and spoke very lovingly to us. He was seated on a couch, and we sat on the floor close by - I held his feet with both hands, and started crying. I had been mixing with bad company lately. Suddenly switching from my austere life of a yogi, who only ate raw fruits and vegetables, I had started consuming meat and alcohol. The pendulum had swung to the other extreme. I had not been meditating sincerely and was overshadowed by guilt.

Still holding his feet, I wept and said, "Bhagwan I've ruined my life. I am eating meat, drinking and gambling. I feel so heavy and dull. I've missed you totally."

Bhagwan stroked my hair and said, "You just attend one ten-day camp and I will totally transform you."

But I was inconsolable. I also told Bhagwan I had been unfortunate enough to miss Mount Abu camp. Bhagwan told me lovingly, "I give you permission to fall as low as you want. I have your hands in mine. I will pull you out of all misery, all sin in one instance, whenever I feel it's about time. I won't allow you to ruin your life."

He reminded me that much work remains to be done in Nepal. I kept sobbing and said that I didn't want to go back to my university and complete my studies. I wanted to live with him in Bombay, translating and transcribing his books like Chinmaya and Maitreya Swami.

In 1969 he had hinted that if I didn't want to study engineering I could drop it. For a person of poetic temperament, engineering was a rather dry subject. But at that time, I didn't have enough courage to do so. Now after much suffering and wastage of time, I could see what he meant. But this time Bhagwan forbade me from doing so. He said, "Now you are in the final year of engineering. You have already spent so much time studying so you might as well complete the course. It is just a matter of a few more months. And, moreover, I will need your civil engineering degree. In the future, I will build many ashrams in Nepal and elsewhere."

Needless to say, my friend was finding it all very weird and was unable to make head nor tail out of our conversation. Half-heartedly and rather fearfully, I asked Bhagwan for *sannyas*, because at that time *sannyas* meant wearing an orange *lungi* and *kurta* all the time, even at the university. To be honest, I didn't have the courage to go to my university in an orange *lungi-kurta*. Nevertheless, with trembling heart, I asked for initiation. Bhagwan could see through me more clearly than I could see myself.

He said, "After *sannyas*, it will be very difficult for you to complete your study. First you complete your studies and build a house in Kathmandu for your parents."

Back then I couldn't understand that the house was going to be the epicenter of the Osho movement in Nepal. I also came to understand what he meant when he said I couldn't complete my study after *sannyas*. Four years later when I finally took *sannyas*, I was blissed out for months, unable to do anything at all.

Miraculously, after the meeting something changed inside me on its own. It was as though I had undergone some alchemy. The old habits left me effortlessly. I stopped smoking, drinking and eating meat. A new lightness descended on my life. I also started doing Dynamic meditation on our college sports ground in the middle of the night.

That *darshan* had lasted for about half an hour. When I came out I was transported into another realm. I was not in a state to return to our accommodation. To regain my composure, I sat down on a couch in the reception area. These meetings with Bhagwan were extraordinarily powerful. During his Woodlands and Pune ashram sojourns, I saw many celebrities like Bijay Anand, Haribansha Rai Bachchan, Mahipal, Hema Malini, Manoj Kumar, Kalyanji Anandji, Binod Khanna, Mahesh Bhatt, and Parveen Babi, among others, come to meet Bhagwan. Before they met him, their faces would be fully made-up, and the entire body would be stiff with a sense of pride. But after a few minutes with him, most of them would walk out of the room drenched in tears, free from the masks of success and make-up, totally sober and soft. They would lie down on the couch, and usually ask for a glass of water or a loving embrace. This was Bhagwan's magic; he could strip off our masks even in such short meetings. Unfortunately, this transformation did not last long for many people. When they went back to their normal lives, they couldn't sustain this transforming experience.

Missing the Chance
of a Lifetime

Acharyashree had promised me during the Dwaraka camp that he would visit Kathmandu five months later in the month of March 1970. He had given me the dates as the 19th to 22nd of March. I still have the letter that Arvind, the then secretary of Acharyashree, had written to me. The letter dictated that I should make arrangements for a first-class train ticket from Jabalpur to Banaras, and a connecting flight ticket from Banaras to Kathmandu, return. Apparently, this was the second letter Arvind had written to me in regards to Acharyashree's visit to Nepal. The first letter never reached me; it was probably lost by the Indian mail.

Acharyashree had attained enlightenment on the 21st of March 1953, but had still not declared anything about it by 1970, so we didn't know that the 21st of March would come to hold a

acharya rajneesh

kamala nehru nagar : jabalapur (m.p.). phone : 2957

प्रिय अरुण भैया,

तुम्हारे पत्र के उत्तर में जो काठमांडू से आया था, मैंने एक पत्र पटना दिया था, आचार्य श्री के कार्यक्रम के संबंध में। पर मालुम पड़ता है, वह तुम्हें मिला नहीं।

निवेदन है कि आचार्य श्री ने काठमांडू कार्यक्रम हेतु १९, २०, २१ एवं २२ मार्च ६० की तिथियाँ निर्धारित की हैं।

आने जाने के लिए — वाराणसी तक Air Conditioned से आया और वहां से ट्रेन द्वारा काठमांडू पहुंचना। इसके लिए तो तुमने उचित व्यवस्था की होगी।

और कोई जानकारी चाहिए हो तो सूचित करना। पत्र शीघ्र देना।

शुभकामनाओं सहित।

जबलपुर
२३/१२.

विनम्र:-
शारदें कुमार

■ *English translation of Osho's letter in Hindi from page no. 80*

Beloved brother Arun,

I sent the reply to the letter that you sent from Kathmandu regarding Acharyashree's programs, to your Patna Address. But it seems that you did not receive it.

Acharyashree has chosen the dates of 19,20,21 and 22 March 1970 for programs in Kathmandu. For his travells you need to make arrangements for AC train tickets till Varanasi and the flight from there to Kathmandu.

Please let me know if you need any more information. Please reply quickly.
With good wishes,

Yours,
Arvind Kumar

special significance for all Acharyashree (Osho) lovers. He became enlightened under the Maulshree tree at Bhawartal Garden in Jabalpur, but only acknowledged it openly eighteen years later in May 1971, when he then called himself Bhagwan Rajneesh. On 26th September 1970, he started the Neo-Sannyas movement. During those eighteen years of unannounced enlightenment, he travelled extensively, giving public talks to gatherings of thousands. Acharyashree's bewitching presence, together with his mesmerizing voice, astute analytical skills and poetic style had connected thousands with him on an intellectual level. But when he saw that mere intellectual understanding wasn't enough to transform people, he decided to devise a new technique to jolt people out of their comfort zones – he started giving *sannyas*. As expected, this caused a furore among those who had simply understood him as a good orator and philosopher. And this was just what he wanted to do. As he said:

"I have chosen it [the name "Bhagwan"] *for a specific purpose, and it has been serving well, because people who used to come to me to gather knowledge, they stopped. The day I called myself "Bhagwan", they stopped. It was too much for them, it was too much for their egos, somebody calling himself "Bhagwan"? It just hurts the ego."*

Many people who had gathered around him simply out of intellectual curiosity felt betrayed by this new move, and immediately started condemning him. In fact, many of them became his staunch critics. But Bhagwan had decided to work on a deeper level. What he had wanted to share couldn't be said in words, it could only be given in a moment of great love and trust. Mind is a mechanism of doubt. So when it comes to analysis, debate, suspicion, mind is very helpful. But if one wants to move into more profound dimensions of existence, it becomes a barrier. It was a delight to listen to Bhagwan, but his words were just baits to hook us into the silent space where all the mysteries of life would unfold. By giving *sannyas* and declaring himself Bhagwan, he was challenging us to connect with him in a deeper and more meaningful way – the way of the heart.

"You ask me: Why do you call yourself Bhagwan? Why do you call yourself God?

Because I am—and because you are. And because only god is. There is no other way, there is no other way to be.

There are only two ways to give a label to life. One is the way of the realist—he calls it matter. The other is the way of the poet, the dreamer—he calls it god.

I am an unashamed poet. I'm not a realist. I call myself god, I call you god, I call rocks god, I call trees god, and the clouds god.... The whole consists of only one stuff and I have chosen to call it god, because with god you can grow, with god you can ride on great tidal waves; you can go to the other shore. God is just a glimpse of your destiny. You give personality to existence.

When I call myself god, I mean to provoke you, to challenge you. I am simply calling myself god so that you can also gather courage to recognize it. If you can recognize it in me, you have taken the first step to recognizing it in yourself.

It will be very difficult for you to recognize it in yourself, because you have always been taught to condemn yourself. You have always been taught that you are a sinner. Here I am to take all that nonsense away. My insistence is that it is only one thing that is missing in you—the courage to recognize who you are.

I call myself god to help you, to give you courage. If this man

*can be a god, why not you? I'm just like you. By calling myself god,
I am not bringing god down, I am bringing you up. I am taking
you for a high journey. I'm simply opening a door towards the
Himalayan peaks..."*

Bhagwan had told us, "I am using this word "Bhagwan"
as a method to disperse the crowd, and when its work is over,
I will drop it as well." In October, 1989 he fulfilled his promise,
and changed his name from Bhagwan Rajneesh to Osho. He often
told the story of Al Hillaj Mansoor, a Sufi mystic, who had been
beheaded simply because he declared himself to be god. This
declaration, of course, did not go down well will the Khalifas. They
chopped off his head and mutilated his body in the grossest way
possible.

Speaking on why he chose to keep quiet about his
enlightenment, Osho has said, *"I have learned much from the past
buddhas. If Jesus had kept a little quieter about being the Son of God
it would have been far more beneficial to humanity. I had made it a
point that until I stopped travelling in the country I was not going
to declare it, otherwise I would have been killed - you would not
be here.*

*Once I had finished with travelling, mixing with the masses,
moving from one town to another... For twenty years continuously
I was moving, and there was not a single bodyguard....*

*If I had declared it, I would have been killed very easily. There
would have been no problem in it; it would have been so simple.
But for twenty years I kept absolutely silent about it. I declared it
only when I saw that now I had gathered enough people who could
understand it. I had gathered enough people who were mine, who
belonged to me. I declared it only when I knew that now I could*

create my own small world and I was no more concerned with the crowds and the masses and the stupid mob."

There was a reason why Bhagwan had wanted to visit Nepal shortly before he initiated the second phase of his work – and that too, on his enlightenment day.

I started making the necessary arrangements. The tickets weren't very expensive. I still remember the plane ticket from Banaras to Kathmandu cost around only five hundred Indian rupees. The train tickets were even less expensive. The total trip could be covered in around three thousand Indian rupees. But unfortunately it was a big amount for a student like me. I asked my parents to support me financially, but they were not particularly happy about my association with Bhagwan and my ever-growing fascination for spirituality. They were scared I might drop my studies and become a full-time monk. So they declined to help me financially.

Eventually, the whole trip couldn't materialize because I couldn't afford to arrange a mere sum of three thousand rupees. I consider it the greatest failure of my life. To this day, I am not free of guilt, and despite Bhagwan's constant consolation, I won't be free of it in this lifetime.

Although we had to cancel the whole trip due to lack of funds, now I understand money wasn't as much of an issue as was my lack of trust and total surrender. Forty-two years after this event, after having built so many ashrams and communes, printed over one hundred twenty Osho books, arranged his seminars and festivals all around the world, and encircled the globe several times with his mission, I have realized when you are totally surrendered to a cause, existence will go out of its way to help you materialize your determination. Money is not an issue. Money has to come; it is the law of existence.

Today, Tapoban is worth millions of dollars. But when we started the commune twenty-seven years ago, I had hardly a few thousand rupees on me. If I had've thought about money, we wouldn't have been able to build this paradise. Recently, we have started Tapoban - Phase II. Its estimated cost is around a hundred million Nepali rupees. I still don't have that much money. But today I know temples are not built on money; they are built on the foundation of trust and devotion.

Had I been total in my surrender, existence would have taken care of everything. There were a few people who were reading Bhagwan's work in Nepal then, and there were a few other well-to-do friends of mine, from whom I could've asked for financial support. Moreover, I knew the place where my parents kept money in our house. I could've simply stolen a few thousand rupees. Had Bhagwan come to Nepal and stayed in our house, it would have not only been a blessing for me and my family, but for the entire country. The possibilities were boundless.

Bhagwan often said in jest that his work would never suffer from lack of funds, because his secretary, Laxmi, was named after the goddess of wealth. And he couldn't have been truer.

I have come to realize that while doing any existential work, if we are hindered by lack of funds, it simply means we are not total in our effort and are not surrendered to the cause. The bad karmas from my past lives had also prevented me from materializing this auspicious plan. I now know that with total surrender and effort one can even dispel the curse of bad karmas. I shall never forgive myself for my lack of determination and courage at that time.

I have seen that although we pay our respects to gurus and masters, unconsciously we go on maintaining a safe distance, because deep down we know that if we come too close to them, our lives will be transformed qualitatively and become full of joy and lightness. Regardless of what we go on saying, all of us are attached to our misery. We hold on to it dearly, as the ego thrives on misery and suffering. As Bhagwan would say, happiness is the greatest rebellion. It is the declaration of one's individuality, of rebellion against the social hypnosis which benefits society by keeping people as miserable and unhappy as possible, so they can be enslaved by the priests and politicians.

In regards to this, I remember one of the incidents from Bhagwan's life:

In his early days, he used to travel extensively around India, conducting meditation camps and giving discourses. During one of his trips, he was on the Allahabad station waiting for a train and talking with his secretary, Ma Madhu. As it often happens on Indian train stations, a beggar came close to them and started disturbing Bhagwan who was deeply involved in his conversation with Ma Madhu. It was one of Bhagwan's unique qualities; whenever he was talking to anybody, he was totally involved with that person. The audience would feel as if the whole world had faded, and that Bhagwan was showering his whole attention on the listener.

When the beggar didn't get any attention from Bhagwan, he started screaming. Bhagwan stopped talking, gazed at the beggar deeply, and asked him, "Tell me, what do you want?"

Bhagwan's unblinking gaze, and the totality with which he had asked the question, suddenly scared the beggar. He started trembling, and moved backwards.

Bhagwan asked him again, "Come forward and tell me what you want."

Then he moved further away, and replied, "I don't want anything."

The atmosphere became grave for a while. Bhagwan closed his eyes and became silent. He broke his silence some time later, only after he was seated on the train. He said, "Great compassion had arisen within me after hearing that beggar's plea. Existence would have given him anything he had asked for. He also had good karmas from his past life. But he was afraid and he ran away. This happens to me every day. I want to give something to people but they become afraid. People are not just greedy to share things, which is understandable, but what I can't comprehend is their inability to accept things. Anyone whose eyes I gaze into and to whom I want to give something, they become afraid and run away."

What happened to this beggar has happened to me, also. Three times I fell into the trap of my mind, and missed the opportunity to accept Bhagwan's invitation to come close to him. Had I not missed those opportunities, they would have transformed my life radically and illuminated my being.

When I met Bhagwan again in 1972, I wept at his feet, and repented for having missed those rare and precious opportunities. I had been so frustrated that I was even ready to end my life.

Bhagwan, incarnation of compassion, has always consoled me and given me faith and courage to live. He said, "No, it is not your fault. You were a student and did not have any money. I understand that it was difficult for you to manage it."

But I was inconsolable. Every time I met him, I was full of regret for those missed opportunities. Once, he said, "Arun, in my previous lives I committed similar blunders. It is natural for an unconscious person to commit mistakes. Just learn from your mistakes and try not to repeat them. Whenever existence gives you a chance in future, don't be afraid. Be ready to take total risk. When you surrender totally, the unknown force will come and support you, and miracles will happen."

This is the greatest teaching I have learned from my beloved master, but I must confess humbly that I couldn't adhere to his advice totally. In spite of his great encouragement and support, and my deepest longing, I still commit mistakes. I have realized while it comes to the Master Disciple relationship, one shouldn't listen to the mind. Mind is the great deceiver.

I told Bhagwan that if he gave me another date, I would definitely organize something in Kathmandu. He replied, "I have started giving *sannyas*. People have started coming to me from around the world and I have stopped travelling. I have to help and work on my *sannyasins* on the astral level as well. This is not possible while travelling, so I have to confine myself to a room."

After starting the Neo-Sannyas movement, Bhagwan confined himself to a room in Woodlands Apartments. He cancelled all his appointments, and conducted only two ten-day meditation camps, in April and October, each year at Mount Abu. This made me even sadder, as it meant that he would never come to Nepal. In one of the *darshans*, I rolled on his feet and started to weep.

Bhagwan put his hand on my head, and said, "Don't cry. I promise you that I will come to Nepal before I leave my body. You have so much love that I will have to come to Nepal. But I cannot come now. You do my work. Make at least a thousand *sannyasins* in Nepal. This way many people will be able to benefit from my visit. Work hard and create the atmosphere where I will be able to work. This is my promise."

When he had said this to me, I had not even taken *sannyas* myself. And he was telling me to make a thousand *sannyasins*!

He repeated his promise on the 30th of June 1985, when I had a private *darshan* at Lao Tzu House in Rajneeshpuram. Rajneeshpuram was the dream city. Now that Bhagwan had moved to America, I couldn't believe he would ever come to Nepal. But the promise of an enlightened master isn't fickle like the promise of a politician, who just manipulates people to win votes and secure a good future for himself. Hoping against all odds, I continued preparing Nepal for his visit, and worked as he had instructed. By a miraculous intervention of existence, Bhagwan fulfilled his promise by coming to Nepal in 1986. By that time, we already had over a thousand *sannyasins* there.

Missing Mount Abu Camp

In those days, I used to write frequently to Bhagwan. One early September morning in 1971, I received a letter which was written in reply to my last one. The letter was dictated by Bhagwan, and written by Swami Yog Chinmaya, who was Bhagwan's secretary then.

"Dear Arun,
Your letter, full of your thirst, anguish and restlessness, reached Bhagwan in time.
He says you should definitely attend the meditation camp at Mount Abu, Rajasthan, from September 25th to October 2nd, 1971.
Bhagwanshree says sannyas initiation is waiting for you. He not only wants to make you his own, as you pleaded in the letter, but to take you into the mysterious realms of the inner journey, which alone can provide solace to all your anguish.

You should start making preparations for the camp. Come to the Mount Abu Camp. You have thirst and longing. But that is not enough. It's time to take a jump. <u>You will encounter a lot of obstacles, but if you surrender yourself totally to existence, you will be able to overcome all obstacles.</u> Surrender to existence, and you will be filled with tremendous energy.

For further information on the camp, please send a blank envelope with your address on it to the following address:

Jeevan Jagriti Kendra
Dye Chem. Corporation
Khadia, Char Rasta
Ahamdaba - 1

If you have not read the book Jin Khoja Tin Paiya, then buy a copy from any Motilal Banarasidas bookshop, and read it.

Don't miss the camp. Immense possibilities are waiting for you.

With the blessings of Bhagwanshree,
Yog Chinmaya
21-08-1971
PS - Bring along a set of ochre clothes for the camp."

I read the letter, and sat stunned for a long time. Bhagwan had asked to underline the part about obstacles. I knew it was about time to take the jump, but I felt uncertain. A strange fear took hold of me. When Bhagwan decided to give initiation, he

prepared names and *malas* for fifty people who he felt certain would take *sannyas*. I had been one of this fifty. This was a rare chance, and demanded great courage, as *sannyas* was an exclusive affair in those days. One year earlier, in September, Bhagwan had

स्वामी योग चिन्मय,
भगवान श्री रजनीश के सचिव.
NEO-SANNYAS INTERNATIONAL
(नव सन्न्यास अन्तर्राष्ट्रीय).

A-1 WOODLAND PEDDAR ROAD BOMBAY 26   PHONE 382184

प्रियवर अरुण,

प्रेम व प्रणाम।

तुम्हारा प्यास, पुकार, पीड़ा व आकुलता से भरा हुआ पत्र भगवान श्री को समय पर ही मिल गया था।

उनका कहना है कि तुम २५ सित० से २अक्टू० १९६१ को माउन्ट आबू (राजस्थान) में हो रहे विशेष ध्यान योग साधना शिविर में अवश्य ही आ जाओ।

भगवान श्री ने यह भी कहा है कि सन्न्यास-दीक्षा भी तुम्हारी प्रतीक्षा कर रहा है।

भगवान श्री न केवल तुम्हें अपनाना ही चाहते हैं वरन् उस गूढ़ व गहन अन्तर्यात्रा में भी ले जाना चाहते हैं जहाँ और केवल जहाँ ही समाधान का स्रोत है।

भगवान श्री की पुकार सुनकर तुम शीघ्र ही शिविर की तैयारी में लग जाओ।

क्योंकि केवल अभीप्सा ही काफी नहीं है, अपने आपको दाँव पर भी लगाना होगा।

अपनी बाधाओं का ख्याल न करना।

प्रभु समर्पण तुम्हें आश्चर्यजनक शक्तियों से भर जायेगा।

शिविर की विस्तृत जानकारी हेतु एक पता लिखा

खाली लिफाफा निम्न पते पर प्रेषित करके
प्राप्त कर लो:

जीवन जागृति केंद्र, डायकेम कार्पोरेशन
खाडिया चार रास्ता, अहमदाबाद-१

यदि 'जिन खोजा तिन पाइयां' न मिले तो
मोतीलाल बनारसी दास की दुकान से खरीद कर
पढ़ना।

शिविर चूकना नहीं।
विराट सम्भावनाएं तुम्हारे लिए प्रतीक्षारत है।

भगवान श्री के शुभ आशीर्षों के साथ

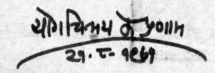

योगचिन्मय के प्रणाम
२१.८.१९६१

उनहरः शिविर में गेरुवा वस्त्र बनवा के लाना।

initiated the first batch of his *sannyasins* at a meditation camp in Manali. But out of those fifty people, only six had been courageous enough to be initiated.

In those days, *sannyas* had tougher rules. The initiates were to wear an ochre *kurta* and *lungi* all the time, even during their college /office hours. I was still a university student, and when Bhagwan summoned me for *sannyas*, I imagined myself going to college in my ochre *lungi-kurta*. Even as I was imagining, I felt embarrassed. I didn't know how I would explain myself to my friends and professors. But as Bhagwan had now called me, I had to go whether I was prepared for it or not.

Apprehensively, I started making preparations for the camp. My mother was visiting her parents at Mujaffarpur, Bihar, in India, at that time. When I disclosed my plan to go to Mount Abu to my parents, something very dramatic happened. In the postscript, Bhagwan had instructed me to bring ochre clothes. My mother had briefly sighted the letter, and had been upset ever since. Now, when I told her of my decision to go to the camp the same day, she had a heart attack. She was a heart patient and she had a few attacks earlier as well. She had always been afraid that if I would embark upon a spiritual path, she would lose her only son forever. Of course, my parents' fear was reasonable, since traditional *sannyas* required the initiate to renounce all worldly affairs, sever all relationships and to meditate in solitude. Bhagwan's vision was to bridge the gap between the mundane and the sacred. He spoke of this new vision of *sannyas*, which combined the art of enjoying the finest pleasures of this world and moving into the finer ecstasy of the otherworld, together, in a harmonious rhythm. His teachings spoke of an ultimate synthesis, which went beyond the dichotomy of flesh and soul. He often gave the example of a

lotus flower to illustrate his teaching. A lotus rises from the marsh, and yet remains untouched by it. When rain lands on its velvety petals, it forms droplets, like mercury, without making the petals wet. This is how, Bhagwan said, a *sannyasin* was to live - amidst the world and yet untouched by it, radiating the grace of the otherworld. But at that time the idea sounded too grand to be true. I couldn't fathom the gravity of his teaching, and it was only natural that my mother would doubt that such a way of life was possible.

When she had heart attack, the event was so cataclysmic that we all were pulled into the vortex, and forgot about my imminent *sannyas* for a while. We had to hospitalise my mother immediately. As I stood in the hospital foyer, reflecting on the situation, I decided to go to the camp regardless – Bhagwan had specifically mentioned that I would encounter a lot of problems but if my determination would be total, I will find way out to reach him.

I walked up to my father, and told him that I had to go. He was visibly disappointed by my decision. He scrutinized me with mute anger, and said, "Why are you such a tyrant?! Your mother has just had a serious heart attack, and you want to pester me with threats of *sannyas*?"

I could totally understand his loathing, but there was no way I could make him understand that what waited me at Mount Abu was what I had been praying for, for lives together. I didn't even understand clearly what it was, but all the same, I knew it was there. Bhagwan had written in the letter, "Immense possibilities are waiting for you." Had I been able to get to that camp, I would have been totally transformed. But sadly, my own karma prevented me from making it. This is one of the biggest regrets of my life.

But it wasn't an easy choice to make. My parents had the fear that if I were to take *sannyas*, they would lose me forever. So, naturally, as time progressed, existence tested my decision to take *sannyas* even more severely. I couldn't bear to meet my father's eyes. I couldn't tell what made him sadder - my mother's heart attack or the fact that I was going to take *sannyas*. I had not intended to hurt them but the choices had to be made. Kabir has sang beautifully that only those who are courageous enough to burn down their own houses could follow him. The older I get, the more I understand how true that statement really is. Of course, Kabir is not asking you to literally burn down the house. He means that unless we can bear to let go of our closest attachments, we cannot tread the path of spirituality. If you want the truth, you must love it above everything. You must be ready to stake everything for it. Naturally, I was most attached to my mother. The fact that I had to brood over the decision of *sannyas* in the hospital, where she was hospitalised for a severe heart attack, is quite symbolic. It wasn't easy for them, but it wasn't easy for me either.

I couldn't sleep at all that night. On the one hand, I was the only son, and my mother was lying unconscious in a hospital bed, and on the other, there was Bhagwan and the unmistakable promise of transformation. I remembered again that he had underscored the line, "You will face a lot of obstacles, but if you surrender yourself to existence, you will be able to overcome *all* obstacles." So he had foreseen that I would be thrown into such a dilemma. I kept tossing and turning the whole night. As dawn broke, I decided it was, indeed, about time I took the jump.

I went to the hospital and told my father I was leaving for Mount Abu. At first, he tried to reason with me to stay back, but when he realized I was unshakable in my decision, he quivered with anger and threw three one-hundred rupee notes in my face, saying, "You are a disgrace to our family. I hope you go and never return."

The words stabbed my heart. I felt weak in the knees. I went to see my mother. She was still lying unconscious.

I walked out of the hospital, and straight to the railway station to catch the train. It was monsoon, and heavy flood had disrupted most of the train service. But I was fortunate enough to find the only train that left for Patna exactly at 8:00 in the morning. From Patna, I had a reservation on the Toofan mail train for Mount Abu. But I had wanted to see my mother for one last time, so before going to the station, I went to the hospital. She had regained consciousness, and was out of danger. I touched her feet and bade her goodbye. Both of us felt betrayed by words; there wasn't much to say to each other.

I arrived at the station half an hour before departure. But as I was sitting on the platform, an idea struck me; since I was going to be with Bhagwan, why don't I carry a camera with me? I remembered that a friend of mine who lived close to the station had a camera, so I went to his place to borrow it. As I was returning from his house and climbing over the bridge, which was two minutes' walk from the station, I saw my train leaving. Usually Indian trains never arrive or depart on time, but strangely enough that day the train left at sharp eight. I ran as fast as my feet could carry me, but soon the train gained momentum and it seemed unlikely I could catch it at all.

As the train went away in its rhythmic, monotonous pace, I reached the threshold of the station, sweaty and panting. I kept staring at the giant locomotive, which became smaller and smaller until it appeared like a small dot on the horizon. I couldn't understand what had just happened. Had I been only fifteen seconds earlier, I would have caught the train, or had I left my suitcase on the platform, I could have managed to get on. I went to the booking office to see if I could catch any other train, but sadly there weren't any other trains leaving for Patna that day because of the flood. I went to a taxi stand to see if I could take a taxi. The taxi driver said he would charge me three hundred rupees, which was all that I had. I should have given him the money and gone to Patna anyway, but this was one among many obstacles Bhagwan was talking about, and this time I failed. I returned home, my parents were overjoyed to see me, and my father said, "See, God doesn't want you to go, either."

I couldn't sleep *that* night either. The next day, I woke up early and caught a train to Patna. When I reached Patna, my friends had already left and my reservation had been cancelled. I tried to enter the carriage for people who were travelling without reservation, but as fate would have it, it was so overcrowded I couldn't manage to get on.

Bhagwan had forewarned me of these obstacles, and clearly told me that if I surrendered myself to existence I could overcome them all. But despite that, I could not gather enough trust. In Buddhist texts they speak of *maar*, an inauspicious external manifestation of one's own fear that prevents meditators from going into deeper states of meditation. I knew that all these obstacles were nothing but the external manifestation of my own deep-seated fear of transformation. Had I been courageous enough, I could have managed one way or another to reach Mount Abu. Many years later, when I remembered a few of my past lives, I gained a deeper insight into this event. In my immediate past life,

I was a maharaja in one of the states of India. During that time, I was a great hunter and had killed hundreds of innocent animals just for fun. I had been shackled by this karma in my spiritual pursuit. Despite my willingness to go to Mount Abu camp, I was still unable to go because I didn't have enough *punya*, or good karma in my account. Bhagwan was aware of this, and therefore had emphasized his communication regarding obstacles. I needed great will power to break out of these shackles, but still I couldn't muster enough of it. Now I know that if you have a great will power, you can overcome all obstacles of past karmas.

Later, Bhagwan told me had I been trusting enough, I would have undergone a great transformation at the Mount Abu camp. Of course, it sounds like a fabrication now, but I cannot say in enough words how I regret this event. It remains the greatest failure of my life. Until I took *sannyas* in 1974 in Poona, I had to go through many torturous events in my life, and I was driven to the verge of suicide. In fact, suicide seemed to be the only solution to all my anguish. It was exactly in this state of absolute helplessness and unspeakable anguish that I met Bhagwan in 1974 in Poona, and took *sannyas*.

PART III

PUNE DIARIES

Pune Diaries

It was in the middle of the seventies when an orange ocean sprang forth in the heart of a small city on the Deccan plateau. In the beginning it looked just like a tiny spring, but it was soon to overflow from the boundaries of this small city, Pune, and later stretch far and wide across the world, bringing back waves of seekers from all over the globe.

During the seventeenth century, Pune was the main seat of the Peshwas of the great Maratha Empire, and was one of the power centres of Hindustan, lasting almost a century, before the British invaded this land of the proud. To this day, Pune sings the glories of its great warriors and rulers who inhabited it. But in 1974, it received a new guest, who was unlike all its former residents, and who changed its course forever, establishing the city as one of the major spiritual centres of the world.

Nobody knows why Bhagwan chose to stay in Pune and establish his first ashram there. Some say it was due to Meher Baba, an enlightened mystic, having made Pune his spiritual abode, and leaving behind an atmosphere of his presence and energy. But whatever the reason, it all started with one house, Lao Tzu House, which was to be Bhagwan's new residence and the seed of the future ashram. It had been purchased from a maharaja and given to Bhagwan by Ma Mukta, a Greek disciple who was the heiress of a rich ship merchant in Greece.

When he first moved there from Bombay, his body didn't respond well to the climate in the city; he fell ill and couldn't talk for a few days. There was a rumour he would go back. So after years of waiting for an ashram, and now having one just in its infancy, the people around Bhagwan were uncertain of its fate. But after a few weeks of rest, one fine evening he asked the residents to gather on the balcony of Lao Tzu House, and he commenced the evening discourse. *My Way, the Way of the White Clouds*, one of my favourite books, was then begun.

The house had been purchased, the master had settled in, and so began the great Orange Revolution. Bhagwan started giving daily discourses, at first in the evening, and later, in the morning, initiating new *sannyasins* on the porch of his carport, designing new meditation techniques, and conducting *darshans* flavoured with his blazing energy. He was giving his total energy as the midwife for the *new man*, while his ashram became the womb.

Never before had a spiritual movement been so juicy and life affirmative. Bhagwan embraced everything that life had to offer, condemning nothing. He didn't project spiritual dreams with promises of meetings with gods, or space in heaven beside his throne. He was creating simple humans who enjoyed all the colours of life, and was teaching a new art of aesthetics, sensitivity and awareness, with which he believed life should be approached, and thus revered. Everything and everyone had a space in Bhagwan's ark, and he left no stone unturned in showing humanity how unconsciously and miserably it was living. Bhagwan spoke on everything from the ancient wisdom of the Upanishads to modern man's most recent dilemmas, from sex to superconsciousness, and from the latest discoveries of science to the most refined and subtle nuances of the esoteric.

Soon the word spread of this new god-man living in Pune, and every heart that had a seed of divine madness was pulled by this magnet. Thousands started pouring in from all over the globe, and it was no longer a surprise to spot an orange-clad Rajneeshee at any airport in the world. Shree Rajneesh Ashram became the haven for the modern man's spiritual quest, and Pune was the place to be

The Dark Clouds
of Karma

On the morning of the 10th of October in 1974, I arrived in Pune, finally ready to jump into the orange wave and dissolve into it forever. But now that I was ready to take *sannyas*, a painful memory of my past flared up before my eyes. The last three years, after I had missed the Mount Abu camp, had been the most difficult days of my life. To be honest, misery had dug its nails so deeply into my life that I often felt suicide was the only way to escape this wretched existence. Bhagwan still shone like a bright moon in the skies of my heart, but the clouds of my karma were so dark they prevented me from seeing his radiance - so dark I couldn't even see a trace of a silver lining.

In 1972, during my meeting with Bhagwan at Woodlands in Bombay, he had given me two clear instructions before he would give me *sannyas*. Firstly, he told me to complete my engineering studies as I was in the final years. He said that after *sannyas* there would be such a drastic change in my life that I might not be able to complete my Degree. Secondly, he told me to build a house in Kathmandu, which, as fate was to have it, became the Mecca for the Osho movement in Nepal.

"After that," he told to me, "you can come and live in my ashram."

I did complete the engineering course, but with enormous difficulty. Engineering hadn't been my subject of choice. I felt daunted by the dry mathematical accuracy it demanded; I didn't have a natural flair for it. On the contrary, I identified more with the poetic fluidity of the romantics. And now that I had started reading Bhagwan's work, my relationship with engineering only soured. Bhagwan addressed my quest directly and intimately. By comparison, engineering seemed far-fetched and alien to the reality of life. But on completion of my course, Bhagwan had promised me that I could finally live with him in the ashram. He had also told me that engineering would come of use in building his future ashrams. These promises were my only drive, but even then, I struggled relentlessly.

In retrospect, I see that if there was anyone to be blamed for my misery, it was only myself. From very early on, I felt disenchanted by the ways of the world; I found no joy in what the world called achievements. In my heart, I was a solitary recluse. I had always found more meaning and nourishment watching the tranquil Ganges, losing myself to the resounding silence of the Himalayan valleys, and wandering alone amidst the dew-kissed wildflowers. By the strange will of destiny, I've been unfortunate when it comes to relationships. I now understand that had I been content in my marriage, I would have been deprived of a deeper spiritual search. It was my destiny to embrace the whole world as my family. But wonderful as it may sound, the sense of universal brotherhood comes at the cost of personal relationships.

Although I knew I could never be content raising a family and being confined within that small boundary of relationships, I had neither enough clarity nor courage to revolt against my parents' will to get me married. I married. And that, combined with my promise to build a house in Kathmandu, suddenly threw me into a vortex of problems. I do not want to write much about my marriage, as every story has two sides to it, and I would not be able to do justice to the story by writing it from my perspective alone.

Osho has often said that a fish in the ocean is not thirsty. Any suffering is merely an indication that we are straying from our path. I suffered much during that time because I was doing everything that was contrary to my nature. Solitude, which had been such a precious part of my life, had been invaded violently by the mundane responsibilities that came with marriage. And I repeat that I alone was to be blamed for this, because I had always known in my heart that my contentment came from meditation. Raising a family without disturbing my inner balance was the art I hadn't yet mastered. Some yogis who have achieved inner centring can partake in the world without much difficulty, but I had not reached that point.

I think if I hadn't met Osho, I would have still managed to drag through the marriage. But in his presence, I had tasted bliss, and this taste was addictive. He had shown me how content and blissful one could be, and now that I'd had a glimpse of that bliss, everything that the world calls achievement paled in comparison.

As I struggled to fit into the patterns of the 'normal' world, my anguish deepened. Like a fish moving further away from the ocean, the more I got entangled in the world and becoming more 'successful', the louder became the song of despair in my heart. Meanwhile, I had started working as a licensed engineer at NCCN, a government construction company, earning barely enough to maintain my family and myself. In accord with Bhagwan's wish, I managed to construct a small two-room house in Tahachal, Kathmandu, with support from my parents. The day we moved into that house, I felt that my conditions were fulfilled, and I should go to my guru. So the next morning I departed on a bus at six o'clock with a month's salary, which was equivalent to four hundred Indian rupees. I had applied for three-month's unpaid leave from my office, and left before it was even approved. I knew they would not approve it readily, so I just lodged the application and left for Pune. When I reached Patna, many of my friends came to receive me. Some had become doctors, and others, engineers. I told them I was going to Pune to take *sannyas*, and eight of them were ready to come with me.

When I left for Pune, the song of despair in my heart had reached its crescendo. Many nights I stayed awake and wept bitterly. I was not doing justice to myself or those around me; I was playing a role I wasn't meant to play. But by then, I had already sunk neck-deep into the marsh, into which I had jumped of my own free will. I saw no way but to accept the slow death or end it all by committing suicide. I had thrown myself into the strom of suffering. The question was, did I want to suffer it the whole way or end it abruptly in the middle? There was no way out.

When I arrived at Pune again in 1974, I reached Bhagwan in this state of utter hopelessness. I had no future, and my past had totally worn me out. I flopped like a dead bird at his feet.

Sannyas:
The New Birth

Bhagwan had already prepared my *sannyas* name four years ago. As he was writing down my name on the *sannyas* certificate, I was weeping uncontrollably. For lives I had searched for peace in my heart, and for lives I had missed it. Sitting close to Bhagwan on the Lao Tzu House carport porch that day, my deepest anguish burst open. It is magical what a master can do to you. He alone can walk through that secret pathway in our heart, which we are afraid of revealing to anyone else. Sitting at his feet, bathed in his grace, my heart, which had sought love in so many places and failed each time, throbbed joyfully in recognition of the beloved.

Bhagwan put the *mala* around my neck and touched my third eye with his thumb. I felt a strong current of energy. It was unlike anything I had felt before in my life. A channel opened

Swami Anand Arun receiving shaktipat from Osho at Pune, India.

through my third eye and a strong wave of energy washed over me. Bhagwan used to wear a plain white robe in those days. But as he touched my forehead, everything around me turned vibrant orange, including Bhagwan's gown and the walls of the porch, which had been painted white. I closed my eyes, the wave of energy repeatedly welling inside me; I had lost all sense of time. The huge dam of repressed traumas had burst open; I kept wailing. My friends who were taking initiation that evening later told me they couldn't hear most of what Bhagwan told them because of my loud and disturbing screams. I wept until the anguish melted and became tears. My whole body became soaked with tears and sweat.

Laxmi and Mukta tried to hold and soothe me. But I was inconsolable. Each cell of my body was weeping. I knew that Bhagwan had caressed my back several times, but that's all I can remember. The carport porch, where Bhagwan used to give *sannyas* then, could accommodate about twenty people only. Apart from Laxmi, Mukta and a few other *sannyasins* who recorded *darshan*, there were nine of us who had come to attend the ten-day meditation camp.

In Pune, there used to be a ten-day meditation camp from the eleventh to the twentieth of every month. The camp charge in those days was one hundred rupees, which covered meditation, Bhagwan's lectures, dormitory accommodation in Somji Estate near the ashram, and three meals a day. All of my eight friends had enrolled in the camp and we stayed together in the dormitory. After the journey there, I had only two hundred rupees left on me, and as I wanted to stay longer, I asked Jayanti Bhai, the camp coordinator, to give me a discount. Ever so kindly, he gave me fifty percent discount for the camp, which was overwhelmingly generous and a great help.

Jayanti Bhai was a very kind-hearted person who had come to dedicate his whole life to Bhagwan. He had been a businessman of great repute from Ahmedabad, but had suffered a troubled marriage, and because of his social stature he daren't look at another woman. Bhagwan was well aware of this, and advised him to find a partner. Sometime later, Jayanti Bhai fell in love with Prem, who was a few decades younger than him. She was in love with him, also, and when Bhagwan came to know of it, he asked them to be together. For the first time in his life, Jayanti Bhai was truly happy, but the relationship became a source of humiliation for him back home. Despite this, he remained selflessly devoted to Bhagwan, and later, when Prem fell in love with another man, he supported both of them openheartedly without any jealousy. Such generosity of heart only comes to those who have experienced love in its fullness. Being with Osho, listening to him, and meditating together, our love should purify every day, and it should be free from jealousy and guilt. Jayanti Bhai was certainly an example of this.

When we returned to Somji Estate where the ashram had set up a dormitory for the regular monthly camp, I was still in a state of trance. Except for Drs. Sunil and Mishra, all the other friends were returning home after the camp. Sunil and Mishra had decided to stay on with me for three months and they were interested in silent retreat.

Sunil mentioned to Bhagwan he had started having a problem with his eyesight while doing Dynamic meditation. Bhagwan suggested he try other meditations, but Sunil loved Dynamic, so Bhagwan asked what his physician's opinion was. "He says I should discontinue Dynamic meditation, but I love it and don't want to drop it."

"So, it means you will end up becoming Surdas," replied Bhagwan. "And Surdas, I love. He was such a beautiful man, so totally devoted to Krishna. Don't worry, and continue Dynamic meditation." Sunil continues to do the meditation to this day, and nothing damaging has happened to his eyesight.

Incidentally, there was yet another friend of mine who was in an even greater dilemma.

"Bhagwan, my family is pressing me to get married. What shall I do?" He asked.

"Who is pressing you?" Bhagwan enquired.

"My mother."

Bhagwan chuckled and said, "My mother, too, is pressing me to marry. Whenever she comes to meet me, she says everything else is fine, but why am I reluctant to get married. Mothers are there to press you, but don't make the mistake of giving in."

Immediately after, another friend also asked, "Bhagwan, shall I get married?"

"Definitely," replied Bhagwan. "You should get married."

The reply surprised him. Bhagwan went on, "If you get a good wife, you will have a very happy life. And if she turns out to be a difficult one, you will become a philosopher like Socrates. So you are in a win-win situation. Marry by all means."

My friend asked, "You just said *you* won't marry, and now you are suggesting to *me* to do so. Why?"

"I am not married, but I don't go around asking anyone whether or not I should get married," Bhagwan smiled and replied. "You are asking me the question and it shows that you have a desire to get married. And when there is desire, it is better to experience it rather than suppressing it and depending upon others' opinion."

rajneesh

SHREE RAJNEESH ASHRAM, 17, KOREGAON PARK POONA 1 ● PHONE: 22845. 28127.

swami anand arun
स्वामी आनन्द अरुण

11.10.1974

Swami Anand Arun's sannyas certificates.

When we walked out of the ashram that day, I was still in a state of bliss. In fact, I was blissed out for the next three months and did not have a total control over my body and mind. I remembered Bhagwan had told me I wouldn't be able to complete engineering after taking *sannyas*. I had not realized why he had said that, but once I took *sannyas*, I became so intoxicated I couldn't even take care of my body; it would have been difficult to complete my studies. I recall that evening a friend of mine, Dubey *jee*, who was obsessed with philosophical questions, had asked a few far-fetched questions of Bhagwan. Bhagwan had cut him short, and said meditators should ask questions related to their growth rather than fabricating far-fetched, philosophical queries. Dubey *jee*'s pride had apparently been hurt, and when we were returning, he threw away the *mala* in anger in the darkness. We looked all around, but couldn't find it that night. The next morning, we found it hanging on a tree.

When I had introduced my eight friends during *darshan* that night, Bhagwan had thrown me a wicked smile, and asked, "Have you all come of your own accord, or has Arun forced you to come here?"

I replied, "They have come of their own accord."

Out of these friends, Sunil and Mishra had already taken *sannyas* at Mount Abu camp. The other six were interested because of us.

Walking down the moonlit paths of Pune, in the shadows of tall, ancient trees, my trance grew sweeter and sweeter. When we reached our dormitory, we were so high and looked so fresh that none of us wanted to sleep, so we talked late into the night about *sannyas* and what Bhagwan had said to us. We were throbbing with ecstasy and uncontrollable joy. I felt a deep contentment within; silently, I offered my gratitude to Bhagwan, and closed my eyes. A fathomless bliss awaited me. As the silence of the night deepened, still drowned in the pool of joy, I fell asleep.

The next morning, I woke up a new man.

Where was the heaviness that had weighed me down all my life?

The next few days were very mystical. One night, when I was resting in the dormitory, unexpectedly, I saw Bhagwan's smiling face on the ceiling. His benevolent smile filled me with joy. This was the first time his image had appeared in front of me, and I felt his intense presence in my room. The pale moonbeams flooded the room. In that hazy, moonlit night, I watched Bhagwan smile at me with enormous love.

To Stay or
to Leave

It was the end of the ten-day camp, my first meditation camp after taking *sannyas*. Those who were leaving for their homes had gathered for the evening leaving *darshan*. We sat in rows, facing Bhagwan. I was beaming ecstatically. It was magical. The soft yellow light of the moon filtered through the trees. After ten days of rigorous meditation, we had all become light and fresh as children. In the beauty of the evening, everybody appeared even more radiant. Just ten days before, on the day of *sannyas*, I was so sad and crying bitterly, disturbing the entire *darshan*. But ten days of meditation had brought about a radical change in my psyche. I was overjoyed for no reason, and I couldn't contain it. Every fibre of my body was dancing in ecstasy. Everybody could feel it. The joy was out of control; it was maddening me. Bhagwan looked at me, called me to sit close to him, and chuckled, "Nepali *Babu* is in ecstasy."

How much had changed in ten days! Those ten days felt like ten years. When I had arrived in Pune, I had been sad, dull and hopeless. A few days in the presence of my master and in his buddhafield, and I was relieved of the pains and anguish of lives. I was bursting with joy. I sat down near his feet as he continued talking to the *sannyasins*. All of my friends had come for the departing *darshan*. All had been transformed in those ten days. I watched Sunil as he asked for Bhagwan's permission to undertake a three-month silent retreat. Tears of gratitude glistened in his eyes. Bhagwan said since there was no space at the ashram, he could go to Lonavala, where a devotee of Bhagwan, Harekrishna Agrawal, had a small ashram in the forest. It was located mid-way between Bombay and Pune, and was a hill station with a great deal of greenery. Bhagwan told Sunil to try silence for just twenty-one days. Sunil nodded happily. Bhagwan called Laxmi Ma to give him the address of the ashram. Harekrishna Agrawal was not only a great devotee of Bhagwan, but also a very charitable person. Bhagwan's *sannyasins* could stay free of charge at his ashram. There was no common mess; either they had to cook their own meal, or eat what the guard of the ashram prepared, which was very basic food. It cost one rupee per meal, which was a very economic option.

Once the camp was over, the attendees had to vacate Somji Estate dormitory. Around sixteen people were living permanently in the ashram. On the weekends, a few visitors would arrive from Pune and Bombay. Since there were now only two buildings in the ashram, Krishna House and Lao Tzu House, the camp attendees and visitors had to manage accommodation on their own once the camp was over.

That morning, we had been told that all participants had to

leave Somji Estate at 7:00 the next morning. I was already short of cash, and had no idea where I would be staying from the next day. Ma Big Prem and her American boyfriend were renting a room in Krishna House. They paid the ashram forty rupees, which included their meals, and they were part-time volunteers there. Over the days, we had bonded well. When they came to know about my situation, they offered to help me. They had a small balcony outside their room, and they said I could sleep there if I liked. Of course, I thought it was a great privilege. After seeing off my friends, I returned to the ashram with my belongings. Both Sunil and Mishra had decided to try a twenty-one-day silent retreat at Lonavala. The other friends had returned to Patna. After the farewell, I suddenly felt a pang of loneliness; I was a stranger in Pune, with nothing but one hundred and fifty rupees and the desire to live with my master forever. My friends were also sad to leave me behind. They gave me their leftover toothpaste, shampoo and whatever else they thought was going to be useful to me. We hugged each other for a long time before they departed.

When I arrived at the ashram gate with my suitcase, I was still quite emotional. Swami Anand Swabhav and Laxmi were in the Krishna House office. It was already evening; the crimson clouds were turning grey. I told Laxmi about Ma Big Prem's offer, and asked her permission. But even before she could answer, Swami Anand Swabhav replied harshly, "No, you can't. You have to make your own arrangements."

I said I was short of funds, and Bhagwan had permitted me to stay at Pune. Swabhav *jee* came from a well-off family. They had a large stake in Nestle India. Sadly, this wealth hadn't allowed him to experience the life of a poor seeker. It had already become dark. On the verge of tears, I told Swabhav *jee* I did not know where I could stay overnight. He was quick to reply, "Go to Lonavala with your friends. You can stay there for free."

I told him Bhagwan hadn't advised me to go for a silent retreat rather he had told me to stay at Pune. So if he would grant me a *darshan* that evening, I could ask for Bhagwan's permission, and leave. Swabhav *jee* replied that Bhagwan was generous to everyone, and did not know the practical details of running the ashram. I should just leave for Lonavala, he repeated.

"But it's already dark. I can only leave tomorrow," I replied meekly.

"There is a night train. Just leave."

I asked Laxmi, saying it would be difficult for me to locate the Lonavala ashram at night. So it would be more practical for me to leave in the morning. Although Swabhav *jee* was adamant I should leave straight away, Laxmi was kind enough to allow me to stay overnight. As I was walking out of the office, Swabhav *jee* repeated, "But make sure you leave the ashram tomorrow morning."

That was my first night in the buddhafield. Ma Big Prem and her boyfriend were very kind and rather surprised by Swabhav *jee's* harshness. They brought their dinner into the room and shared it with me. It was not allowed that food be shared with the visitors in the ashram. Although I was very happy to be in the buddhafield, I was very sad and uncertain about my future. I had given up everything to be able to live in Bhagwan's presence, but the encounter with Swabhav *jee* had left me disheartened and feeling hopeless. The next morning, Big Prem shared morning tea with me, which again wasn't permitted in the ashram. I went to attend Bhagwan's discourse with a very heavy and sad heart. The discourse was on the upper verandah of Lao Tzu House. I

could not enjoy it at all because of my fear and the uncertainty of the future. I cried through the entire discourse, after which, still tearful, I left the ashram for Lonavala.

It was about a two-hour train ride there. Lonavala looked like Nepal. It was a sparsely-populated mountainous town, surrounded by a lush green forest. I hired a curricle, and headed for Harekrishna Agrawal Ashram. The driver was a friendly man who loved chatting. I was still very sad. He asked me why I was going there. Finding a kindred spirit, I recounted my story briefly to him. When we arrived at the ashram gate, I took out fifty paisa and handed it to the man. He rubbed his hands hesitantly and said, "Please allow me to do this service for you. I will consider myself fortunate for being able to help a seeker like you."

I urged him to take the money, but he refused. I was so touched by the kindness of this poor driver, who then said, "Give me a blessing instead of money."

The curricle driver had more love in his heart than did Swabhav *jee*. This has surprised me continuously that many Osho *sannyasins* who have been meditating for a long time, and traditional *sannyasins* as well, some of whom even claim to be enlightened, when it comes to the crunch, don't have a drop of compassion for people in need. The practice of dry and automaton-like meditation will not bear fruit, if our hearts are just dead seeds.

Haunted Silence
at Lonavala

Both Drs. Sunil and Mishra were happy to welcome me at Lonavala ashram. All three of us had been feeling lonely, and we were delighted to meet each other. The ashram, in the middle of a dense, tropical forest, had no canteen; everyone was supposed to cook their meals in their own rooms. Alternatively, the ashram guard, who prepared simple meals in his own quarters for himself, was ready to serve any interested visitors who were unable to cook on their own, for one rupee per *thali* (platter). We had to arrange for breakfast, tea, and snacks on our own. So on the first day, we went to the market and bought supplies...including a teapot. It was a very simple and quiet market. All the essentials were available, without a city crowd. Lonavala was a sleepy, sparsely-populated town with empty streets, and a thick forest surrounding it. The climate was mild, and I found the place ideal for meditation. From the core of my heart, I felt grateful to Harekrishna Agrawal, who had selflessly built the ashram in this beautiful town, for meditators. Not only was he allowing people to stay for no charge, but Sunil *jee* told me he also supported the meditators financially, whenever they approached him for help.

We had a simple routine: every day we did Dynamic and Kundalini meditations in our rooms, and for the rest of the day we had nothing to do, so we practiced witnessing. No books or writing materials were allowed. In fact, we were not even allowed to use a mirror. The purpose was to remove all sources of distraction so we could continually witness our minds. Dr Mishra couldn't sustain this hardship, and after a few days he wrote us a note saying he was leaving. I asked him to lend me some cash if he had any spare; he gave me three hundred rupees. The farewell was sad, and it was difficult for us to part.

Throughout the silence, I constantly remembered that Bhagwan had advised me to stay at the ashram in Pune, and I was feeling guilty. Whenever I looked at his picture, I had the distinct feeling he was calling me back. I thought I even heard him say, "I told you to stay here, why have you gone to Lonavala?"

The huts were scattered far apart, making it ideal for a silent retreat, but during the night-time, we could hear the sounds of jackles and other animals in the forest. The night-time experience became very frightening. As the darkness deepened, my repressed fears and traumas started surfacing. Lying on my bed with closed eyes, I would hear the rustle of clothes, as though someone was standing close by. When I'd open my eyes, there'd be no-one there. It got worse as the nights progressed. I heard the sound of footsteps on the porch, outside my window, on the roof

- everywhere. These strange sounds in the darkness, combined with my absolute solitude, had me conjuring up unknown spirits, which haunted me day and night. I kept feeling an eerie presence in my room. If I looked in one direction, I felt the apparition move swiftly behind my back. I became so frightened that I moved my bed to one corner of the room, and sat with my back against the wall all night, depriving the imaginary ghost any space for a hideaway. Some nights, I would manage to doze. But just as I was about to fall asleep, I would hear something crawling under my bed. I slept with the lights on, and yet nothing seemed to ease this terror. There were nights when I thought I was going to die of fear. The presence was so indubitable, that after the first few days, I could no longer fall asleep at night. In the daytime, I would catch up on sleep.

Every night, I crawled into bed, huddling myself, and waited for the dawn. When dawn broke, it brought me some comfort; I felt I had survived yet another night. In the morning, I would bathe, do Dynamic meditation, and have some fruit and tea. After a light breakfast, and comforted by the daylight, I would fall asleep. At around 1:00 pm, the guard would knock on my door, bringing lunch. It was instructed that I should open the door some time after the knock, so I wouldn't see anyone. The food was plain and tasteless. The chapatis were crusty and hard, it was a rare fortune to find a few lentils in the watery *daal*, and the curry was so spicy it burnt my tongue. Yet I'd be so hungry, I'd relish every morsel. But the guard also brought a small piece of *sakhhar*, caramel candy, which was the only dessert I could afford. I would eat the chapati with the *sakhhar*.

During those days there, I realized that my hunger and many of my fears were merely psychological in nature. Despite eating plenty every day, and knowing there was an ample food supply, I was preoccupied with the thought of food and sex most of the time. Since I was not doing any physical activity, my mind was more active. In the absence of a real problem, my mind started fabricating pseudo-problems. At 7:00 each evening, I'd have the last meal for the day. As soon as I had eaten, the mind knew that there was nothing more to think about food for the day, so it would bring out ghosts and apparitions from strange places. The sound of the wind in the forest would awaken monsters that paralyzed me with fear. Before this, I wasn't even aware of the latent, repressed fears within me. Perhaps there is a reason why they say an empty mind is the devil's workshop; left unoccupied, many fears from my unconscious mind started surfacing. The sounds and the shadows of the forest roused fears I had pushed deep down into the darkest chambers of my mind. Usually, we are so engrossed in our daily lives that we don't have enough time to contemplate or reflect upon ourselves. And sadly, many of us die without finding a moment of reflection. Later, I spoke of these fears with Sunil and other meditators, who all shared that they, too had had similar experiences during the silent retreat.

Apart from the food and sex obsession, and the fears, I was haunted by yet another thought constantly: Bhagwan had told me to stay in Pune. I left Pune because Swabhav *jee* had insisted I go to Lonavala for silence, but in the heart of my heart, I had wanted to live near my master. Later I heard that the day I left Pune, Bhagwan had inquired of Laxmi about me. She told him that on Swabhav *jee*'s advice, I had left for Lonavala. Apparently, Bhagwan scolded Laxmi, then summoned Swabhav *jee*, and forbade him from telling any *sannyasin* to do twenty-one days of silence without his instruction.

I stayed at the Lonavala ashram for seven days, but did not have any fruitful experience during that time. The conviction that Bhagwan was calling me back kept getting louder. It was on the seventh day I decided I should leave. I had only a few hundred rupees left, but I realized that at that moment, the only place I belonged to was with my master. Those seven days had strengthened my determination to stay with him. That day, I wrote a note to Dr Sunil, who was in silence about my wish to go back to Pune. A strange clarity had come to me the moment I decided to return to Pune, all my problems simply dissolved, and I felt very light and happy. This time, I had gathered enough courage and clarity. Perhaps the whole Lonavala chapter was meant for me to realize how much fear, sex, and disturbance was ingrained in my unconscious mind.

When I returned to Pune, I noticed a few hippies around the ashram. I made friends with them, and not surprisingly, they were very resourceful when it came to information about the cheapest accommodation and eateries. With the help of one of these friends, I managed to rent a dormitory space at Hotel Mobokos, for three rupees per night. In those days, most of the visitors with a tight budget used to live at Mobokos, the only hotel close to the ashram, about a twenty-minute walk away. Koregaon Park used to be the summer retreat for the wealthy, the old maharajas and royals of India. It was much cooler, quieter and greener than Bombay. Pune, Dehradun and Bangalore were reputedly the best residential cities in India. Staying in Pune was my first experience of living in a well-to-do metropolitan region, and I was absolutely enchanted by it.

Hotel Mobokos itself was also once part of a princely state. This double-story hotel was a huge complex, but had only a few bedrooms. These rooms, however, were king-sized, with luxurious en-suites. The rent per room ranged from forty to sixty rupees a day, which was quite expensive. When more and more *sannyasins* began arriving and requesting cheap accommodation, the hotel management decided to convert a considerably big drawing room into a dormitory. They charged each person three rupees per day, and provided a mattress and pillow for each of us, but we had to use the servants' bathroom, which was crowded and not very comfortable. Any other provisions we had to manage on our own. Outside the hotel, there was a cafe where we could buy inexpensive treats. Many of my roommates from that dormitory later became famous group leaders, gurus and therapists. I remember Radha, the pretty Italian ma living with us in the dormitory, who later became Bhagwan's medium. She was very popular among the *sannyasins*.

After settling in at the Mobokos dormitory, the next morning I had a shower and went to Bhagwan's discourse. I paid three rupees, the entry fee for the lecture, and sat down. When I saw Bhagwan, I was overwhelmed with joy and soon soaked in tears.

After the discourse, I saw Laxmi at the entrance leading to Bhagwan's room. When she saw me, she called me over and said, "Good, Arun, that you came back. Meet me in my office; I will issue you with the free pass for the discourses."

The news made me so happy that I bowed down at her feet again and again. In her office, she gave me a pass that allowed me free entry to Bhagwan's daily discourse for a month, and said if I decided to stay longer, it would be renewed.

What a relief that was! Now I only needed three rupees per day for my accommodation, and a few more rupees to buy some cheap food. I asked my hippie friends where I could find the cheapest food, as they were experts on everything cheap around town. They'd done all the research, and would pass on the knowledge to anyone looking for a budget lifestyle. One hippie turned *sannyasin* friend said, "There is a restaurant close to Pune railway station, where the rickshaw-pullers and porters eat. Each meal costs only seventy-five paisa per *thali*: that's the cheapest lunch you can buy in town. You cannot find anything cheaper than that."

So I went there. The food was served on an aluminum platter, with aluminium bowls. The chapatti was served with a small bowl of *daal*, a runny curry, a cup of buttermilk, and a miserable portion of rice. I decided that seeing as I couldn't get a better deal for that price, I'd have to settle for the place. It was more than three kilometres from the ashram. As I was short of cash, I was only eating one meal a day, at noon. In the evening, I would just have a snack in a cheap eatery.

In spite of it all, my days were wonderful; I would go early in the morning for Dynamic meditation and then Bhagwan's discourse. After that, I'd have lunch at the railway station. By the time I returned to the dormitory, half the day was gone. I would try to rest for a while, despite the noise there, then I'd shower and get ready for Kundalini meditation. In those days, we didn't have a meditation hall; meditation was done in any open space available in the ashram. So every day I would go to the ashram, and have to find the place where the meditations were happening for that day. Teertha, who was the meditation coordinator then, would come with the tape recorder, and walk around the ashram to find the appropriate space, and we would all follow him. Construction was in full swing in the ashram. Some days, we would come to the lawn, only to find heaps of bricks had been unloaded there, so we would have to go and find another space. But those were some of the most blissful days of my life. I went deeper and deeper into meditation every day.

One night, when I was resting in the dormitory, unexpectedly I saw Bhagwan's smiling face on the ceiling. His benevolent smile filled me with joy. This was the second time his image had appeared in front of me and I had felt his intense presence in my room. The pale moonbeams flooded the room. In that hazy, moonlit night I watched Bhagwan smile at me with enormous love. That vision was enough to keep me intoxicated for weeks.

After about a month, one day, I checked my pocket, and realized I only had two five-rupee notes and a few one-rupee coins left on me. We had to pay for three days in advance at Mobokos. After paying the nine-rupee board, I only had a one-rupee note, and a few coins left. I counted the coins once again - five rupees.

I went and sat down, deep in thought, in a small garden at Mobokos and counted the money again. I did not want to leave Pune as long as Bhagwan was there. But I couldn't even survive for three days on that amount, and here I was planning for eternity.

The Taste of Satori

T he next morning we went to Dynamic meditation, which began at 6:00. Back then, there were only three daily sessions: Dynamic, Bhagwan's discourse at 8:00am and Kundalini meditation at 5:00pm. At 7:00pm was *darshan*, where selected people were given private audience with Bhagwan by appointment, and those who were interested in initiation were given *sannyas*.

In this life, this was my first experience of spending time in a buddhafield, and an unknown bliss filled me to the brim. Every day, listening to Bhagwan and meditating, I was gently falling back into my heart-space. My thoughts were gradually settling, a new clarity arose, and awe filled my heart. It was during this time that I had started having several esoteric experiences and frequent glimpses of *satori*.

One evening, after Kundalini meditation, I fell into a trance-like state. I remained in that state until late into the night. At that time, we were doing Kundalini meditation on a lawn at the ashram, where they built Radha auditorium later. As the night closed in, and the mist started settling on the grass, it became chilly. I knew my shawl was lying somewhere close by. If only I could cover myself, I would be just fine. But, try as I might, I couldn't move my hands. I had fallen into a state of trance. I was to have many such experiences, but when it happened for the first time in the ashram, it totally stupefied me. I was consciousness. I could hear the faint sound of people passing by me, the noise of the crickets and the sound of wind in the trees. I wished somebody would take notice and cover my body with the shawl. But back then the ashram was almost empty, and nobody took any notice of me.

The evening mist was falling gently all over my body. The crickets grew louder. I did recall Bhagwan saying that when one falls into such states, one needs to take deep and long breaths. I tried to take deep breaths, but I didn't have control over my breath either. My breathing was very subtle. It was as if I wasn't breathing at all. After a conscious effort for some time to come back to my body, I slowly regained control of it. I got up slowly and sat in the lotus posture. The warmth of the shawl was nourishing.

When I woke up fully, I started walking toward Mobokos, but I was floating, not walking. It took me thirty minutes to get there: I hadn't fully recovered from the trance. I had no sense of the body, including hunger. Out of habit, I looked for a roll of biscuits, which I ate with a glass of water.

Back in 1972, during my meeting with Bhagwan at Woodlands Apartment, I had told him it was with great repentance that I had not managed to bring him to Kathmandu, nor make it to the Mount Abu camps. He had assured me then by saying, "You are a ripe fruit. A little effort and you are ready to let go. Attend one camp. Much can happen on your very first camp."

As Bhagwan had promised, I was totally transformed on my very first camp. I had been an unhappy man for a long time, and sadness had scarred me deeply. But in his presence, suddenly, they lost their weightiness. The chain that tied me to my past had been broken. I was free to soar high into the unknown skies of bliss. And Bhagwan kept on taking me higher and higher. "Enlightenment has a beginning, but no end," Bhagwan had once said.

I had received the first glimpse into eternity.

Miracles Unfold

I had no plans for the future; I could no longer afford to have plans. But just when I had given up all hope, the miracles started to unfold.

I had already lived in Pune for more than a month, but the series of events that happened in the second month of my Pune stay with nothing but five rupees, changed my entire perspective on life. I realized that as long as our faith rests on our own arrangement for survival, existence doesn't intervene. But the moment you surrender yourself, existence finds miraculous ways to support you, to nurture and nourish you.

While I was still playing with the coins in Mobokos garden, a hippie *sannyasin* came running and said, "I have been looking for you everywhere. What are you doing here? Laxmi has sent for you. She said she has some urgent work for you."

I ran to Laxmi's office. She said, "Arun, the ashram has purchased a building to start a Press Office, but nobody has stayed there for the last few years. The house is very dirty and unmaintained, and we need someone to clean and guard it. I have heard that you don't have a place to stay. If you want, we can let you stay there for free."

I couldn't believe my ears.

She told me, "But there is no bathroom there. You will have to make do with the municipal toilet. But there is water connection and a tap in the building. The ashram will provide you with a bucket and a mug so you can bathe there. But the place is very dirty; it will take you a few days to clean it." She gave me two tungsten bulbs, the key to the house, a bucket, a mug and a broom.

When I arrived there, after about a fifteen-minute walk from the ashram, I discovered that the whole building was just one big room. There was a small partition behind what looked like a kitchen and washing space. The roof was covered with clay tiles. Nobody had stayed there for the last few years, and rumour had it the house was haunted. The room was full of cobwebs, and the floor was carpeted by a thick layer of dust. Laxmi had forewarned me that it would take me at least a few days to clean the place. My problem was I didn't have anywhere to stay overnight, since I had run out of money.

As I had only one orange outfit (*lungi* and *kurta*), I took it off, and went into the building in my underwear. First, I removed all the cobwebs with the broom. I saw there was a big, wooden cupboard in one corner of the room. That day, my plan was to clean just a small corner so I could make a space to sleep overnight. I asked for help from a *sannyasin* who I had met outside the ashram, and together we moved the cupboard to create a corner for sleeping. I collected around three buckets of dust while cleaning just that small corner. Once it was clean, I laid down my yoga mat and my old sleeping bag, and turned my suitcase into a pillow. I fitted the bulbs so at least I had light in the building. Then I put the light on, and fell asleep. In the middle of the night, I woke up to find a swarm of spiders crawling all over my body. I looked at the army of spiders in horror. At least I had left the light on. I jumped up and shook the tiny monsters off me. Then I tried to sleep, but with no success. In the morning, I was faced with yet another problem - finding a toilet!

I got out of bed at four in the morning and went to the municipal toilet. But nothing had prepared me for the horror that waited for me there. It's alley, around six metres long, was entirely covered with defecation. The stench was intolerable. I couldn't even walk up to the toilet. I flushed the alley with several buckets of water, and only then could I walk through it. This flushing, by the way, became my daily routine for the coming months. There was no latch on the toilet door, so you had to sing out to let others know that you were inside. Beggars and street-vendors used the toilet; you couldn't take enough time, as someone would come knocking. It was a great torture to go to the toilet in the morning - every morning. Thankfully, there was a tap in the building so I could bathe and clean myself after that painful exercise.

But after I had done Dynamic meditation and attended Bhagwan's morning discourse, I was in bliss again. While listening to him, after Dynamic meditation, I was literally stoned.

Thanks to Bhagwan, my accommodation and discourse attendance was taken care of. Now the only problem was food. I had a few coins left on me. The cheapest edibles I could find were bananas. The bananas from Bhusawal were famous in the area.

They were fragrant, delicious and inexpensive. It cost around half a rupee for a dozen. I used to buy half a dozen for a quarter. I could only eat four in one go, and would keep two for later. That was the cheapest way I could survive. If I ate a *thali*, it would cost me three quarters, and I would have run out of my meager savings in no time. Some days, when I was fed up with eating bananas and wanted to eat something salty, I would eat *aloochop*, spicy potato fritters, from a street vendor who sold two for a quarter. My budget was a quarter per day. After that, I would fill my stomach with water from the municipality tap. That was how I survived until I ran out of money. In between, I tried a few other experiments to get free meals. One of my hippy friends, who had mastered the art of frugal living, said that at Budhwar Peth market a businessman was giving free lunches to the beggars and monks. It was a few kilometres' walk from the ashram, and one had to stand in a queue in the scorching sun to get a helping of two thick rotis and a bowl of *daal* or curry. My friend said he sometimes ate there and that the food was good, as well as filling. One day I went to see what it was like. I had done so many things in my life, yet I had still not begged for living. So I was a bit embarrassed to be standing there, and Bhagwan knew all about it. He had planned to test me in the harshest possible way. The man who was serving the food came by, and thrust two chapattis in my hand, then was about to pour *daal* over them even though I had nothing to contain the *daal* with. My hippie friend, on the other hand, was better prepared. He produced an old cup from his bag for the *daal*. I have to say, the cup looked like he had picked it up from the road somewhere. The server filled the mug with *daal*, and the two of us shared his *daal* roti.

I realized that I could eat free food there every day, but

there were two problems with this setup. One was that it was too far from the ashram, and the other, and more important issue for me, was that although I was penniless, I felt very uncomfortable standing in a line with beggars for food. My whole being revolted against it.

While I was looking for ways to solve my food problems, another hippy-turned-*sannyasin* friend of mine told me a businessman served food to the traditional *sannyasins* with great love and respect in the basement of a business house. The businessman didn't allow foreigners, but since I already had a beard and wore orange clothes like a yogi, my friend told me, I qualified to eat there.

When I arrived, I saw that only Hindu yogis and *sannyasins* were allowed inside. I had climbed down the stairs into the kitchen; the room was filled with the aroma of fragrant delicacies. I could smell *puri* (fried, puffed bread), a variety of curries, and halwa (dense, sweet confectionery). The setup was magnificent, and the food was being served on shiny, steel plates. The yogis and *sannyasins* had sat down in two rows, facing each other. I took a seat by a not-so-friendly-looking yogi, and attempted a feeble smile. Someone came and put a plate in front of me. Another man followed with a big bowl of hot *puris*, and placed them on my plate. I felt intoxicated by their aroma; it had been days since I had eaten such delicacies. Next came a man with curry, but as soon as he saw me and my *mala*, he said, "What? A Rajneesh disciple? You guys have enough money to listen to the discourses of your rich guru, you perform all types of nonsense on the streets, and yet don't have money to eat? Get up! Get up and leave right now! This is place is only for traditional *sanyasins* and not for a hippy like you."

It seemed as though he'd had a very bad experience with some hippy *sannyasin*. But the whole event was quite embarrassing, and painful. Some of the *sannyasins* took pity on me. Since I had already sat down, the *sannyasins* requested that I be allowed to eat at least on that day. But the whole situation was so insulting that I just stood up and left. Once I was outside, I couldn't help but cry, and I cried for a while.

I went back to my banana diet. One day, I counted my money, and it turned out I was down to my last quarter. I bought six bananas with it, and had no money left for the next day. Yet I was neither scared or worried, nor did I want to return to Nepal. I was so high on meditation and Bhagwan's energy that I walked along the street as if I owned it.

I had visited Laxmi several times asking for some work in the ashram, but she kept saying she had to ask Bhagwan. And Bhagwan told her that I was too blissed out to be able to work. That was true as well. Despite my financial difficulties, I felt like I was the most blissful person on the planet at the time.

By then I had already cleaned the future Press building. Now it was very habitable. Every morning I would go there after Bhagwan's discourse, and as I had only one set of orange clothing, I would wash the *lungi* and *kurta* every day after the discourse. While the clothes dried, I would wrap a towel around my waist, lie down on the lawn and read books.

As more and more *sannyasins* came, the ashram needed more staff, and Laxmi decided to use the Press building as a dormitory for the newly-appointed ashram staff. My first room-mates were Swami Chaitanya Keerti and Ma Krishna Priya. One Muslim *sanyasin* joined us later. Keerti immediately got the job as the editor of *Rajneesh Times*, which meant he received all the facilities of a resident including food pass. The other two also had food passes, as they were working in the ashram; I was the only one who didn't. I had a free-entry pass and free ashram accommodation, and so was treated as a half-ashramite. Pune ashram was not very financially stable in those days. All the staff members were given a cup of tea in the morning after Dynamic meditation. They had to work from ten until eleven o'clock, when they were given brunch. They were always served chapati, rice, *daal* and a curry for both brunch and dinner. After brunch, they would go back to work, and meet again at three o'clock for a cup of tea. Dinner was served after Kundalini meditation in the evening. Apart from the camp days, we only had Dynamic meditation in the morning and Kundalini in the evening. The ashram did not have enough funds for breakfast or to expand the menu in any way. But as I didn't have a food pass, I couldn't even eat the food or drink the tea in the ashram.

My room-mates at the Press building told the management that they couldn't manage time to drink the morning tea in the ashram so they asked for a stove, tea, milk, and sugar so they could make their morning tea in the building itself. They were provided with the supplies and I, too, had the privilege of enjoying hot morning tea with them. But their condition was that I had to prepare the tea and do the dishes. But Ma Krishna Priya had her own problem; she had a very jealous and complaining mind. She couldn't tolerate this harmless happiness of mine, and went to the kitchen in-charge staff member, complaining that I was drinking tea without a food pass. So I was called in, and forbidden to drink the tea without a food pass, after receiving a good verbal-thrashing session.

I have always been a tea lover, and yet with so little money left, I couldn't even afford this simple pleasure for many days.

But the day I ran out of money completely, everything changed. When I walked out of the ashram after the morning discourse, I was penniless, but my mind was totally vacant and I was walking along in a meditative state. Mind thrives on duality. The day you cannot make any choice, the mind simply dies. There was no fear that I might have to remain hungry that day. Just as I had come out through the ashram gate and was walking along the street in Koregaon Park, a car came by and stopped right in front of me. Inside, was Manik Bafna *jee*, who later became a dear friend of mine.

He peeped out of the car window and said, "Oh Swami *jee*, you walk like you are absolutely blissed out. Where are you from?"

I said I was from Nepal. He then asked me what my profession was and I told him I was an engineer.

We talked for a while, and he then said kindly, "There is a feast at my house today. Are you free to come along for lunch with me?"

"I sure am," I replied, even before I had time to think about it.

He said that lunch would be ready at one o'clock, and I was free to finish my work before going there for lunch. He gave me his house address, and said it was in a place called Sadal Baba. I told him I had nothing to do before lunch, so he invited me to go there with him in the car, which I did. When we arrived, Sohan *ma* had already prepared a Gujarati feast. Before the Pune ashram was established, Osho used to stay at their house during his Pune visits. Sohan *ma* had the good fortune of serving him many times. Osho had written her many letters, and had given her many of his personal belongings as gifts, and so her house was filled with his fragrance. The whole place felt like a temple. I have experienced that in a place where Osho has stayed, even for one night, there is a special energy which remains. It continues to throb, creating a mini buddhafield. And all those who cooked for Osho had magic in their hands. Whatever they touched, tasted divine.

At Bafna *jee*'s house I was served a variety of delicious foods, and I ate to my delight. I hadn't eaten properly for months, and I gorged on the food shamelessly. After lunch, we talked for a while, and Sohan *ma* showed me the hundreds of letters Bhagwan had written to her and the gifts given by him. She also told me detailed stories of the times when Bhagwan stayed at her house. In this very first meeting, we became quite intimate. When we were finished, my hosts showed me a room where I could have rest. I woke up refreshed, had a wonderful cup of tea, and walked back to the ashram for Kundalini meditation in the evening.

The next day the miracle repeated itself. Just as I was walking out through the ashram gate, a car came and stopped in front of me. A man wound down the window and asked about me. I still remember his name: Ramkrishna Agrawal. I told him a little about myself. He was one of the prominent industrialists of Pune, and had his own pharmaceutical business. Like the previous day, I was asked where I was going, and if I had any engagements.

"The only engagement I have is the evening Kundalini. Otherwise, I am totally free," I replied.

Handing me his business card, he said, "Can you please have lunch with me at one o'clock?"

I nodded my head. He gave me his address and then left. I didn't know what to do until one, so I thought I should just walk up to his place rather than roaming around. I arrived there at ten thirty, but as nobody knew me there, I didn't dare to go inside. I found a nice, cozy place in the shade of a large tree outside his compound. I laid down my yoga mat and slept with utmost ease, as I didn't have to worry about the day's meal. Absurd are the ways of existence. While I had *some* money, although paltry, I had to find strange ways to make a living. But the day I ran out of money completely, jumping trust fully into the arms of the unknown, all my problems vanished.

At one o'clock, Agrawal *jee* arrived and found me sleeping soundly outside his house. He woke me up and asked, "Swami *jee*, when did you arrive?"

When I said "Ten thirty", he looked at me in surprise, and asked, "Then why didn't you go inside?"

I just smiled gingerly. We went inside together.

Agrawal *jee* was a bachelor and an unusual man. He was one of the richest people in Pune. He had several residences in the city alone. Unlike all his brothers, who were married and settled, he had remained single. Because of my friendship, he started coming daily to the discourses, and reading Bhagwan's work. After few years, he took *sannyas*, and became Swami Ramkrishna. He treated me with heartfelt affection and respect and often insisted that I was his spiritual guide. I had introduced him to meditation and yoga.

I received royal treatment in his house. The food was exceptionally tasty. Agrawal *jee* was a man of taste. He was also romantic by nature, and had many female friends. His house was lavish and well appointed. It's curious that when I had a little money, I lived like a beggar, and now that I had no money whatsoever, suddenly I was being treated to a sumptuous meal every day, and travelling around the city in a luxurious car.

After lunch, Agrawal *jee* said if I had any work to do, he would drive me back to the ashram. When I said I had nothing to do until Kundalini at five o'clock, he showed me his guest room, and said I could rest there as long as I liked. The room had a music system, a small library and an en-suite. I was not just *feeling* like an emperor, but living like one.

He invited me to stay over at his house, but the problem was, if I were to leave the Press building, even for a single night, Laxmi would expel me, and might withdraw the entry pass. So despite all discomfort, the Press building was by far more precious to me; it held my entry to Bhagwan. And for this intimacy, I was ready to pay any price.

During lunch, Agrawal *jee* confided,"Swami *jee*, I have a sleep problem. I have undergone a lot of different treatments, but nothing has worked so far."

I said I could try some yoga and meditation techniques with him. I did a few relaxation techniques like *yoga nidra* and *Savasana,* which I knew helped people sleep. During the session, I suggested he relax different parts of his body for a few minutes, and meditate on some mantra. He soon fell asleep and slept like a baby. I went to the guest room and rested. At four thirty, when I got up to go to Kundalini, he was still asleep, so I left for the ashram.

The next morning, he came to pick me up from outside the ashram gate, where he hugged me joyfully, and said, "Swami *jee*, I have not slept like that in my whole life. You have done magic. Please spare some time for me, and if it is not too much to ask, please have lunch with me as often as you can. And please introduce me to the world of yoga and meditation, and bless me with deep sleep."

He would come to pick me up every morning after Bhagwan's discourse, and take me to his house. Someday, I was offered a sumptuous breakfast of fruits, and his refrigerator was always full of fruits and sweets. Every day I had one guaranteed royal lunch and someday if I was lucky enough, I would also enjoy breakfast occasionally. After breakfast, he would go to his factory, and I had free time, so I would read his books. He had a wonderful collection of books and music, and I was welcome to take any book home. Between one and two o'clock, he would come back from the factory, and we would eat lunch together. In the evening, after Kundalini, I would return to the Press building. I couldn't have asked for a better life.

Everything at Agrawal *jee*'s was perfect, except that his servant disliked me from the very beginning because his master was paying too much attention and respect to a vagabond yogi; he stared at my tattered clothes in disgust. Apart from that, the arrangement was ideal, and after a few days, I began to put on weight.

Meanwhile, Sunil *jee* returned, having finished two sessions of twenty-one days of silent retreat. I was well fed and had grown healthier and more radiant. When he saw me, he thought I must have been living very comfortably, and probably had a lot of money. He said, "I am sick of eating the dry chapatis at Lonavala, and have run out of money. Why don't you take me out for a good dinner?"

I didn't even have a penny. I was wearing a *kurta*, so I flipped out my pockets, and showed him I had nothing on me. I said, "It's been a month since I have touched any money."

He was surprised and also concerned. He complained that I hadn't informed him earlier of my situation. He said he could've asked his family to send some money. He asked, "How have you been managing without money?"

I shrugged my shoulders and said, "I survive on the grace of Bhagwan, and he has been very gracious so far."

Later that evening, *he* took *me* to a restaurant and treated me to dinner.

Overnight, these miraculous divine interventions had become part of my life. Somehow, I was always taken care of.

One day, Agrawal *jee* told me he was going to Singapore for two weeks. "Why don't you continue coming to my place for lunch," he said. The image of his servant flashed through my mind. Well-fed Agrawal *jee*, I used to over eat. I didn't have enough courage to face his disrespectful looks on my own, so I politely declined the offer. Agrawal *jee* assumed that since I was an engineer, I had enough money to support myself, so he said goodbye and that he hoped to see me when he returned. He had no idea I was penniless. My hungry days, I thought, had resumed again.

I had an American friend named Sucheta, who had been a hippy before she took *sannyas*. She was a paying guest in a Gujarati household. For three hundred rupees a month, she was given a bed and lunch daily. As Gujarati food is spicy, she didn't particularly enjoy it, so she would pack it in a lunchbox, and after the discourse, sell it at the ashram gate for two rupees. For a few days, she gave me the food for free. Kind-hearted though she was, Sucheta also was running out of money. So she came up with an idea that benefited both of us.

"Why don't you sell this food," she said one day. "If it sells, you can keep fifty paisa, and if it doesn't, you can eat it."

This was a good deal for me. If it got sold, I could buy some bananas or whatever else I could afford with fifty paisa. If not, I would have the good fortune of enjoying the Gujarati lunch. So my work was to stay outside the ashram gate after the discourse and try to sell the meal. As Sucheta used to do the same before she conferred the business on me, I already had a few customers.

Most of my potential customers were poor *sannyasins* or former hippies. Whenever somebody came and showed any interest in buying the food, my heart sank. If they decided to buy, I had to survive on bananas. So if any foreigner came looking to buy it, I would warn them that it was very spicy, which discouraged most of them. This routine continued for fifteen days until Agrawal *jee* returned.

With Agrawal *jee* back home, of course, my royal routine started again. Unfortunately for me, he often had to travel on business trips. Whenever he left town, anxiety would haunt me. However, for the next four months I lived in Pune, and survived without any money. Agrawal *jee* was grateful to me for introducing him to Bhagwan and helping him resolve his sleep disorder. He often expressed his gratitude by indulging me gloriously.

The Orange Sweater
and Coca Cola

I had never been more happy or healthy in my whole life as I was in those four months. But December came with its winter chill, and found me without any warm clothes. I had plenty to eat, but I wasn't prepared for winter. I wished I had at least a sweater.

Big Prem's American boyfriend, who lived in the ashram, was a good friend of mine. As I hardly had any engagements, people would often ask me to tag along whenever they needed company to go shopping, or get a haircut or anything. I would most gladly accompany them because I would get free snacks or a meal. I was their handyman.

One day, Big Prem's boyfriend took me to the market, as he needed to buy a sweater. He bought a beautiful orange sweater, and afterwards, we went to a Madrasi restaurant for South Indian delicacies.

He had bought the sweater according to his size, but hadn't tried it on. So when we returned to the ashram, he tried to get into it, and found that, although the size was right, the neck was too small and he couldn't get his head through. He decided to return it. The next day we went to the shop, but since he had already peeled off the tag, the shopkeeper refused to refund him. I tried to argue with the Indian shopkeeper, but he wouldn't listen to me. He didn't have a bigger size in the same colour, either, so we couldn't exchange it. On our way back, we each had a milkshake, which cooled us down. "Oh!" Exclaimed Big Prem's boyfriend. "This might fit you, why don't you try it on?"

And he was right. It was a perfect fit. Miracles kept me grateful, but ceased to surprise me anymore. I saw that miracles unfolded everywhere, all the time. We ourselves hinder them by being too self-reliant or self-sufficient. When you let yourself sink completely into the hands of existence, the greater intelligence takes care of you. I had so much to be thankful for every day. If my shoes were torn, someone would come and give me a pair of sandals. Whatever I needed would always come to me. During these months, living a carefree existence, not a single desire of mine remained unfulfilled.

One day as I was passing by the petrol pump, which is on the next corner along from the ashram, I saw a huge billboard with a picture of a Coca-Cola bottle on it. It was the middle of a hot summer's day, and I had been sweating profusely. The frosted bottle, emanating a thin cloud of cool mist around it, looked inviting. Suddenly, all I wanted to do was drink Coke.

I think Coca-Cola used to cost about seventy-five paisa in those days. Of course, I couldn't afford to buy it, but stare I could. I was greedily staring at the picture, when a *sannyasin* appeared out of the blue and started chatting with me. I was not too interested in this casual stranger, except he was insistent that we have a cup of tea together. He was very gracious, but I didn't feel like drinking tea at all. Not far away was a small tea stall by the road, so we went to have tea anyway. The tea vendor said, "There is no milk so I can only serve a cup of black tea."

I told him I didn't like black tea at all. Then the *sannyasin* said he didn't like it either. Then he said, "Let's try another shop", but there was no other tea vendor around. As we left the stall and were walking towards the petrol pump, he suddenly changed his mind, and said, "Forget about tea. Let's have a Coke."

I acted nonchalantly, and said, "Oh, might as well then"!

The Spark of Madness

We were living in a fairy tale. Every little thing we did was saturated with great love and purposefulness. Slowly, silently we were all growing in meditation every day. Bhagwan took us deeper and deeper into the silence of our hearts. I experienced a profound restfulness such as I had never experienced before. While listening to Bhagwan every morning, I would go into a deep trance. There were only a few people living in the ashram then, each of whom was deeply in love with the master. It was a very loving and intimate gathering.

Bhagwan had told me that he often visited his disciples in dreams to guide them, so I kept a diary in which I wrote all the dreams related to Bhagwan. One night, I had a lucid dream in which Bhagwan was speaking on Nanak and the set of verses called *Japji Sahib*. In the most poetic way, Bhagwan described how Nanak attained the ultimate through songs and poetry. He spoke for about five minutes. When I woke up, I could still recall his words. I immediately wrote down what I remembered. I had heard about Nanak, but I didn't know anything about his verses, *Japji Saheb*. But soon afterwards, I forgot all about the dream.

Bhagwan gave discourses in Hindi and English, and switched languages on the eleventh of every month. The regular ten-day meditation camp would also start on the eleventh of each month, which was attended by new visitors. During these camps, the whole ashram would become more festive with four meditations a day. A temporary tea and snacks stall would also open during this time. Jayanti Bhai used to come from Ahmedabad to coordinate each camp. I cannot recall the month, but that day, when I arrived for the morning discourse, Bhagwan had switched to Hindi. As he began the discourse on Guru Nanak's *Japji Sahib*, I started to sweat profusely. I couldn't believe my ears. I had already heard what he was saying in my dream, word for word. He had spoken the same words in my dream a month earlier. I was at a loss. Bhagwan never prepared for his discourse, he always spoke spontaneously and extemporaneously. He himself wouldn't know what he would say a month later, and here I was unconsciously catching a thread of the future.

And this was just one example. During those golden days in Pune, I had many psychic experiences. I now understand why Bhagwan didn't allow me to work in the ashram. All spiritual experiences happen in a very relaxed and unoccupied state of being. This is one reason why a lot of yogis often retreat to secluded spots. When your mind is freed from its patterns, it gradually becomes liquid and receptive. In this state of no-pattern, your inner wisdom and intuitive faculties become sharp and active. This intuitive wisdom is the ground for spiritual growth. By relieving me from all kinds of responsibilities, Bhagwan was untangling my patterns. I did Dynamic meditation every morning, and Kundalini meditation every evening. Throughout the day I enjoyed myself with a newfound spontaneity. As I didn't have money or any work, there wasn't much to plan or think about. I was totally present in each moment, and in this totality, I entered a new dimension of being. Some days, I would be walking aimlessly or just sitting silently in the room, when suddenly a cloud of intoxicating perfume would envelop me. Sometimes, during the meditation, a torrential rain of light would bathe me. One day, I heard the subtle *naad* (sound), playing deep within my being.

There is a discourse series by Osho called *Peevat Ramras Lagi Khumari*. *Khumari* means intoxication, but not the kind that is chemically induced. Metaphysical poets have often used the term as a metaphor to describe the state of being drunk on the divine. It is the state when one has become so harmonious and unified with existence, one's being is in a perpetual state of bliss. There is no conflict with the whole; one's total being becomes attuned to the great law of nature, or dhamma, Tao, or whatever one may want to call it. By the grace of my master, I was in the state of *Khumari* most of the time. After the discourse, I had to walk to the train station, to save the fifteen-paisa bus fare, and get my seventy-five paisa *thali*. But I was so deep in a trance, that I would feel like I was floating in the air. My steps had an unusual grace and lightness. As I slowly floated through the bustling traffic of Pune, with a strangely radiant face, the passers-by often scrutinized me quizzically, and asked, "What is he high on?"

Chuang Tzu Auditorium had been inaugurated on the 21st

of March 1975, which had coincided with my second Pune visit. Bhagwan began giving morning discourses and evening *darshans* in Chuang Tzu. Once the morning discourse was over, a *sannyasin* would come and mop the floor. We were supposed to leave the hall before the cleaning started. Osho's discourses have been, and remain, a source of the most meditative experiences for me. A kind *sannyasin*, who was in charge of the hall, knew of this. She often came and whispered gently in my ear, "Swami *jee*, it is time to clean the hall. Please get up." She knew my situation well, and dealt with me very sensitively. One day, after the morning discourse I sat entranced for a long time. This *sannyasin* had come a few times and left me alone. After sometime I heard her footsteps again, so I decided to make an effort and walk out of the hall. With much difficulty I stood up and walked out. When I reached the ashram gate, the guard started laughing uproariously. I looked at him and suddenly started to laugh myself. Soon, a small group of *sannyasins* gathered around us and they all looked at me and broke into peals of laughter. Encouraged, I laughed even louder. I had no idea why they were laughing, but couldn't care less! I was totally enjoying the whole scene with them. When I walked up to the main gate, called Gateless Gate, the guard, who was also a friend of mine, walked up to me and said amidst the laughter, "What's going on? What is this?" He was pointing towards the lower part of my body. I looked down and saw that I was stark naked below the waist. I had apparently left my *lungi* in the hall. I ran to Chuang Tzu, but the Lao Tzu House guard stopped me and said, "The gate is closed, I am not supposed to allow anybody in without permission from Laxmi."

How was I supposed to go to Laxmi in this state! I pleaded with him to help me out.

The guard, who was a German, said, "I don't know how. This is your problem. I have to obey my orders." Except during the morning discourse and evening *darshan*, nobody could enter Lao Tzu House without permission.

I asked him to at least fetch the *lungi* for me if I was not allowed in. He absolutely refused. Then I pleaded with him to let me use the intercom to call Laxmi. At first he said that was not allowed as well, but in the end he acquiesced.

I called her and explained my condition, which made her laugh out loud as well. She said, "It seems you have totally lost it!"

Laxmi was aware of my *khumari*. She told the guard to let me in to get my *lungi*. This was not the end, but just the beginning of the divine madness that stayed with me when I was close to Osho.

The Madman Saga
Continues

It so happened that one day after the morning discourse, my face just froze. Try as I might, I couldn't move the muscles of my face. They had all become rigid, immobile. I walked out of the hall in the faint hope that once I was outside the ashram, this rigidity would gradually ease. I walked all the way to the restaurant by the train station. I was a regular there, the waiters knew me well, and as soon as I sat down, one of them came with my seventy-five paisa *thali* and banged it on the table. Now that the food was on the table, I tried to open my mouth forcibly, but to no avail. One of the waiters, who was observing my absurd theatrical movements with fascination, walked up to me and said, "Why aren't you eating? The food is getting cold. Eat!"

I looked at the *thali*; there was no way I was going to be able to chew the chapati. But I could at least try to gulp down some buttermilk and *daal*. I held the bowl of buttermilk in one hand and force opened my mouth with the other hand. Then I poured the liquid into my mouth and swallowed. I did the same with *daal*. At two o'clock, the restaurant would be closed for the afternoon. While I was still struggling with the food, a waiter signaled me to leave. Whether I could eat the food or not, I still had to pay seventy-five paisa. And if I couldn't eat it, I'd be hungry for the whole day because that was my daily budget, spent. Despite my best attempts, my face remained frozen for the entire day, and I remained hungry. Nonetheless, I was blissed out.

Many times, my consciousness was not rooted in my body. I could hear and understand what people were saying but I couldn't respond, as my body had no connection with my mind. Once somebody asked my name, but when I wanted to reply, I discovered I couldn't remember anything, including my name. So I had to take out my entrance pass from my pocket to find out my name. As I mentioned earlier, the patterns of my mind were dissolving, and a nebulous chaos was filling the mind before becoming crystallized in non-dual clarity. During this time, I constantly pestered Laxmi asking her to give me some work so I could get some support from the ashram. Bhagwan was aware that I couldn't do any work during this phase. The only way to pass through it was by resting in absolute non-activity. But I didn't understand that, back then. Laxmi would say that she had to get Bhagwan's permission to give me any work. But one day, to my surprise, Laxmi me asked me if I could transcribe a series of Hindi lectures entitled *Sahaj Samadhi Bhali.*

I was overjoyed to receive this work, as it meant that I could listen to Bhagwan all the time. The ashram provided a tape player and the tapes of the discourses. In those days, tape players were

Osho guiding Swami Anand Arun for his work in Nepal during darshan at the Pune Ashram.

not a common thing, so it was a luxury to have one. Laxmi also said that I'd be paid twenty rupees for transcribing each discourse. That was a good deal of money. Normally, people took three days to complete the transcription of a discourse. But those who skipped meditation, and devoted their entire time to transcribing, finished the work in two days.

It was an entirely different case with me; every time I listened to Bhagwan, I went into a trance. I would be completely blissed out, and forget totally that I had to write down what I was listening to. It took me more than seven days to complete even one discourse. Swami Anand Maitreya was in charge of the Publication department. Laxmi asked me to submit what I had completed. It took me more than double the allocated time to just finish one discourse. I used to take part in all the meditation sessions, and so the time I could spare for the discourses was limited. But even then, the time that I spent with the tape player was not productive in terms of producing the transcriptions. But I was enjoying immensely listening to Bhagwan, and wanted to listen more and more.

I was summoned to Laxmi's office, and was asked about the delay.

I had finished only one lecture. I handed over the few pages that I had transcribed to Laxmi. She perused the work, and remarked, "Arun, you have very good handwriting but you are very lazy."

The delay was not acceptable to the Publications department. Bhagwan was very particular about the deadlines that he set for the publication of his books, and at my speed there was no way that they could be met. The maximum time that they could give me was three days per discourse. I told them about my condition, and said, "I'm afraid I won't be able to complete one in three days' time." Although the Ashram was very liberal about individual freedom, it was very particular about the productivity and deadlines. Once, Swami Chinmaya had also faced a similar problem during Bhagwan's Woodlands stay. He had said that while listening to Bhagwan's discourses, he would get drunk on his words, and couldn't submit assignments on time because he would be in a trance. When the matter was reported to Bhagwan, the answer came, "Stop Chinmaya's entry into discourses until he finishes his work." Bhagwan said the ashram is an institution that thrives on the creativity of its members. If they are not productive, the ashram becomes unsustainable." He didn't appreciate a lethargic approach to work. He is not against lazy people, but such an institution as an ashram needs productivity for its sustainable growth. He had said, "Lazy people should find out their own way of making a living, and should vacate the ashrams pace to make room for those who were more productive." When it came to work, he was a hard taskmaster.

When Laxmi reported my inefficiency to Bhagwan, he said there was a reason why he did not want to assign me any work. In my state, my mind was not ready to do any intellectual work. As long as the work was manual and did not involve intellect, I could manage, but when it came to intellectual work, I simply couldn't do it on time. However, the ashram was providing me with free accommodation and a free pass to discourses, therefore it was obliged to give me some work - so I became the ashram's handyman. In this way, Bhagwan allowed me to live in the state of complete no-mind for as long as I lived with him during that time.

In that golden period, I listened to extraordinary discourse series by Osho such as *Ashtavakra Mahageeta,* the 16th chapter of the *Bhagavad Gita, Ek Omkar Satnam, And the Flowers Showered* and *When the Shoe Fits.*

I still remember during *And the Flowers Showered* series, Osho had spoken on death, and given a clear instruction of how his body should be treated after his death. On the fifth discourse of the series, given on the 4th of November 1974, Osho had instructed that his body be preserved after his death.

He had said, "When I am dead, don't bury my body, don't burn it, because I will be involved in you, many of you. And if you can feel, then a sage remains alive for many years, sometimes thousands of years, because life is not only of the body. Life is an energy phenomenon. It depends on the involvement, on how many persons he was involved in. And a person like Buddha is not only involved with persons, he is involved even with trees, birds, animals; his involvement is so deep that if he dies, his death will take at least five hundred years."

It's unfortunate that, despite his clear guidance, his body was cremated in haste. When I received the news of his death, I called a few members of the Pune ashram management, and read them this chapter -but in vain. Osho's body was burned with a strange urgency. If his body had been kept, even for a day, millions of his lovers and disciples would have gathered from all over the world to have his last *darshan*. The Pune management fabricated the story that Osho had instructed them to burn the body immediately. *Sannyasins* in Pune city itself couldn't even have his last *darshan*.

It was always doubtful whether Osho died a natural death, but with the recent development since Dr. Gokul Gokani, who was pressed to sign Osho's death certificate without being allowing to be at the time of death and without performing necessary examinations of the body, has been rekindled after twenty-five years. The Indian media and thousands of *sannyasins* have requested an investigation be conducted into this suspicious matter. In this context, Dr Gokani's recent revelation about Osho's death in ABP News has provided threads to the unsolved mysteries around the death. Many Osho *sanyasins* who were living in Pune and were very close to the management or even the ones that had been the members of Inner Circle then, have spoken to me and other *sanyasins* in private about the conspiracy behind Osho's death. But they are scared to speak about it in public. Ma Yog Neelam, who was Osho's secretary then, has made similar revelations in the same interview. According to her, when she first broke the news of Osho's death to Osho's mother, she exclaimed with grief and certainty, "They have murdered him!"

165

Dr. Gokani has shared with me, in the company of a few American *sannyasins*, that the events surrounding Osho's death were suspicious and mysterious. At midnight, he was told that Osho was dying. He said that Osho needed to be taken to the hospital, but the ashram management refused. As soon as Osho's dead body was brought to the Chuang Tzu Auditorium, it was hurriedly taken to the burning ghats. Strangely, gallons of kerosene were poured over the pyre to burn the body quickly.

Laxmi and I had repeatedly told Osho over some period of time that management were plotting to murder him. After his death, we consulted lawyers all over India with our gathered evidence, but they said we did not have enough evidence to sustain the case. There are *sannyasins* who are aware of the whole conspiracy, and could reveal it, but they've chosen to keep quiet. I have since contacted many oracles and Tibetan mystics about Osho's death. They all confirmed that it was not a natural death. Dr R K Karanjia had reported on Osho's death in three consecutive issues of *Blitz*, which was one of the famous weekly tabloids of India then, and had mentioned that Osho had been murdered by his close disciples for their benefit.

In spite of it all, Osho's death remains a mystery to this day. But I am certain that sooner or later, the truth will come to the fore. And I hope it will be sooner rather than later.

Time to Leave

While I was still fully drunk on Bhagwan's presence, I received a telegram from my father, which announced the death of my grandfather. I had also been fired from my job as I had overstayed my one-month leave. My parents knew that my grandfather's death was a good excuse to call me back; I could detect their intention in between the lines.

Laxmi called me to her office and handed me the telegram. "Your grandfather has died," she said, and looked at me searchingly. "Your father has called you back home. What do you want to do?"

I took the telegram, but to be honest, I couldn't connect with it at all. I read the message several times, but it failed to make any impression on me. I didn't feel grief for my deceased grandfather. I just held the letter dispassionately. After reading it once again, I folded it and put it in my pocket, not knowing how to respond.

Laxmi suggested I make a decision as to whether or not I would return, and that I should send a telegram to my father either way. I had neither the money nor the willingness to send a telegram. During those few months with Osho, a new void had opened up within me. In that space, I became acquainted with my solitude for the first time. My personality, which had been shaped conveniently by the crowd, was crumbling. In its place, an individual was emerging. An identity which did not belong to the past, but sprang from the core of "herenow", was taking hold of me. Against this backdrop, the telegram seemed like a memento from the remote past to which I did not connect anymore. My family belonged to this faded memory. I was now so thoroughly engrossed in the present, that I had forgotten my past.

Laxmi relayed to Bhagwan the news of the telegram, and how it had failed to make any impression upon me. Bhagwan summoned me the next evening for *darshan*. This news thrilled me.

It had been a few months since I had touched any money. I had survived on the foresight of kind-hearted *sannyasins* for food, and still only had one outfit of *lungi* and *kurta* after many months, until Swami Chaitanya Keerti gave me another one. He had a tattered *lungi* and *kurta*, which he was generous enough to give me than throwing it away. I treasured the present very much; for the first time in many months, I didn't have to wear wet clothes on cloudy days. I cannot describe in enough words what relief the gift brought me. And yet despite all the hardship, I was as happy as ever. The fact that I was to meet Bhagwan in the evening only made me happier. But the first thing Bhagwan asked me was, "Which day did your grandfather leave his body?"

Of course, I did not remember the date. I took the telegram out of my pocket and checked the date. He remarked, "So, the twelve days of funeral rites are not over yet? You should go home for that."

Amongst the Hindus in India and Nepal, it takes twelve days after the cremation of a deceased one for the funeral rituals to be concluded. I had no desire to go home at all. I said, "Bhagwan, I don't feel like going back."

"No, you should," replied Bhagwan. "Your grandfather has passed away, and your father is worried about you. You have already stayed here for a long time. Now it is time for you to return home."

I was stunned: This was unexpected. I objected, "Bhagwan I don't want to go back to Nepal. I am so blissful here. If I go back, I will be miserable again."

By this stage, I was confident I could survive without money. I had a place to sleep and a free entry-pass for discourses, and I knew that existence would supply me with food and essentials one way or another.

Bhagwan then said, "There are a lot of people in Nepal who are waiting for me. Since I couldn't visit the country, and now I have stopped travelling, you need to be my contact person in Nepal. Nepal lies between India and Tibet, the two ancient mystical lands, and has a great spiritual potential. It is as ready for me as Tibet was ready for Buddhism when Padmasambhava visited the country. Now you have to fan my fire of revolution in that Himalayan Kingdom."

Osho had told me the same thing in October, 1969, during my first personal meeting with him at the Dwaraka camp. I couldn't understand the significance of his prophecy then, but forty-seven years later, this prophecy is materializing miraculously. Now Osho has become a household name in Nepal. There are over eighty-five active meditation centres and fourteen Osho communes in this small country. There are at least twenty active meditation centres in Kathmandu valley alone. Whenever you are moving around the country, it is a common sight to spot Osho *sannyasins* with *malas* wherever you go. Amusingly enough, whenever we are travelling we see billboards advertising Osho Hotel, Osho Restaurant, Osho Dental Clinic, Osho Pharmacy, Osho Travels, Osho Transport Company, Osho Finance and sometimes even Osho Barber Shop. The Osho movement has become a thriving spiritual force in Nepal, with the intelligentsia of the country reading or listening to Osho regularly. Surprisingly, he is more widely recognized in Nepal than in the country where he was born, travelled extensively, and conducted meditation camps and seminars throughout his life. Nepalese communes are inaugurated by the presidents and prime ministers of the country, and have become a spiritual hub for the intelligentsia of Nepal. Hundreds of meditation camps, seminars and *satsangs* are conducted every year there, and a significant number of people from eighty different countries participate in them. Around two thousand people are initiated into Osho Neo-Sannyas every year – they wear the Osho *mala*, and have photos of Osho displayed in their homes and work places. Unfortunately, many people have been misled into believing that Osho had asked *sannyasins* to drop their *malas*, and remove his pictures from everywhere. This unfounded rumour is a part of the well planned and thoroughly fabricated conspiracy to efface Osho's legacy, and erase the memory of him from people's minds entirely. But by Osho's grace, Nepal remains untouched by this. Recently, Osho Tapoban was featured as the major destination globally for spiritual tourism by The Huffington Post. I am humbled by my master's grace every day, and surprised how he could foresee it forty-seven years ago with such confidence and clarity when I was the only Osho disciple in the country. Osho Meditation teachers trained at Tapoban are invited to conduct meditation camps around the globe.

These days during my meditation, when I express my job satisfaction, gratitude and awe, Osho tells me, "This is just the trailer; the movie hasn't even started yet. What I have told you 47 years ago will materialize a 100 percent in the days to come"

So during the *darshan*, Bhagwan instructed me to go back to Nepal and start a meditation centre for his work. I was so overwhelmed, I wept.

"Don't cry," Bhagwan said. "You need not worry. I will keep on calling you here. And whenever you have the wish to come here, existence will help you. But now is the time to go back."

During the months there, I had undergone a remarkable change. I have always been an emotionally driven person, which meant my moods fluctuated continuously, and I floated perpetually in a sea of fleeting emotions. I had never experienced a neutral space, a peaceful space within me. But during my stay with my master in Pune had helped me to locate this space. Bhagwan had told me that now I was ready to face the challenges of the world, and he was right in saying that. But I clung to him like a child clings to its mother in a crowd of strangers; so precious, so nourishing was his presence.

"Now that you have a house in Kathmandu, you will open a meditation centre there." He passed the verdict, picked up his letterhead and wrote down the name of the centre; first in Hindi, then below it, in English:

Asheesh Rajneesh Meditation Centre.

Once he had written the name down, I felt the weight of the imminent responsibility. Of course, I wasn't ready for it. "Bhagwan, there are only two rooms in my house," I immediately protested.

Bhagwan asked, "But you will, at least, have one room for yourself, won't you?"

"Yes, I will."

"Then open the centre in that room itself," he said with a radiant smile.

I loved my carefree life too much to let go of it that easily. My mind immediately began fabricating excuses.

"Bhagwan, my house is in the suburbs, and nobody will come there to meditate," I persisted.

"That is not your problem; it is mine. You just put the signboard outside your house, and start the centre," he said.

"Bhagwan, I am a very disturbed person, and have only begun meditation. I cannot run a centre at all. All I want to do is stay with you." I said.

"No, no, I will call you here whenever you need, and whenever you feel the urge to come here. But now I need a centre in Nepal. "

"Bhagwan, my family doesn't like the fact that I am a *sannyasin*, and I am not ready in any way to run a centre, nor do I have the capacity to do so. I have so many financial and family problems, that I cannot possibly do it."

He was handing me the letterhead with the name of the centre on it, but I was refusing to take it. He said sternly, "First, hold this certificate."

I held the certificate.

"Listen to what I am saying, and do as I say. Go to Kathmandu," he said.

Still not convinced, I countered, "But where will I find people that will come and meditate?"

"People will come. That is not your concern. You just go and open a centre, and do at least one meditation daily. Place a signboard for the centre outside your house. Leave everything else to me. People will come, and they will come looking for you. You will not have to look for anyone. You just meditate and remain in bliss," he explained.

I resisted a few more times, but he took no heed. He kept saying, "Something wonderful will happen in Nepal. You just trust me and do as I say."

Although Bhagwan had told me to open a centre, I had no money, no job, and no idea of how to begin. Running a centre would bring a new set of responsibilities, and require infrastructure. I was afraid I wouldn't be able to equip it at that stage. I needed a tape recorder, tapes and books, just to begin with. But I did have some old books that some of my hippy friends had given me. Mukti and Narendra were kind enough to give me two overused tapes with Bhagwan's discourses on the Tao Upanishad that they had brought back from the *kirtanmandali* (a touring group spreading Bhagwan's teachings). The sound quality was very poor, but something was better than nothing.

I then informed everyone that I was leaving, but I had no idea how I'd be travelling. Sunil *jee* said he would go back with me, and another *sannyasin* from Nepal, Krishnarayan Bharati, who has recently left his body, also said he would join me. He was proud to announce that he was the second Nepali *sannyasin* - yet another beautiful madman.

The price of the ticket from Pune to Patna was eighty-eight rupees. Ramkrishna Agrawal paid for my second-class sleeper coach ride. He also gave me a one-hundred rupee note for my travelling expenses. I bought a tape of Dynamic and Kundalini meditations instead, with the money.

So I left Pune that winter with the meditation tape, two old Tao Upanishad tapes and the few old books donated by my hippie friends. Though my possessions amounted to little, the treasure Bhagwan had given me was immense. Enriched by this treasure, I set out on the mission Bhagwan had entrusted to me.

PART IV

BACK TO NEPAL

Back to Nepal

First I went to Janakpur for my grandfather's death rituals. Clad in orange clothes and a *mala*, and sporting a long beard, I became a spectacle in my village. The rumour spread quickly that I had renounced the world and become a yogi. Soon the whole village came to see my new persona.

A rumour spread in the village that now I would no more work as an engineer and that I would be a celibate and would not live with my family but would instead go back to my Guru. People came to our place to get blessings from this new holy man that had arrived in the village. The elderly people demanded me to give a sermon and I obliged with their request. They would ask me all kinds of questions whether I would watch the cinema or not, whether I would eat in restaurants or not. Just the change of the color of my clothes had given birth to new expectations in the simple village people. A man in an orange clad those days had to go through all kinds of scrutiny that age old traditions and rules of *sannyas* had established.

After the twelve-day death rituals were over, I returned to Kathmandu with my parents, who had been more relieved than happy to see me. They had thought they'd lost me forever, and had feared I might not return from Pune. But now that I was back, they returned to their normal routine with the same old mechanical efficiency. Naturally, after a few weeks in Kathmandu, my ecstasy turned dull. I had come back to the normal plane, where I had to start thinking about money and career.

I went back to the National Construction Company Nepal (NCCN), my old office, with a job application. As I had overstayed my leave by months, naturally the whole management was very unwelcoming of me. The Works Manager, to whom I had handed my leave application last time, dismissed me without a thought.

Before passing my file onto the General Manager, he wrote on it that I was an unreliable employee; I had overstayed my leave by many months, and he strongly suggested that the company not hire me. So he wrote, "Not fit for the post," and sent the file to B P Shah, the General Manager.

B P Shah knew me well, as he was a family friend. Our fathers were friends. He was known to be a tough administrator. He looked at my file and saw it was full of bad recommendations. He then called me to his office, showed me the file and said, "See it for yourself, no one has any trust in you. What is your intention? Do you want to work or run away to Pune again?"

I said, "No sir, I want to work."

He then said, "Ok, I will grant you one last chance. If you run away again,then even I won't be able to help you."

So, I resumed my position as an engineer at NCCN.

And I opened the centre at my house. I made a small signboard that said *Asheesh Rajneesh Meditation Centre,* and hung it outside my house. My parents didn't like it; they were very proud of their only possession, and had built that house with meager savings and a considerable struggle. They were afraid I would turn it into a *dharmashala* (a religious sanctuary, or inn), and eventually, their fear came true. By Osho's grace, *Asheesh* has become the epicenter of the Osho movement in Nepal, and one of the oldest meditation centres in the world. Again and again, my parents had tried to sell the house, but mysteriously, it wasn't within their control to sell it. Osho had initially told me that unless I built a house, he wouldn't give me *sannyas.* I now understand that, that house is an anchor for Osho's energy in Nepal.

After opening the centre, every morning I would leave for the office, and then my parents would remove the signboard and throw it in the backyard. We had a large compound, so every evening after returning from the office, I had to search the whole area, looking for the signboard. Strangely enough, they chose some of the most unlikely places to hide it: sometimes it would be shoved behind the banana grove, sometimes at the far end of the kitchen garden, and other times, under bushes at random around the property. Some days, it would take me more than an hour to locate it, after which I would re-erect it in the front. This enraged my parents. They accused me of turning their home into a public inn, which wasn't entirely untrue. But I had my own problems to deal with. Firstly, I had three cassette tapes, but no tape player. Secondly, nobody really turned up at the centre to meditate. So

I decided that the best way to spread the message was to set up a make shift book stall on the footpath beside the street in downtown New Road, in the heart of the city.

Bhagwan's books were not available then in Kathmandu; they had to be brought all the way from Pune. I had a friend, Sudheer, a mechanical engineer who used to work in the Trolley Bus Department. He had fallen in love with Bhagwan, and was one of the few early frequenters of the Asheesh meditation centre. He told me he had some savings, and was ready to invest five thousand rupees to buy books by Bhagwan. I had no idea then that we could order books for delivery by transport or post, so I said to Sudheer we should go to Pune to get them. We set out for Pune to coincide with the 21st of March enlightenment day celebrations.

In Pune, we participated in the celebrations and bought books with the entire five thousand rupees, which gave us a large quantity. They were not expensive in Pune at that time, and the Pune ashram also gave a forty-percent discount to all meditation centres. We bought mostly the cheaper books so we'd be able to sell them easily. But as their number was so large, we faced some difficulty in getting them back to Kathmandu; we had to bribe the railway employees all along the way to get them there.

We were full of excitement coming back with the books. From April 1975, I started selling books under the Peepal tree in New Road. After my office hours were over, I would spread a bed sheet on the footpath and display the books. I would also set up a picture of Bhagwan, and burn some incense in front of it. Then I would wait for my customers.

My only constant company in this lone affair was a young and literate shoe-polisher, who also had his little stall under the tree as well. The two of us became good friends. He would polish my shoes for free, and in return, I allowed him to read Bhagwan's books for free. Sometimes when he needed to go somewhere, he would leave his shoe polishing paraphernalia in my care, and would reciprocate if I had to go somewhere. Most days, Swami Sudheer would also join me. As I was a new engineer then, my company did not provide me with a car, but would send a company vehicle every day to pick me up from, and drop me back home to Tahachal. But after I started the footpath stall, I asked that I be dropped off in New Road. It took me two weeks to persuade the office management, as they were adamant they could only drop me off from where they picked me up in the morning. They said allowing the driver to drop me off at random places was against the company's rules. But eventually, I swayed them.

I used to stay in the stall until dark. For many days in the beginning, I didn't sell one book. Most of the visitors came to my stall out of curiosity, flipped through a few pages, and put the book down. I started to notice the pattern of the readers, so I devised a trick. I made a little signboard in my office, and wrote on it that anyone could take a book on trial, and if they didn't like it they could return it within seven days and get their money back. The free-trial trick worked; people began taking them on trial. Most of them came back with the book, pretending they didn't like it, but when I went to refund them, they said they would try another book instead. I could see that they had been fascinated by Bhagwan. I smiled inwardly, and replaced the book. I was happy that people were at least reading Bhagwan's work. Gradually, young people started coming to my stall.

Among the first of these customers were Rameshwor Rai Yadav and Rajendra Mahato. They were studying at the Law

College in Tahachal, and staying in the hostel there. Later they became well-known politicians, and even served as ministers many times in the government of Nepal. Today they are among the senior most politicians of Nepal. They joined me at the Asheesh centre and started helping me to sell the books as well. Later, they also took *sannyas*.

In those days, there weren't any theatres or other means of entertainment in Kathmandu. New Road was the social hub then, the meeting place for everyone in town. Every evening, people gathered there for tea and a chit chat. That was the only place where people could purchase newspapers. Even my father used to visit New Road on daily basis but he was very ashamed that his son was selling books on the footpath so he would avoid my lane and the area where I used to sell. Dr. Durga Prasad Bhandari, who was the head of the English Department at Tribhuwan University, and who later became the Vice-Chancellor there, started coming regularly to my stall. Bhandari was very vocal about his admiration for Bhagwan, and often bought several books.

Gradually, more and more distinguished people started visiting my stall. Bishwabandhu Thapa, the politician who was known as the architect of the Panchayat System in Nepal, was one who came and bought books. Then came Renu Lal Singh, the principal secretary to His Majesty the King.

From our very first meeting, Renu Lal *jee* and I were destined to be very close friends, despite him being senior to me in age, position and spiritual quest. He was a devotee of Shri Shivapuri Baba. He had been brought to my stall by a very unique circumstance. The late king Birendra, Bishwabandhu Thapa and Renu Lal *jee* had taken a short trip to the Shivapuri Hills, where Shivapuri Baba used to live. The king was on a horse, and the other two were walking. Renu Lal *jee* began talking about Shivapuri Baba and spirituality in general. As Bishwabandhu Thapa had started reading Bhagwan's work, he commented on how astounded he was by Bhagwan's immense understanding of spirituality. This didn't go down well with Prof. Renu Lal Singh, who had heard many unflattering rumours about this new "guru" in India.

"Stop praising a fraud!" He said angrily. "How can someone who declares himself Bhagwan, a God, and who preaches sex, as a pathway to the superconciousness, be a spiritual guru?"

Bishwabandhu Thapa looked at him sternly, and said, "Sir, have you read him?"

"I have no intentions of reading books by such a fraud!" Singh replied.

"How have you got any right to call him a fraud without reading him? I thought you knew better than to judge somebody without having read his books," Thapa retaliated.

Renu Lal *jee* was a thoroughly honest man. Thapa's words made sense to him, and he realized his mistake. He immediately asked where he could buy Bhagwan's books. Thapa informed him, "They are not available in any bookshop in Kathmandu. A young engineer sells them every evening for two hours under the Peepal tree in New Road. That's the only place you can buy them."

Bishwabandhu Thapa had begun to admire Bhagwan, and really appreciated what I was doing. He was one of the prominent thinkers in Nepal, and had a strong literary sense. He had convinced Renu Lal *jee* that he shouldn't denounce Bhagwan without having read his work.

So one evening, Renu Lal *jee* arrived at my stall. He was a high brow officer and a man of few words. He looked at the books, and said, "Which book do you recommend? I have not read

Bhagwan yet." I picked out *Antaryatra, Sadhana Path* and a few other pocket books for him. He bought them all.

He had come with two associates from the palace. One of them said to me, "Don't you recognize him? He is Professor Renu Lal Singh, the king's secretary."

I said, "I have heard of him, but I did not know him in person."

Some time ago, I had come across a book, *Right Life*, on Shivapuri Baba's teachings. Renu Lal *jee* had written it. His beautifully written preface had left a deep impression on me. It was a simple, honest account of a disciple who was deeply in love with his master. He had said in the preface that there were many books in the world which might have a higher literary value, but he had written the book to share what he realized after meeting Shivapuri Baba, which was the worth and beauty of this rare enlightened mystic. Nobody except John G Bennett had previously written about Baba, but it would have been unjust to know Baba and not to relay this experience with people. He had written it with such simplicity and honesty that it left me teary-eyed.

Although I was brought up in Kathmandu, I had never heard of Shivapuri Baba, who had lived in Kathmandu, for thirty -seven years. When I was leaving Pune after my first stay there, I received a note from Bhagwan saying I should visit Shivapuri Baba's *Samadhi* in Kathmandu. In the note, he laid down clear instructions on how I should get there. He said that behind the Kathmandu airport there is an army barracks surrounded by dense forest, and inside the barracks is the hut where Shivapuri Baba lived. His body is buried there. Bhagwan said that visiting the *samadhi*, I would receive spiritual energy from the place.

When I returned to Nepal, I searched for books on Baba, and found only two: one by Bennett, and the other by Renu Lal Singh. After visiting the *samadhi*, and reading those books, I fell in deep rapport with Baba; he began appearing in my dreams. Later, in one of the dreams, he told me that Singh was a true devotee and would guide me.

When Renu Lal *jee*'s associates told me his name, I suddenly remembered the book. Excited, I yelled at the top of my lungs, "Aren't you the one who wrote *Right Life* on Shivapuri Baba?"

Maintaining his serious demeanour, he replied indifferently, "I am."

I was so overwhelmed to have met him in person that I hugged him, despite the stern looks from his associates.

"You have written amazingly about Shivapuri Baba. It touched my heart, and left me teary-eyed," I said.

For a while he didn't say anything and kept staring at me awkwardly. After a while he asked, "Where do you live?"

I said in Tahachal, where I had made a meditation centre in my house. He asked about my job and office.

"I work for NCCN, and now I am overseeing the construction of the Royal Drugs building at Babarmahal," I replied.

He nodded and left without saying anything else.

That night he had a dream about Shivapuri Baba. Much later, he conveyed to me that Shivapuri Baba had told him that I was an authentic seeker, and instructed him to help me out in any way possible. In the spiritual world, dreams have a special significance. During sleep, our conscious mind relaxes, and our intuitive faculties become sharper and more active. Our conscious mind has a very limited concept of what 'reality' is. Anything that exceeds or contradicts our narrow vision of reality is immediately rejected by the mind. Therefore, masters often use dreams as the medium for communicating higher truths and insights.

Particularly in Tibet, a great deal of study has been done on dreams. The *tulkus* and those reincarnated often have the secrets of their next incarnation revealed in dreams. A comprehensive glossary of dream symbols has been developed in Tibet to understand and imbibe the guidance received through dreams. And interestingly, not just the lamas and high monks benefit from this astral guidance, but there are many other Tibetans who, for example, forecast the unpredictable weather of Tibet according to their dreams. It is said that if one dreams of the death of a beloved one, it will inevitably rain during the following days.

In Mahabharata, the well-known Hindu epic, Karna is said to have had a prophetic vision. Long before the battle of Mahabharata, he had already foreseen the fate of the Kauravas in his dreams. Similar incidents have also been cited in a range of diverse spiritual literature.

However, these kinds of prophetic dreams and visions are experienced not only by meditators; scientists, artists, writers and visionaries have accidentally made discoveries or stumbled upon inspiration in dreams. Dimitri Mendeleev, for example, had been trying to arrange all the chemical elements in a table, but without success, as he couldn't detect a linear pattern. One afternoon, he fell asleep at his desk, and in his dream, in a flash, he saw the periodic table. He has said, "In a dream, I saw a table where all the elements fell into place as required. Upon awakening, I immediately wrote it down on a piece of paper."

This is just an example. For years, meditators have always known the significance of dreams and used them to communicate messages from the astral plane.

The next day, Renu Lal *jee* came to my site office at the Royal Drugs construction. He asked me if he could talk with me for a while. He was an officer of high standing, and the whole construction site was abuzz with talk of his arrival. Everyone was wondering what had brought the king's secretary to the site.

I, too, was taken aback by his surprise visit. "Of course you can talk with me," I replied hastily.

It was late afternoon; I ordered tea, and we began talking. But as we both opened up, we discovered we had a lot to talk about regarding our respective gurus and our spiritual experiences. We became so engrossed in the conversation, that it was late evening before we realized we had to go home. He had said, "It's utterly strange, but I don't feel like leaving your company."

I felt the same. It was as if I was meeting a long-lost friend to whom I could pour my heart out.

The office vehicle that ferried me every day had left hours ago. The driver had asked me, "It's so late, how will you get home?"

"I'll walk home, it's not a problem." I said. Renu Lal *jee* had said he would love to drop me home.

Needless to say, we became very close friends. After that meeting, I was longing to meet him again, but I didn't know how I could do so. Apparently, he was feeling the same, and so he turned up at Asheesh the following Saturday.

On Saturdays, I used to borrow a tape recorder from a neighbour, and play fifteen minutes of one of Bhagwan's discourses. People asked me to play them longer, but with only two tapes, I would have had to repeat them too often. So with my fifteen-minute trick, I could play the discourses for weeks before repeating them. After the discourse, I would play Kundalini meditation for those who had come.

Renu Lal *jee* listened to Bhagwan's discourse, and stayed for Kundalini meditation. After it was over, I introduced him to my father. They had heard of each other, as both of them were in the administrative services. My father was very pleased that the king's secretary had graced our house, and the two of them got along very well.

From that day, Renu Lal *jee* came to my house quite frequently. The news of his visits became the talk of the town. Many people started coming to Asheesh on Saturdays because of him; some out of curiosity, and others to meet him. He told me many times that Shivapuri Baba constantly inspired him to help me out. Indirectly, Shivapuri Baba has contributed greatly in establishing Osho in Nepal.

Sometimes Renu Lal *jee* and I would have a difference of opinion regarding spiritual matters, and an argument would break out. He was a stubborn man, and there were times when we didn't speak for months. But because there was a deep spiritual connection between us, he would come back to my place, and say, "I was a bit harsh on you last time. Forgive me."

He was a straight forward man, and was very overt about his admiration for Bhagwan. He was the first man to openly endorse Bhagwan in the early days. I couldn't have done much without his support. He would get constant visions of Shivapuri Baba, who kept him connected with me. Baba also guided me in my dreams.

One Saturday morning, Renu Lal *jee* arrived with Dr Mrigendra Raj Pandey, and asked me if I recognized him.

Of course, I didn't.

"Well, this is Dr Mrigendra Raj Pandey, the royal physician," Renu Lal *jee* said, introducing him to me.

Dr Pandey asked me to play Bhagwan's discourse, so I

played the fifteen-minute quota. After it was over, he insisted I tell him more about Bhagwan. Of course, nothing pleased me more than to speak about my master. Dr Pandey listened patiently, and with apparent admiration. He has been my friend and an Osho lover ever since. He is a residential member at Osho Tapoban, and continues to visit the commune regularly. After that meeting, he gave my mother, who was a heart patient, a consultation, and then left with Renu Lal *jee*.

The weekly meditation programmes I conducted on a Saturday were at 3:00pm. One day as I was about to begin, Dr. Pandey arrived on his own. He sat quietly through the discourse, and stayed for Kundalini meditation, and then left. But at eight o'clock he came back again, this time with his wife. Osho has mesmerized Dr Pandey right from those early days, and he continues to visit us regularly.

Another Saturday, Renu Lal *jee* brought yet another distinguished person to Asheesh in his Volkswagen Beetle, which he had received as a gift from the king. Every time I went to Pune, he would take me to and from the airport in that car. That day, as Renu Lal *jee* stepped out of his car with the other man, he asked me, "Do you recognize him?"

As usual, I said, "No."

"Oh! You are such an idiot. Don't you know Ranjan Raj! The whole of Nepal is dying to meet him and you don't even know him! He is the chief personal secretary to the king." He said jovially.

My parents knew him well, and as the word spread that Ranjan Raj *jee* was there, the whole neighbourhood turned up at my place to see him. Renu Lal *jee* had praised me generously to him; in private, Renu Lal *jee* was quite stern and straightforward with me, but he always praised me wholeheartedly to others.

There was a time when Renu Lal *jee* was on a trip to Trishuli with King Birendra. While they were talking, the king said, "*Mastersaab*, I hear that you have left Shivapuri Baba, and have become a devotee of Bhagwan."

"No, I haven't left Shivapuri Baba, but I have started reading Bhagwan, and I find him brilliant."

Throughout their two days in Trishuli, Renu Lal *jee* has said that whenever they met up, the king would ask him about Bhagwan. He said they spoke at length about Bhagwan, and about me and my meditation centre in Tahachal.

"You speak of this man with such fondness. What is he like?" King Birendra inquired.

Renu Lal *jee* replied in his usual fearless manner, "How much does His Majesty's government give to the Tribhuvan University every year? A few million rupees? Well let me tell you this much - this young man from Tahachal, alone is spreading more knowledge than your university."

The king was impressed by what Renu Lal *jee* had said about Bhagwan and me, and he asked for a book by Bhagwan.

When Renu Lal *jee* came to Asheesh after this trip, he took me over to the bookstall and said, "Take out a clean book. Make sure there's no stains on it."

Renu Lal *jee* chose *The Book of Secrets*. Before choosing it, he went through the shelf and examined each book carefully. He had never been so particular about buying a book, so I asked him what was the matter. He said he was going to present the book to the king. It cost eighty rupees, which was a good sum then. When I heard that he was looking for a royal present, I said I would like to present the book to the king myself. Renu Lal *jee* flipped open the book to its first leaf, and said, "Then write "At the feet of His Majesty the King"."

It was the year 1977. Renu Lal *jee* also asked for a tape of Bhagwan's discourse. From my meager collection, I found a tape on which Bhagwan described his enlightenment. After listening to it very meditatively, he said, "A lot of masters have described enlightenment, but no one has done it like your guru. Make me a clean copy of this."

He gave the book and tape to King Birendra, and after a few days he asked him what he thought of the discourse.

King Birendra, honest as he was, replied, "*Mastersaab*, I didn't understand a thing."

Renu Lal *jee* was also the king's English teacher, so when he heard his reply, he was enraged. He admonished the king, "No wonder! I have been telling His Majesty to read good literature. All you read is *Newsweek* and *Time*; how do you expect to understand Bhagwan?"

Nobody else would have dared to admonish the king like that. Ranjan Raj *jee* recounted the story later, and said, "Had he not been the king's own, he would have been fired from his job that instant. The king is extraordinarily generous to Renu Lal *jee*, and all his mistakes are forgiven at the palace. Had it been me, I would have been fired immediately."

It was not a mere coincidence that King Birendra was interested in spiritual gurus like Khaptad Baba, Shivapuri Baba, Swami Rama and Osho; he also had a keen interest in meditation and tantra. I had always found him as having an exceedingly charismatic and admirable personality. But in my meditation, I gradually became aware of his spiritual background which extended across his past lives. In many lives, he had lived as a monk or a yogi.

In fact, I have come to realize, all rich, successful or famous people have a spiritual background; they come to achieve fame, wealth, or grace from the sheer power of good karmas they have accumulated over lives. During the clairvoyant moments of meditation, I can see through the lives of many charismatic and successful people, and without exception, they have all gone through severe austerity, and practiced asceticism in their previous lives. Some of them were great yogis, devoted disciples or had selflessly donated a huge sum of money to a spiritual cause.

I would like to reveal a very mysterious law of nature. There are a few things in the world which can be attained through human effort in this life. For instance, a poor man can become rich with effort, an illiterate can acquire a university Degree, or with plastic surgery, one can enhance the facial structure. But there are other things which one cannot attain through effort alone. Natural beauty, innate predisposition to fame, power or wealth, or charismatic personality can only come through the good karmas and *punya* of past lives.

By the grace and regular guidance of my guru, I have seen into my own past life and also the lives of many charismatic personalities that included royals, a famous actor and actresses, successful politicians, business tycoons, writers and artists. Late Maharani Gayatri Devi of Jaipur, for instance, was the epitome of grace. There was something otherworldly about her beauty; you couldn't ignore the grace when you were in her presence. The same was true with Pandit Nehru, Rajeev Gandhi, Waheeda Rehman, King Birendra, Amitabh Bachhan, and Aishwarya Rai, to name a few. They have a presence which demands attention and admiration, and brightens up the whole atmosphere.

In the 41stverse of the 6thchapter of Bhagavad Gita, Shree Krishna has said, "The unsuccessful yogi, after many years of enjoyment on the planets of the pious living entities, is born into a family of righteous people, or into a family of rich aristocracy." This is also my observation that if a great yogi, at the moment of his death, has some unfulfilled material desire lurking in the back of his mind, he is born into great fame, wealth, beauty, grace and power in his next life. Nothing is accidental in this world; everything is causal.

But when you have this insight, a big question arises: Why aren't these people, who had led such austere and spiritual lives, attracted to true spirituality in this life?

My own understanding is that mind functions like a pendulum – it always moves in extremes. And while moving into one extreme, it gains momentum to return to the other. Osho has explained beautifully the psychology of indulgence and repression.

He says, "The mind moves to the other extreme very easily, because the lower opening only functions in two ways: suppression or indulgence. They appear to be polar opposites, but they are not. They help each other very mysteriously, like friends in a deep conspiracy. If you indulge too much then you will be pulled automatically toward the so-called opposite, suppression – and vice versa."

I have been a victim of the same pendulum effect in a series of past lives, and have experienced both extremes, yog and bhog, of going from palatial pleasure to the extreme penance of an ascetic.

195

The other reason that hinders the spiritual quest of such people is their environment. Famous people are always surrounded by their admirers or flatterers, who constantly boost their ego. And ego is the greatest hindrance on the path of truth. Sadly, in most cases, success just strengthens the ego, which in turn, makes one more miserable instead of joyous. Osho has said, "Nothing fails like success." Most so-called successful people become victims of their own ego. It takes them into the cloud of imagination, and the world of delusion. It is very difficult to be humble when one is successful, because the ego finds many excuses to assert itself. This is why whenever someone becomes successful or charismatic, or attains power, fame or wealth, they are blinded and numbed by the glamour. And unfortunately, this is also what prevents them from bowing down at the feet of authentic spiritual masters, because a master is not interested in boosting your ego. He is interested in your soul, and one can only get glimpses into one's soul when one is ready to dissolve one's ego.

Sometimes they might even go to so-called gurus, who are not enlightened themselves, and go on embellishing their egos further for their own benefit. A real master will see right through our masks, and tear down the false walls of ego straight away. Therefore, pseudo-masters seem to be more successful than the authentic ones, because the pseudo masters are always ready to strengthen your ego. There is no harm; he cannot expose you. A real master will strip you of all your personas, and expose you to the naked truth of your being.

But sometimes, if these people are really fortunate, a rare miracle happens – they recognize real masters. And since these people have already accumulated an immense spiritual heritage in their past lives, much can happen on the very first meeting.

The cruel emperor, Prachanda Ashoka, transformed into the benevolent Priyadarshi Ashok after just one meeting with his master. Amrapali, the famous beauty of her time, became a Buddhist *bhikkhuni* merely after seeing Buddha. Kings Bimbisara and Prasenjita bowed down at the feet of Buddha. Rajarshi Janak of Mithila bowed down at the feet of a twelve-year-old, deformed child, Astavakra, and attained enlightenment in the first meeting itself. Alexander the Great was transformed by his meeting with Diogenes. Indira Gandhi became the disciple of Anandamayi Ma and was deeply interested in Osho and Krishnamurti. Queen Victoria was mesmerized by Shivapuri Baba from the beginning and housed him as a royal guest and her spiritual guide at Buckingham Palace for four years. The king of Khetri surrendered to Swami Vivekananda, and became his disciple. The same was true of the king of Tehri, who became Swami Ramateertha's devotee.

More recently, superstar, Vinod Khanna, became Vinod Bharati, who left his stardom and was content to work as a gardener in his master Osho's garden. The prince of Hanover bowed down at the feet of Osho, became Swami Vimalkirti, and eventually attained enlightenment. Alfred Ford, grandson of the famous Henry Ford became the disciple of Pravupada and was known as Ambarish Das.

But these are exceptional cases where fame, wealth, power or charisma didn't hinder these people from recognizing enlightened masters. If such people come into contact with an authentic master and can surrender themselves, the absolute transformation can happen in a miraculously short period of time. But as I said earlier, it is exceptional. Most successful people are blinded by their own success, and do not have the courage to see beyond the immediate allure of power. It is difficult for them to come down from their high pedestal and to be on the plane of reality, which is where spiritual transformation is possible.

Existence had a similar plan for King Birendra. Without troubling your skeptical mind too much, I would like to share a fact which was revealed to me during meditation: King Birendra had lived as an ascetic and a yogi in his many past lives. He had been so intense and so sincere in his quest that he had earned a heritage of enormous *punya*. My master had assured me that if a personal meeting could be arranged between him and me, his spiritual *sanskara* could have been awakened. Unfortunately, this private meeting couldn't be arranged.

Several times, we had crossed paths and seen each other briefly during a few formal events, but an intimate meeting was due. Every time he saw me, I could detect admiration in his eyes, and they glowed with a sense of recognition. Sadly, he was massacred before this meeting could happen. But I am fully assured that in his next life he will continue his journey as a sincere spiritual seeker, and attain ultimate liberation in no time at all. Another person for whom I have a similar insight is Rajeev Gandhi.

The Unusual Friendship

Osho's revolutionary teaching, combined with his unparalleled wit and poetic appeal, drew a wide range of admirers. As I started sharing his vision in Nepal, I met some of the most remarkable people, from literary giants, poets, artists, and the elite to illiterates, outlaws and bandits.

Our understanding of an individual is so ambition-driven, that generally we evaluate a person's worth in terms of their profession, wealth or intelligence. If we are stripped naked of all personalities, with no rank, recognition or credential to certify our worth, our existence becomes meaningless, unworthy of appreciation. But Osho, like other enlightened masters, was not interested in this show of masks and personalities.

Osho embodies compassion to release all sensitive human

beings from their bondage of misery. And misery, I have come to understand, makes no distinction between rich and poor or scholar and illiterate.

Naval Kishore was a friend who enabled me to understand this precious teaching. He was a close relative of Swami Rakesh, who had helped me to set up the book stall at Peepal Bot. He lived in Bihar, India, and was visiting Swami Rakesh. As Swami Rakesh was a regular at Asheesh, Naval Kishore met me, and in his own words, "fell in love [with me]."

He was a sturdy, well-built man with a remarkably pleasant and easy-going personality. In no time, we became very good friends. He became a regular at the centre and was meditating with us. I have to admit, there was something very childlike and innocent about him that inspired immediate trust. Since he had plenty of leisure time, he also began helping me out with the bookstall. Some days, when I had to work late into the evening, he would open the stall and run it alone.

When one looked at this man with his bright, innocent eyes, one could hardly imagine that he had a notorious past. But as we became more intimate friends, he revealed to me that he had belonged to a famous gang of bandits in Bihar. He told me interesting inside stories about the lives of bandits and their meticulous dedication and devotion to their profession. He said that before they broke into a house, they spent months studying the nature and temperament of the potential clients, their relationship with the neighbours, whether the neighbours were friendly and could possibly intervene during the operation, whether there were firearms in the house, the distance of the house from the closest police station, etc.

Most of the time, the local police officers were taken into

confidence, and there was a general agreement between the police and the bandits that the police were to arrive only when the operation was over. For this, the police officers would receive a good portion of the loot. His stories about police partnership and political protection were intriguing. According to him, politicians were given a handsome sum at election time by the bandits, who also assisted the politicians by capturing election booths, creating riots, kidnapping rivals, and carrying out other routine political crimes. In return, they were rewarded with political protection. If these bandits were arrested accidentally, they would be given immediate bail or minimal punishment.

When I heard his stories about police-criminal compliance, I was terribly upset for days. As a young, idealistic man, I couldn't believe that police, who were supposed to be the custodians of the citizens, were undercover partners in crime. This friendship with Naval Kishore gave me penetrating insights into the dark underbelly of our so-called democratic societies. The whole of humanity suffers from limitless hunger for power. Over the years, I have reflected a great deal over his deep-rooted hankering for power. It is difficult to find a man who is not interested in becoming more powerful. It is insignificant whether this quest for power takes him deeper into the world or into the sublime realms of the spirit. Why is there such a desire for power?

Power is an ability to influence. Until we realize ourselves, our sense of self-worth depends upon the opinions of the masses. Power is simply a tool to manipulate the opinions of others, either through charisma or through oppression, in one's favour. In this mad hunt for power, one has to sell the parts of one's soul piece by piece, because the one who seeks to be appreciated by others cannot be oneself. He must mould himself to the public's liking.

In this way, those in pursuit of power, end up soulless, and not surprisingly, lose their sense of right and wrong.

If we want to establish a truly democratic system, our leaders must be trained in the art of meditation. Only the man who has come to realize complete fulfillment within himself, will not exploit the other. He alone can protect and nurture those who come to his refuge. Therefore, if we envision a welfare society, the basis should be meditation. If one day, society comes to this realization, and I am very optimistic that that day will come sooner rather than later, it would be ready for the teachings of Osho, who is, himself, the blueprint for the future humanity.

Naval Kishor's stories gave me as much insight as they did intrigue. He also told me about hashish smuggling. Marijuana trafficking is one of the oldest and most profitable trades between Nepal and India, and my friend had also been a part of several of these adventurous smuggling entourages. He related many telling tales about the trade. The band of smugglers moved with a caravan that had a stash of money and firearms. They travelled ahead of the band and informed them of any impending danger. There would be a small group carrying pistols and daggers that followed the main group. Usually, there was a prior agreement among the smugglers, local police and local excise authorities, and so the smugglers could cross the border without any problems. But sometimes there was an unforeseen raid from the police or excise headquarters. If the party would be agreeable they would try to negotiate with cash, but if that seemed improbable they would even open fire.

Only accidentally, if there were honest officers, were the smugglers taken into custody. Then, of course, the smugglers' political connections were called for to ensure, most of the time, they would receive minimum punishment or be released on bail.

Outlaws as they were, Naval Kishore told me, the bandits had strict professional ethics. The veterans and ethical leaders forbade their gangs from displaying any unnecessary show of power, and they were particular about leaving the women and children untouched. Some young and rowdy bandits *would* rape or assault women, but that was a matter of shame for those with ethics. Also, they were given strict instructions from the police to avoid murdering anyone during an operation, as it would draw the attention of the media and higher authorities.

Oscar Wilde has said, "The only difference between a saint and a sinner, is every saint has a past, and every sinner, a future." Naval Kishore's perpetual enthusiasm, devotion and innocence inspired me. He meditated regularly with totality, and this gave him great relaxation and depth. Later, he took *sannyas* with Bhagwan, and became a *sannyasin*. Bhagwan even gave Naval his personal handkerchief, which was a precious and rare gift. He had been so inspired by Bhagwan, that later he went back to his gang leader with a few of Bhagwan's books. The leader, too, was transformed by the books, abandoned his career as a bandit, and entered politics and became an Assembly Member. According to Naval, he served his constituency with remarkable honesty and selflessness.

Note: *Both the names have been changed for the sake of privacy.*

The Silent Explosion

I
n 1975, Nepal was under the Panchayat System, the authoritarian monarchical regime. In 1960, King Mahendra had used his emergency powers to dissolve the democratically elected parliament, and took charge of the state's affairs. Civil liberties were curtailed and press freedom was largely compromised. Underneath the ever-vigilant eyes of the state, however, the voices of dissent and the talk of revolution had quietly started brewing.

Naturally, when our Peepal Bot bookstall began attracting a lot of young university students and the thinkers and advisors of the capital, the government's secret service agents took notice of us. For a long time, I didn't know we were under constant surveillance, and neither did I recognize the secret service agents, who had been visiting us in disguise. Our bookstall had become a thriving hub for young, curious minds, who found nourishment and inspiration in Bhagwan's literature. We gathered every evening and spontaneous debates on love, life, freedom and such followed. Durga Prasad Bhandari, who was the Head of the Department of English at Tribhuvan University, was famous for his rebellious and libertine views. He often shared with me that he felt stupefied and humbled by Bhagwan's brilliance and courage. He was one of the earliest intellectuals of the country who endorsed Osho openly. This demanded courage and brilliance in its own right, because in the early days, Osho had been widely misunderstood as the 'Sex Guru', due to his thought-provoking discourses on sex energy and the art of transcendence. These discourses have been compiled into the book *From Sex to Superconsciousness.*

For thousands of years, we have ignored the fundamental topic of sex, turning a deaf ear as though it did not exist. It was Osho who addressed questions on sex for the first time, and with unmatched brilliance and courage. The book immediately earned him critics, who sadly, never went beyond the title of the book. If anyone is to read that book with an unprejudiced mind, one cannot help but be overwhelmed by the truth it contains. Many people, who had brought that book from our stall, had been astonished. They told me they had expected to find erotic content, whereas the book was in fact a treatise on the art of *samadhi.*

Like all geniuses, Osho was born ahead of his time. While the world was still trying to bypass the questions of sexuality, either through over-indulgence as it happened in the West, or through the repressive techniques of the East, Osho addressed the crux of the problem. He saw no contradiction between a spiritual pursuit and normal human sex. We need not bypass one to enjoy the other. Rather, he said, these were two rungs of the same ladder.

One starts from sex, and if it flowers properly, it sublimates and becomes the fragrance, prayer. He says:

The simple truth is that sex is the starting point of love. Sex is the beginning of the journey to love. The origin, the Gangotri of the Ganges of love, is sex, passion -and everybody behaves like its enemy. Every culture, every religion, every guru, every seer has attacked this Gangotri, this source, and the river has remained bottled up. The hue and cry has always been, "Sex is sin. Sex is irreligious. Sex is poison," but we never seem to realize that ultimately it is the sex energy itself that travels to and reaches the inner ocean of love. Love is the transformation of sex energy. The flowering of love is from the seed of sex.

Looking at coal, it would never strike you that when coal is transformed it becomes diamonds. The elements in a lump of coal are the same as those in a diamond. Essentially, there is no basic difference between them. After passing through a process taking thousands of years, coal becomes diamonds.

But coal is not considered important. When coal is kept in a house it is stored in a place where it may not be seen by guests, whereas diamonds are worn around the neck or on the bosom so that everybody can see them. Diamonds and coal are the same: they are two points on a journey by the same element. If you are against coal because it has nothing more to offer than black soot at first glance, the possibility of its transformation into a diamond ends right there. The coal itself could have been transformed into a diamond. But we ignore coal. And so, the possibility of any progress ends.

If his fiery words earned him fanatic critics, it also won him the admiration of some of the most brilliant minds of the time, who made no mistake in recognizing the worth of this modern messiah in whom spirituality had attained a new glory and maturity. Osho was not interested in acting in accord with tradition. He never sought any validation or confirmation. He spoke the naked truth, and offered no consolation.

It seems that there has been a conspiracy, going on for centuries, of mediocre people against the genius. And of course, the mediocre people are in the majority – they have all the power. They have the government, they have the military, they have the police, they have the nuclear weapons. The genius has nothing except his intelligence, and intelligence is basically revolutionary; it cannot be otherwise. It's very quality, its intrinsic quality, is rebellion – rebellion against darkness, rebellion against untruth, rebellion against slavery, rebellion against everything that prevents man from becoming his total, grown-up self.

Osho personified this rebellion. He spoke the inconvenient truth, and invited us to drop our masks to find the real answer, and not be content with the ready-made answers supplied to us. I sympathise with people who feel offended by Osho's invitation, because to drop what we have believed to be our identity, and move towards the unknown, requires great courage. I am not surprised that many of us cannot muster up this courage, and in defense, criticise his teaching. But Osho has heralded a new age, and so divided history into two distinct eras: Before Osho and After Osho.

It was not surprising that the young and rebellious folks were among the earliest admirers of Osho in Nepal, too. Dr. Bhandari was visiting our stall regularly, and gave extemporaneous talks on liberty and love. But during that time, any kind of radicalism or revolutionary ideas were viewed cautiously, with mistrust. Interestingly, the secret service agents mistook the titles of Bhagwan's books such as *Women's Revolution, Youth and Rebellion, Beware of Socialism*, and the like, to be politically driven books.

So they reported that I was selling political books, and that our stall encouraged public debate on sensitive issues. They began keeping tabs on our activities. Eventually, when they spotted *The Silent Explosion* on our shelf, all hell broke loose.

Bishnu Pratap Shah, who was the zonal commissioner of Bagmati zone at that time, was reported that a young engineer had been selling books on how to make explosives, silently. He immediately issued warrants for both my arrest and that of my aide, Naval Kishore, who they had judged to be equally dangerous.

It was a pleasant autumn evening. The offices had closed for the day, and New Road was slowly coming to life. There were very few vehicles in those days. The big, golden sun was rolling down slowly, staining the clouds with a frail cherry pink. The weather was warm and pleasant. A group of university students had gathered as usual, when out of the blue, two security personnel appeared and said authoritatively, "Let's go to the police station."

We all stood there, stunned.

"But why, surely we haven't committed any crime?" I said.

The man replied, "I have been ordered to take you to the police station. You can give your justification there. We don't owe you any explanation."

I broke into a cold sweat. On closer inspection, I realized that the man who had come to arrest us had been visiting our stall in civilian clothes almost every day. It was my first encounter with police, and I was uncertain why we were being arrested. Naval Kishore, on the other hand, was in his element. They informed us that all the books were being seized, as they were dangerous for the state. They ordered us to pack them all up, and forced us to carry them on our backs. Naval Kishore did it with impressive efficiency and calm. But I was stupefied by the whole situation. As we carried the books along the road, ironically, I remembered a statement by Bhagwan, "For your whole life, you've been carrying the burden of scriptures that doesn't allow you to roam freely beneath the skies of freedom."

I smiled feebly to myself. Soon, a big crowd gathered around us. Everyone was surprised to learn we'd been arrested. Some of my friends protested, but the police were stern, and repeated, "You can give your justification at the station. Right now, you must walk there with us."

We carried the books on our backs, and walked towards the Janaseva police station in New Road. A small procession of young friends and sympathisers followed us. By the time we arrived, and it had not taken us long to walk from our stall, I was a little scared. Our friends, who had followed us all the way, were not allowed inside. I appealed to the officers, saying that we had been wrongfully arrested, as we had not committed any crime. The truth was, I did not even know *why* we had been arrested. Much to my frustration, the Sub-Inspector, who was the officer on duty, informed us that Her Majesty the Queen was attending a reception in their area that day, and the police inspector, who was in charge and could listen to our appeal, was out on security duty. We had to wait at least until he arrived. That day, apart from the two of us, about a dozen young men had been arrested for petty robbery, pick pocketing and other minor crimes. The whole atmosphere was strangely dehumanizing. If anyone had to attend to nature's call, all of us had to march together to the compound wall, and urinate under the surveillance of several policemen, who continued scrutinizing us with detest and suspicion.

Every evening at eight o'clock, the detainees would receive a routine beating. That evening too, the head constable, a well built man and also the holder of a black belt in Karate, entered the cell. All of us stood up in terror. He started punching the detainees one by one. The police had to attend martial arts training every morning, and in the evening, they got to practice their skills on the detainees. We were all standing in a circle. As the police came nearer, I began to tremble. I grabbed my *mala*, and prayed to Bhagwan. The aggressor moved right in front of me, stood there and stared at me. I kept trembling and praying to Bhagwan. Just as he was about to punch me, the police constable to whom I had related my entire story, intervened and said, "Sir, he hasn't committed any crime. He was simply selling books, and he is a qualified government engineer."

Miraculously, we were saved at the last moment. When the police moved away from me, I pulled Naval Kishore aside, and he too was spared. I sighed. The police beat the person standing next to us with double the vengeance.

The inspector returned at two o'clock in the morning, after the royal dinner. He was blissfully drunk, and in no state to hear anything. Later that morning, when he had sobered up, I went and showed him my official identity card, and explained that I was only selling religious books.

He replied, "It was the order of the zonal commissioner. His office opens at ten o'clock, and you can appeal to him. I've been ordered to present you before him."

At ten o'clock, with the books on our backs, we were about to head off for the commissioner's office at Ranipokhari. As his office was quite some distance away, and the books were heavy, we asked the police to get us a taxi. They replied shrewdly that if we were prepared to pay the fare, a taxi could be arranged. And so we travelled to the commissioner's office by taxi.

When we arrived, the police handed over a small note, announcing our arrival. We were kept waiting outside the commissioner's office for the whole day, but did not hear anything from him. Fortunately, I met Mr Shrestha, who was a retired zonal commissioner, and family friend of ours. He was surprised to see me with the police and the confiscated books. He asked me about the situation, so I told him the whole story. He went inside the office and checked my file, then he came out and explained to us that we had been arrested for "selling political and revolutionary books". It was unbelievable.

After hearing my story, he went inside the commissioner's office again, assured them that he knew me *and* my parents, and that I was not up to any criminal activity. He also told them I came from a reputable family and that I wouldn't be involved in anything that would pose a threat to the present system. We were released on bail for the night, on the written condition to appear at the office at ten o'clock sharp the next morning. I was grateful to learn that we wouldn't have to spend another painful night in police custody.

But the troubles had not ended there. When I arrived home, I discovered that my parents had been panicking for the last twenty-four hours, as I had vanished without a trace. They didn't know anything about the arrest. They were already unhappy that I was a disciple of Bhagwan and spending my whole time spreading his message. If I told them about the arrest, they would simply go crazy, so I had to lie that I had spent the night at my friend's place. The next day, I had to face my manager at work, who was also angry because I had been absent without prior notice. I immediately wrote a leave application, and left for the commissioner's office. After going there again, we had to wait until five o'clock in the evening, then sign a document ensuring we would return at ten o'clock the next morning. The same routine continued for the next fourteen days. It was quite an experience for me. We were kept like prisoners in the office. Naturally, this was very troublesome because I couldn't go to work, and I would often meet acquaintances and relatives, in the commissioner's office, who were surprised to see me there. On the fifteenth day, Mr Dawadi, the assistant zonal commissioner was appointed to read and censure the books and look into the case. He prepared a report stating he had looked through all the books and found them to be harmless and non-political.

As I found out later, Mr Dawadi was a religious person. Reading the books, he was stunned by Bhagwan's marvellous commentaries on the *Bhagavad Gita, Upanishads, Shiva Sutra* and other spiritual works. He wrote in his report that the books were purely spiritual and were not politically motivated and he recommended that everybody should read them.

In fact, he did not want to part with them, so when he called me to his office, he said, "I found nothing objectionable in the books. But by selling the books without them being censored by the government, you have violated the present laws of the country."

During the monarchy, it was mandatory for every book in the country to be censored, by the relevant authority, before it could be distributed or sold.

Mr Dawadi said, "So we will keep two copies of each book

for censoring, and if you get any new books, get them censored by us before you start selling them." So if I wanted to sell them, it was mandatory to have all the books reviewed first.

I understood that Mr Dawadi loved the books and wanted to read them.

I asked him if I could start selling the books again in the same spot. He said he was not in a position to say yes or no; that was up to me to decide.

It took us a few days to recover from the shock. We had gone through a great financial loss because our stock for book was very limited and we had lost the greater number of our books, but we began selling them again at Peepal Bot. Through the stall, many people had already become connected with Asheesh Meditation Centre and had started visiting the centre on weekends. After some time, we decided that the bookstall had served its purpose, and people were now coming to the centre for the evening Kundalini meditation, so we focused all our energy and time on the centre.

Four years later, when I was working at the Pune ashram, I saw Mr Dawadi come through the gates. Surprised to see him there, I said, "Mr Dawadi, what brings you here?"

"Don't act so naive. It is all your doing. I read all the books that we had confiscated, and I have become his fan," he said smiling.

He met Bhagwan, and related the entire story to him. Later, he began frequenting Asheesh, and became a good friend. Many times, he also provided official support to the centre. And so it was that existence played a strange trick which connected me with Mr Dawadi, who became a good friend of mine and a great support to our ashram.

Soon the who's who of Kathmandu began pouring into the ashram. After selling Bhagwan's books in New Road for two years, many Kathmanduites became aware of Bhagwan, and I would often find myself welcoming strangers to Asheesh - strangers who came looking for the centre, just as Bhagwan had promised.

The Princess Arrives

To our surprise, one Saturday afternoon during the weekly *satsang*, a royal procession arrived at our centre, with a fanfare and a big silver tray of fresh roses. The lane outside Asheesh had suddenly come alive with music and activity. I looked outside and saw a princess walking with a regal gait onto our property. Following her was Mr Dawadi, who was visibly in a very good mood.

"Meet Her Highness Princess Princep Shah," Mr Dawadi said, introducing me.

She smiled cordially and returned my namaste. We were all surprised by this unexpected royal visit. Princep Shah was then King Birendra's aunt. She lived in a private palace at Tahachal, which was quite close to our centre. Mr Dawadi used to visit the palace in the capacity of Assistant Zonal Commissioner, and was Princep Shah's favourite administrator. Gradually, he had come to realize that the princess had an interest in religion and spirituality, as he himself did. He began telling her about Bhagwan and our meditation centre at Tahachal. As he was full of praise for Bhagwan and his teachings, the princess became curious and decided to visit the centre.

Naturally I was nervous, because we were in the middle of afternoon *satsang*, and I didn't know how to receive a princess. But Princep Shah was very gracious, unpretentious and simple. She said she would sit down on the floor like the rest of us, and listen to Bhagwan's discourse. I played a discourse which I chose at random from my small collection. It was one I hadn't heard before. Miraculously, in that particular discourse, Bhagwan was denouncing Jayaprakash Narayan's political advertisement details, the denouncement of which was in agreement with the princess's political standing, and so it pleased her. Rupchandra Bista, who initiated the *Thaha* movement, was also a regular visitor at the centre at that time. He later congratulated me for being clever enough to choose a discourse of the princess's liking but it was only a coincidence.

After the meditation session, Princep Shah met my mother. As my mother had a political background and a good connection with the palace, they bonded well. The princess was filled with appreciation for Bhagwan's ground breaking and profound political analysis and his wit. She was very gracious to me, and praised me freely for running a spiritual centre. As she left, she asked me to visit her private palace with some of Bhagwan's books. She wanted to hear more about him and meditation, and asked me to visit her during my free time. A few days later, I went to the palace with some books. But I was too shy to meet the princess, so I left the books with the courtiers, and returned home.

Princep Shah was drawn towards Bhagwan; she read a few of his books with interest. One fine day, the then queen of Nepal, Aishwarya Rajya Laxmi Shah, was visiting Princep Shah. After spending some time with the queen, the princess told her about her recent visit to Asheesh Meditation Centre at Tahachal, and about Bhagwan and me, for both of whom she was full of praises. The queen wanted to know more about Bhagwan, so they sent someone to fetch my mother - I had gone to work.

The queen had reservations about Bhagwan, as she had read articles that projected him as a "Sex Guru", who preached a libertine and promiscuous lifestyle. It is incredible to see how Bhagwan had been so misunderstood by the media. As the famous author, Tom Robbins, wrote in the *Seattle Post-Intelligencer*, "I am not, nor have I ever been, a disciple of Bhagwan Shree Rajneesh, but I've read enough of his brilliant books to be convinced that he was the greatest spiritual teacher of the twentieth century - and I've read enough vicious propaganda and slanted reports to suspect that he was one of the most maligned figures in history."

The queen had also read this propaganda, but Princep Shah convinced her that Bhagwan was a phenomenal guru and his lectures were worth listening to.

My mother arrived at Princep Shah's palace. She had taken a copy the *English bi-monthly Sannyas magazine. Rajneesh Times* magazine, in English. When the queen and the princess asked her to tell them about Osho, she gave them the copy of the magazine. Accidentally, the magazine had some pictures from a Tantra group therapy session. The queen was already prejudiced against Osho, and these pictures only strengthened her view. She looked at the pictures and said, "This is why I have reservations against Osho."

My mother, who had already become a *sannyasin*, tried to defend the magazine, but as she was a new initiate, she didn't do so well. Moreover, she had chosen the wrong magazine, as an introduction to Osho's teaching, for the queen. Nevertheless, the queen was still intrigued by Osho. "Why didn't you bring your son, he could have explained Osho's teachings better," she said. She also asked my mother to come to the royal palace someday with *me*, to explain more about Osho and his teaching. Unfortunately, that day never came.

PART V

PUNE AGAIN

Pune Again

It was early 1979, and Pune still maintained its glory as the exotic city, the retreat of the maharajas. The crisp Indian weather with its tropical flavour leaves one nostalgic. There, one can almost smell the fragrance of the earth. Like the aroma of an Indian dish, the vibration of this country is as subtle as it is spicy. It is a country where the visible and the invisible both have equal roles to play in forming it. The coexistence of the heavy presence of life and the acknowledgement of death is what makes it so special. Everything in India is an expansion of this very concept; poets, artists, romantics and seekers couldn't agree more with me.

I am still reminded of the beautiful Pune evenings, the bustling traffic and the noise of trains passing by, the wearying city life and the peacefulness of its outskirts, and through all of it, running like a thread, the subtle presence of the mystic residing there. This mystic was my master, known to the world as Bhagwan Shree Rajneesh, and his presence in the city made Pune the abode of my heart and being.

My heavenly romance with Bhagwan was destined to be there, or to be more precise, in Koregaon Park where his ashram was located. With large bungalows of former maharajas, surrounded by vast stretches of green lawns that extended out to well-maintained streets lined with ancient trees, Koregaon Park was one of the prestigious areas of Pune, and still speaks of the prestige and glory of the maharajas' lifestyle in India. All the bungalows there were owned by various maharajas and rich businessmen, and were vacant most of the time except during the horse-racing season when the royals would visit the city. However, what I experienced at the feet of my master during the year 1979 was far from a royal experience.

In her book, *Pilgrims of the Stars*, Indira Devi says, "True gurus are very rare in this world, but true disciples are still rarer." Bhagwan has stated this fact in his lectures many a times. The task of a real master is not an easy one. He has to design tests of one's mettle for the disciples, and constantly work upon the disciple's ego so that one day it can be totally dissolved. Sometimes the master has to be really hard on the disciple, and there is a great chance the disciple will misinterpret and misunderstand the master's compassion.

The hammering can be so painful that sometimes we disciples find it easier to leave than to endure the surgery upon what is so dear to us, our egos. This is why many disciples are like fair-weather friends; while the master is loving and sweet, they stay with him, but as soon as the master begins doing his real work, the disciples drop him and flee.

1979 was my year of the test of my mettle. I always wanted to stay with my master and every time I asked for permission, he would send me back to Nepal after I had stayed in Pune for three or four months, saying that much work had to be done in the Himalayan kingdom, and I was to put my total energy into it. Fully expecting the same answer, again I made my old request via Bhagwan's office through which the message would be conveyed, and Bhagwan's answer returned. Bhagwan was no longer speaking during the *darshans*. *Darshan* literally means to get a view, but usually refers to holy people and holy places, in which context it means anauspicious view. Every evening, the *darshan* was held at Chuang Tzu Auditorium in Bhagwan's residence, Lao Tzu House. And it is there that Osho's samadhi was later built.

A visiting *sannyasin* would generally get two *darshans*, one on arrival, which was known as the *arrival darshan*, and one before departing, known as the *leaving darshan*. From 1978, these *darshans* became energy *darshans*, during which Bhagwan spoke less with words and conveyed more with his energy, giving direct *shaktipat* to those who came to see him, with the help of his twelve mediums, while the orchestrated live music played wildly in the background, and lights flickered as Bhagwan controlled them with the switch under his feet. It was almost theatrical and heavenly at the same time; Bhagwan was a perfectionist and a great artist, he made the best use of the available technology, and with his great aesthetic flair, nothing was, or could ever be, boring. After receiving an energy *darshan*, one had to wait three months for the next one. During the energy *darshan* the whole ashram had to be blacked out and all works were stopped. Except for the guards everybody was to sit in meditation for half an hour. Even disciples residing outside Pune were requested to sit in silence for half an hour so that Bhagwan could channelize his energy.

During *darshans*, Bhagwan sat at the front in his swivel chair, while one by one, the gathering of *sannyasins* would move up to him as their names were called. Apart from the guests, the regular audience for the verbal *darshans* were also seated around Bhagwan. This included Bhagwan's secretary, Ma Yoga Laxmi, his caretaker, Ma Yoga Vivek, his gardener, Ma Mukta, the Greek heiress who gave Lao Tzu House to Bhagwan, his bodyguard, Shiva, who later betrayed him, and Ma Maneesha, who used to record the *darshans* in which Bhagwan spoke. These recordings were later transcribed into volumes of beautiful books with images, called *darshan Diaries*. During the verbal *darshans*, one could touch his feet, talk to him, or ask him personal questions about their life, relationships and other matters. I remember, during these personal meetings, people even asking him what lentils they should eat or how many cups of tea was good for their health. Bhagwan also initiated interested seekers into *sannyas* during these *darshans*.

The energy *darshans* had a completely different flavour. Twelve young and beautiful *sannyasin ma*, who Bhagwan had chosen as his energy mediums, would sit beside Bhagwan and assist during *shaktipat*. The work of these mediums was to channel Bhagwan's energy and pass it on to the receiving guest who had come for the *darshan*. All the mediums lived in close proximity to Bhagwan's house, and lived a very strict life, unlike the other *sannyasins* in the ashram. It was compulsory for all mediums to do daily meditation in order to be constantly in tune with Bhagwan's energy. Even before choosing a boyfriend, they first had to consult Bhagwan for permission, as the person might not be right for them and a wrong person can disturb the psyche of the medium. These mediums were given very meditative schedule and Bhagwan was very particular about what they ate. They were asked to remain strictly vegetarian and not to touch alcohol or tobacco. Once it happened that Bhagwan was feeling difficulty in passing his energy through one of his mediums. Bhagwan was also wondering why she was not allowing the free flow of his energy. He checked her routine and her food menu and he said that it was because she was eating eggs and that heaviness obstructed the flow of energy.

During the energy *darshan*, Bhagwan would call the mediums over and position them around the guest, asking them to support the guest from the back or to touch a certain energy centre of the guest, while he would do *shaktipat* by touching the third eye of the guest with one hand and that of the medium with the other hand. There was no specific rule on how Bhagwan orchestrated the energy *darshan*; everything was arranged according to his intuition and his consideration of the guest who was sitting in front of him. The lights in the whole ashram would be switched off, and everybody was asked to merge into the energy from wherever they were in the ashram. Later, all centres around the world were asked to join in by sitting in meditation at the same time. We also participated at Asheesh meditation centre in Nepal. Musicians would play wild music as *sannyasins* swayed with it and drowned in Bhagwan's energy. It was quite something to be in receipt of Bhagwan's *shaktipat*. People's response took on different expressions; some would cry, scream, or laugh, while others would just fall down. These people had to be carried back to their places, supported by other *sannyasins*, as they were unable to stand up alone. Bhagwan was carrying out a great experiment, which continued until the 10th of April, 1981, after which he stopped giving energy *darshans* and *sannyas* by himself.

That evening, sitting on the chair, wearing his spotless, long-sleeved, long white gown, Bhagwan looked majestic. His olive skin glistened in the evening light, and his long, greying hair would move slightly, nudged by the soft Pune evening breeze. It was an experience to sit in front of Bhagwan. Despite his majestic appearance, he was a very simple man, the simplest you could ask for. Whoever was in front of him received his total attention as he would pour all his energy into that person. As he moved, his well-manicured hands would make the most artistic gestures, while his eyebrows made 'mountains' every time he enlarged his eyes to emphasize something.

When my turn came, I went up to him and sat at the front. I was happy to be back with my master. He was a like a great ancient mountain, wise and enormous. His energy field was so strong that one felt intoxicated with bliss. I always felt a thick cloud of energy covering me every time I was in his vicinity. Sitting near him was like sitting near the giant H*imalay*as covered in white snow. That evening I received my energy *darshan* as Bhagwan tapped my third eye and poured his energy into me. It was unbearable for me; I screamed and cried, and screamed some more. I used to have this experience even before the energy *darshans* started. Whenever Bhagwan touched my forehead I used to feel a great electric shock and my whole body used to tremble and I used to cry so loudly that everybody in the ashram knew that I was getting *shaktipat*. Thanks to Bhagwan that he is doing it again through me and each time when *sannyas* happens at Tapoban or wherever I conduct meditation camps Bhagwan gives energy *darshan* using my body and people go into the same trance and they cry and scream out of ecstasy. I could clearly visualize that Bhagwan is playing his game again. Many early *sannyasins* who have lived in Pune I have similar experience. The music whizzed and rumbled round the room, and the lights flickered frantically as the bodies of the mediums swayed like spindly trees in the wind. Every time I had an energy *darshan*, the effect of it lasted for days. I felt drugged and drunk the whole time. That night I had a deep sleep, and when I woke up the next morning, the sweet drunkenness from the evening before still lingered.

I went to the ashram where good news was waiting for me. To my utmost surprise, Bhagwan granted my wish, and allowed me to stay and work in the Pune ashram. Little did I know of the divine conspiracy that he had mischievously designed for me, which would not only challenge me physically, but would also test my mental, spiritual and emotional states, and bring it all to a boiling point.

The First Blow

Back home, I had been serving the Nepalese government as an engineer, and slowly my lifestyle had been improving. The Pune ashram was expanding and a great deal of construction work was happening there. I was totally confident I would get some work related to my engineering skills, or something to do with my experience as the meditation centre leader back in Nepal. The first blow: I was not allowed to work in the construction department or in the office. Instead, I was given the work of a cook. The second blow: I was not allowed to work in the main ashram building, but was assigned to the ashram restaurant and health centre, away from the ashram, commonly known as "74", which was the number of the building. There, I had to cook Indian food.

The restaurant was called *His Place*. It was located

at 74 Koregaon Park, about 500 metres behind the main ashram building, and was where hundreds of people would eat. I had never worked in a restaurant kitchen, and had no experience as a cook, so the recipes and menu looked very strange to me. There were other cooks there who made continental food, but my task was that of curry and spice. Although working in the kitchen was not my dream job at the ashram, I was still happy; my joy knew no bounds, as I could finally be with my master, staying near him. Now I would easily glide through all adversities and fulfill every challenge my master was to place in front of me, or so I thought. How unaware I was of the difficult months ahead.

It is not an easy task to feed people. The kitchen is a complex institution, and a large kitchen is a large, complex institution. At the ashram, the kitchen and the cleaning section are the most active and difficult departments, and have to be in constant function throughout the day. The kitchen staff is always busy either cooking or preparing for the next cooking session. My work at *His Place* included cooking all kinds of Indian dishes.

It was easy to make rice, and learning to make *daal*-fry was not that difficult. Even today when I am travelling in the West, sometimes I love to make *daal*-fry, and everyone enjoys it. Little do they know that I am a seasoned alumnus of His Place. I could also make the *halva* easily. The most difficult things to make were the chapatis and *dosa*; thank god, the chappatis were made by a team of Gujarati Mas working under Ma Sohan. But what really tested my tolerance and perseverance were the Indian *dosas*, pancakes made from rice flour and pulses.

Cooking the unfamiliar menu was not the only thing that tested me at *His Place*. If being in the boiling hot, oven-like room was not enough, there was the timing system, designed perfectly to keep me away from my master. My kitchen duty schedule was 7:00am to 1:00pm, and 5:00pm to 10:00pm, which usually used to get extended up to 11:00pm for cleaning. So my break was from 2:00pm to 5:00pm. Bhagwan would give his discourses at 8:00am, by which time I would be already busy making *dal-fry* in the 'cooking factory'.

That was not the end of my woes. Bhagwan's ashram was a cosmopolitan society, a New Age ashram where the efficiency of each culture was put to best use. So the management of the ashram was in the hands of the Europeans, and mostly Germans, the best managers one could find in the world. Most of the coordinators at *His Place* were Germans. It was utmost discipline and punctuality that ruled the kitchen. Even being one minute late was considered as eternal delay, and would be marked in red. Being brought up in Nepal, a fifteen-minute delay is not considered late at all, so sometimes I would argue with my supervisors, and ask them, "How can one minute be considered as being late?

They would say, "You should come a minute before. Why can't you come at 6:59?"

Such was the strict discipline and I had never worked under such a draconian order before. My work would never finish on time, and most of the days, I would be working until the late hours. I used to wear shorts, as I had to stand throughout every shift. But this was not all that was in store for me. The next problem was accommodation.

Somji Estate building was about five hundred metres from the ashram on the other side, and had been turned into a dormitory for the workers, so the management allowed me to stay there. All my life, I'd had my own room, and was never comfortable in sharing a room with another person. Now here I was in an overcrowded dormitory, trying to find sleeping space and I had to pay six rupees per night for it. To my relief, I was told that I could share another room with four women; it was better than living in a crowded dormitory. It was a short-lived joy, however, because when I entered my room there were four hippie girls sleeping in the four corners of the small room which had no windows or ventilation. I had to sleep in the middle of the room, and we had to keep the door open all the time for ventilation. That was the only ventilation in our room. It was a torture living with those four European hippies. They kept the room very dirty and in the name of cleanliness they had no traits whatsoever. Apart from that, they would talk loudly during the night, and sometimes even shout and fight. It was the first time in my life that I was among such unsophisticated, wild women.

The ashram's atmosphere was very open, and Bhagwan allowed his *sannyasins* to have relationships. The four *mas* had active sex lives. Their boyfriends would visit them once in a while and they would make love in that same room. That was the first time I was sleeping in a room where couples were making love around me. They had no inhibitions, and would freely express their emotions loudly. The rule at that time was that the lights in the whole of Somji Estate, except in the toilet, were to be switched off right at 11:00pm. Usually, 11:00pm to 12:00am was the peak hour of romance, and one could hear the sounds of ecstasy coming from the lovemaking couples. It was a challenge for a single Nepali man to sleep surrounded by all this romantic music being played loudly around me. It was not only in my room, but also the whole dormitory would be filled with the sounds of couples having sex. There was no escape, except the toilet. So usually I'd take a book and stay in the toilet for ages until everything quietened down, and generally it took one-two hours before everything settled down to silence. It was a blessing in disguise, however, that I could finish reading during this period. After my 'toilet meditation', I had to return to my sleeping place. It was a torture to live in that non-ventilated room. I could not sleep well for many nights, and I was working very hard during the day. When it became too much, I finally decided to leave Somji Estate and find some cheap accommodation in town, but even the cheapest accommodation was expensive for my pocket.

The unventilated, crowded room having become impossible for me to live in, I packed my bag, and was moving out when Mahesh saw me. He was the in-charge of the dormitory, and I had asked him several times to give me a better place, but he was deaf to my requests. When he saw that I was actually leaving, he softened and gave me a space on the verandah. It was an open verandah and well ventilated. Still I was sharing the space with others out there, but I could see the sky and trees outside, so it felt like paradise to me. I stayed there for many months, quite happy. Had it not been for the contrast of the torturous, unventilated room with the hippies, I would not have enjoyed my newly found shelter beneath the sky.

I was happy with my free accommodation on the verandah. I had very limited funds on me, as I had not come prepared to live there for long. I was sure Bhagwan would again send me back, so I had planned for ten days only. I had to pay six rupees a day for my accommodation, and ten rupees every day to enter the ashram. The entry fee was to be made free after one month, but only if they liked my work. This was the general rule.

I fed hundreds of people at the restaurant, but I couldn't

afford to eat there. The minimum price of any dish was above my means. So in order for me to stretch the funds for my longer stay in Pune, I looked for the cheapest meals available. Sometimes I would eat cheap unhealthy food from street vendors, and other times I would eat at the railway station. The cheapest meal there cost two rupees, and the place was frequented by the rickshaw *wallahs*. The rickshaw fare to the station was four rupees, which was out of the question for me. So in the beginning, I would walk to the bus depot, catch the bus to a certain stop, and again walk for a while to the train station. The bus fare was fifteen paisa. Later, when my savings were almost finished, I would walk the entire four kilometres just to get my lunch. It was a matter of great irony that I was feeding hundreds of people at the restaurant, but could never eat there.

I was slowly running out of money, and could see it wouldn't be long before I'd be unable to pay for my accommodation and ashram entry. I went to the management to ask for free food passes, but was told they were provided only after six months of satisfactory work in the ashram, and that, too, on the recommendation of my coordinator. I had to figure out something. There used to be plenty of leftovers in the restaurant. The kitchen staff had the privilege of eating them once working hours were over. I no longer had to go for the cheap food alternatives; I began eating there - but had to wait until our duties were over.

However, eating the leftovers was quite an awkward task. Some days there would be only vegetables, and other days, just rice. One day I would eat just salad, while another day I had to gulp down the remaining *daal*. I would be hungry from the morning on, so at night I would drink bowls and bowls of *daal*. In adversity, one learns to adapt to anything that is available. In hunger, any food is a great delicacy. Today it all seems like a faraway dream to me, but that was my reality in those days. I realized how privileged I had been as a cook, only when I was transferred to other departments.

So in the kitchen, the food that would keep until the next day would be packed up, and only the produce that would go off overnight would be given to us. Although they were meager leftovers and weird combinations of food, it was still a great blessing to me; I no longer had to hunt for cheap food stalls.

All my friends would console me, saying that after one month my department will be changed and all my troubles will come to an end. Finally, that decisive day came when I completed my hard penance as the Indian Cook at *His Place*. I couldn't wait to move on to the new department. The department coordinator called me to the office where a surprise awaited me.

One lesson to be learnt in Pune with Bhagwan was that life could never be predicted, and expectations never fulfilled. Maybe I had not learnt my lesson well enough during this month in the kitchen, so Bhagwan had planned more classes for me in the coming days.

"Is This What I Came For?"

Working in the hot Indian kitchen for thirty days wore me out, body and brain. What I had thought would be the beginning of a great spiritual adventure was nothing but confinement within the walls of the busy cooking factory of *His Place*. My life was rolling between cumin and coriander and the vast maze of other Indian spices. Of course, it *was* the beginning of my spiritual adventure, but it was to take a good deal of time before I figured this out.

Life was mocking me. On one hand, all the physical work I was doing had increased my appetite tremendously, and I was amidst a great abundance of food, but the bitter irony on the other hand was that my access and freedom to devour it was equally constrained. For me, this period was that of my death in many ways: the death of a disciple's expectations, the death of an

237

engineer and center leader's ego and the death of my limitations to survive. It was also the birth of acceptance and surrender, and the birth of a confidence that now I could go anywhere in the world and do anything to survive.

When I went to my coordinator after completing a month as the Indian cook, I had great hopes. I was fully assured that I had passed my litmus test successfully and would now be given an easier and respectable task. Somewhere vaguely inside, I was hopeful that now I would be resurrected to a respectful engineering role or any other white collar job. The coordinator announced my next job; I was transferred to the Pot Washing department.

I couldn't believe what I was hearing. From a cook, I was now demoted to the pot washer. Back then, the kingdom of Nepal was a very class-conscious society. Pot washing was looked upon as work done by the lower class and poor people, and to some extent I was not free from this conditioning either. For someone with an honorable engineering job in the government and the position of a center leader, it was a great insult to have to wash pots. But I swallowed my pride, cursed my fate, and accepted my verdict. If washing pots was what I needed to do to be around my master, then so be it.

The kitchen used to be a very 'happening' place. There were many other *sannyasins* working along with me, so I was never alone in the kitchen. Of course the work was demanding and kept one occupied, but with so many *sannyasins* in one place there were lots of hugs and jokes, and laughter and gossip flying every minute that kept one entertained. The first thing that hit me in my new job was that now I was all alone. In that damp windowless room, my only company were the human-sized, greasy pots that kept on coming from different kitchens in the ashram to be scrubbed and washed. Some of them were so big that I could not even lift them alone.

The pots needed a huge amount of elbow grease and grinding of my bones, in fact it demanded all of my body pressure, to scrub the grease and oil from those gigantic metal containers. Sometimes just one pot would require hours of scrubbing. The room was a dark cell with no opening for light, so even in the daytime the lights had to remain on. For a whole month, I could not see how the day was passing. It was a cold, damp place, and most of the time I had to stand knee-deep in water that used to collect in the washing room due to the blocked drain. I would sit on a plastic stool while I scrubbed and washed the pots, and wearing only shorts and a vest during my working hours, every night I would have a cold from being in the damp room for too long, and my arms would be aching because of the tedious scrubbing. Many times, I thought of returning home where I was earning a good salary and didn't have to labor in so much discomfort. I used to keep on questioning myself, "Is this what I came for?"

As I was not working in the kitchen anymore, I didn't have the privilege of eating the leftovers at *His Place*. Again, the big problem was how to arrange for my food. I only had a one-hour lunch break, which meant I could no longer walk to the stalls for cheap food. So I went back to eating the inexpensive food sold by the street vendors. This included the famous Maharashtrian pavbhaji, vadapav, pakoras and potato chops. Sometimes I just ate bananas and other fruits. The owner of Prem Restaurant had just opened his venue, and he was a good friend of mine. After much pleading, I finally persuaded him to include a cheap *thali* on his menu for people like me.

The cheap *thali* still cost five rupees, so it was not as cheap as I had expected. Whenever I'd had enough of my impoverished life, I would benevolently treat myself with the five-rupee *thali* at Prem's, and this was a lavish dinner for me. Sometimes a generous friend would arrive there and ordered the grilled cheese sandwich or mango lassi for me. Only I know how happy it would make me. In intense hunger, one realizes that food can be the source of the greatest joy, and it is such a privilege to be able to have the food of one's taste. The human mind is a very creative organism; in great adversity it invents a variety of tactics so one can survive. I had friends who used to handle the ice cream in the kitchen. I convinced them to send me over the residual layer of ice cream on the walls of the jars that they sent for cleaning. At the very sight of those jars that contained my heavenly delight, I would jump on them, scraping them out with my fingers and a spoon, and lick every last drop off them. One should have seen the sight of my contentment. That was the only source of energy I had to sustain me for hours of heavy friction, pushing slimy grease off metal surfaces.

Now that my duty hours were from 10:00am to 6:00pm, I had the privilege of attending the evening dance and the morning lectures. The other privilege I had while working as the Pot Washer was that after working for six days, I would get a day off during which I'd catch up on sleep, do my laundry and clean the bedding. Through this period, amidst all the physical and mental torment, I learnt great lessons of life. One of which is that I learnt to value small privileges and small joys: the free hot showers with a bar of free soap that I used to get at the ashram after washing the pots, the rare opportunities when I got to eat the food of my choice at Prem's - nothing could be taken for granted.

After showering and changing into a fresh gown, I would be in bliss experiencing the condensed energy of the buddhafield and Bhagwan, and the evenings there were of great celebration. Once the clean gown was on, I felt like an emperor. All the discomfort I was going through created the backdrop for me to enjoy every small delight that was available. My mornings were free for the discourse, and my evenings were free for the music group. Although I had the time to do the dynamic meditation I had no energy available to entertain this idea. To see Bhagwan after a month and to attend the morning lectures were however a matter of great delight. When I saw Bhagwan after a month I remember crying out of ecstasy.

Two months had passed since the disciple had begun struggling to stay around the master. While the disciple was washing the cooking pots, the master was cooking up in his own cosmic pot. And nobody knew what new ingredients he would add to the mix.

The Dishwasher
Becomes the Boss!

D uring my stint as the ashram's dishwasher, there was an unexpected change in my fate. This time it was a good one. Although it was a short-lived luxury, it was the most joyful moment of my stay. The ashram's purchaser had gone home, and someone new was required to fill the role. The management suddenly transferred me from my department, and made me the new purchaser. My work was to buy vegetables, fruits and other essentials needed in the ashram. The Purchase department was the most lavish department in the ashram, and the purchaser could be handling thousands of rupees every day.

The ashram used a very systematic and progressive method of purchasing. Each department would make a list of its requirements, and put it in my pigeonhole. My work was to collect the lists, analyze them and calculate the required budget, and then place the request in the pigeon hole of the accounting department. The accountant and the purchaser never met, but the money would always be there in the pigeon hole of the accounting department. There were only two keys to open the pigeon hole, one with me and the other with the accounts section. I just had to put the unspent amount and receipts back in the pigeon hole after the purchase was made. The whole process was based totally on trust.

As Purchaser, I was given a vehicle, a three-wheeler Tempo, to use to make my purchases. The only problem was that I didn't know how to drive it. I had driven a car and a motorbike, but never a trike, and an unsophisticated one at that. It was very difficult to maneuver this three-wheeled beast on the road. So I asked one of my Indian friends who had been a purchaser to teach me. For the first two days, I asked him to drive it while I sat by his side; I had no confidence driving it on the busy Indian streets of Pune. Negotiating the haphazard traffic was just another difficulty. I tried my best to learn, and followed my friend keenly in his technique of maneuvering the machine.

We made my first big purchase of vegetables and groceries, in which my friend was of immense help as he had prior experience. Everything had to be purchased in considerable bulk, and there were so many items to be purchased that we could not waste any time in bargaining. I noticed that as soon as our Tempo arrived at the shops, the shopkeepers' faces would glow with happiness. They would leave all the other clients and come and attend to us.

On our way back to the ashram after my first purchase, we were stopped by a police constable. He looked exactly like a constable out of a Bollywood movie. We were both sitting in the front seat, and he told us in a rude tone that we had broken the rule because only one person could sit in the driver's seat. With every sentence, he banged his baton on the ground. This is the signature style of Indian police constables to scare the offenders. He was furious with us, and said that while we were going along he had given us a signal to stop. But we hadn't noticed, so he had been waiting in anger, and now wanted to take us into custody for this offence.

Being in my first purchase trip, I became very nervous. My friend, on the other hand, was very calm and composed. He was well accustomed to the Indian Police, and in a very relaxed tone he told me to give ten rupees to the constable. That was a very big sum for me. As there was no other alternative, I reluctantly handed a ten-rupee note to the constable. He wasn't ready to accept it, which scared me even more, as I thought that now he would also charge me for bribery. Then my friend, again with the same calmness, told me to hand over another ten-rupee note. I couldn't believe it; one ten-rupee note was already hard on my pocket, and now I had to double it. But there was no option, so I handed an additional ten rupee note to the constable.

As if by magic, the constable immediately changed his gestalt, and became nice and polite. He happily accepted the money, and told me to sit in the back. That small space was so full of fruit and vegetables, there was hardly any space for me to fit in. It was covered with thin iron grills, and I had to manage amidst the stack of groceries and other purchases. My friend drove the rickshaw back to the ashram. That was the ride of my life; whenever the Tempo stopped at the traffic signals, all the vegetables would be tossed around, and I would get hit on the head by large pumpkins, cucumbers and gourds.

Apart from having to take the rough ride, I also lost twenty rupees from my meager budget. There was no allowance for the bribery, so I had to take it from my own pocket. My friend who drove the Tempo advised me that I could cover it in the purchase bill, but my conscience didn't allow me to do so. Nobody really checked the bill at the ashram, and later, many people embezzled a lot of money this way. I was in considerable financial hardship at the time, but I couldn't give in to the idea of selling my soul for money.

I quickly learnt the art of driving the Tempo, and soon was acquainted with the pros and cons of being the ashram purchaser. Apart from not being able to listen to Bhagwan's discourses in the morning, the role of purchaser was immensely beneficial for me. I had ample time to rest, and could also do Kundalini in the evening, and participate in the evening dance. I was very happy, and thought finally Bhagwan had heard my prayers, and that he loved me very much.

The perk of being the ashram purchaser was that the shopkeepers loved you and would do anything to keep you happy. This was evident on the very first day we went to purchase; no sooner had the shopkeeper caught sight of us, then he left all his other customers and rushed over to us, because the ashram purchasers were the best buyers, never bargaining like other Indian buyers. Also, we bought in bulk, and always paid in cash. They would say, "Swami *jee*, what would you like to drink? Coca-Cola or *lassi*?" They really pampered us and treated us with great affected respect. I needed to buy toothpaste, and after purchasing for the ashram, I asked the shopkeeper to give me a small tube of toothpaste that cost only one rupee, and not to put it on the ashram bill as it was for my personal use. I handed him the money which he immediately returned, and said as if greatly embarrassed, and in a very exaggerated dramatic tone, "What are you doing Swami *jee*? How can I take money from you?"

He shouted to his assistant, "Chotu, get two king-sized tubes of toothpaste for Swami *jee*!"

He handed the toothpaste to me, and with a cheeky smile on his face, said, "This is on us, Swami *jee*."

I felt this was okay, as I was not cheating the ashram in any way. Soon I realized that this favour didn't end with toothpaste; I could get anything there I wanted for free.

When I was making the next purchase for the ashram, I asked the shopkeeper to give me one towel for my personal use. I knew he would not take the money, which of course I handed to him.

Again, he immediately returned it, saying, "This is a gift for you Swami *jee*, don't worry about the money." He brought out all the king-sized towels, and asked me to choose the best ones among them.

Even when I didn't want anything, the shopkeepers would still give me an extra gift. I started taking advantage of this. I would make a list of the supplies I needed: slippers, towel, soap, toothpaste -whatever I needed it came for free. Every time I went to purchase, the shopkeepers would feed me snacks and sweets. If I had to buy fruit for the ashram, they would hand me an extra bag full of fruit for myself. In no time, my cupboard in the dormitory was filled with fresh and dried fruits, juice and a variety of snacks. I used to share all this with my friends in the dormitory, so they were also very happy with my new job. I would ask them if they needed anything, and would get it for them for free. For a penniless man like me, this was godsend. I became the generous, popular friend for all the members of the dormitory, including pretty girls who wanted the free shampoos, soaps and slippers.

These were my golden days during my stay in Pune at that time. Life was luxurious, and I felt like a boss. Overnight, my poverty had transformed into affluence. Unfortunately, it did not last long; just when I thought my days of struggle were over, I was again summoned to the coordinator's office, where sad news awaited me.

She told me in a very soft voice, "You are very lucky, Arun; Bhagwan knows you personally and is concerned for your growth."

"Why? What happened?" I asked her.

"When Bhagwan came to know that we had changed your department, and that you had been made Purchaser, he called Laxmi and said he was not happy with this change."

He asked Laxmi, "Why did you change Arun's department? He will lose all his energy by remaining in the market for the major part of the day."

"But we frequently change people's department," said the coordinator, "and I have never seen such concern from Bhagwan, so you are very fortunate."

She tried to console me by saying, "Bhagwan wants you to remain in the buddhafield the whole day and not waste your precious energy in the market, shopping is a tiring job and it sucks all your energy. We have already found a new manager for the Purchase department, and you shall go back to dishwashing."

I left the office with a very heavy heart. I had fallen from my ivory tower, and all my love for and gratitude to Bhagwan again turned sour. Even my friends in the dormitory were sad when they came to know of my transfer.

Later I realized that by transferring my department,

Bhagwan not only saved me from losing energy, but also from forming the bad habit of receiving free gifts. If I had stayed in that department for a long time, I would have been completely spoilt. I had no money of my own, but had the power to spend thousands of rupees every day. Later, I witnessed that of all those who had access to the ashram's money, the majority could not remain honest. It happened on a larger scale in Rajneeshpuram, where Sheela and her group embezzled large sums of the ashram's money. And this culture is prevalent even today in the Pune ashram. When people who do not have enough personal money are exposed to large sums, most of them cannot resist the temptation. Once a person becomes dishonest, there is no limit to their greed.

A greedy mind always wants more, and this is one of the main reasons behind the great drama surrounding the trademark, copyrights, and forged will of Osho, and the banning of thousands of *sannyasins* from entry into the Pune ashram by the current management there. Beneath all their justifications, fabrications and deceptive rationale, lying at the very root of it all, is the unquenchable thirst for money, power, sex and intoxicants. The temptation of these things is the greatest human weakness.

The whole world today is governed by the cult of intelligence and conspiracy, and the existence of such organizations as CIA, RAW, ISI, KGB, and MI5 function by exploitation, using these eternal temptations. It is an open secret that all secret agencies are based on the manipulation of these very weaknesses and it is very rare to find someone who is beyond these temptations. In the training programs of all secret service agencies the agents are trained to find the weakness of their target and are taught how to manipulate a person being based on these eternal temptations. When they find someone who is free from these earthly temptations, may be that is the reason why they make the verdict that the person is unfit to live on earth anymore and assassinate them. I have had the opportunity to meet a few people, who were actually beyond these lures and almost always they all suffered the same failure and tragic endings. We all know of Osho's prosecution and his assassination for being a man who could not be manipulated. I have also known a few other individuals like Nepali politician Late Sri Krishna Prasad Bhattarai who could not be lured into these temptations. Despite of his successful political career, many opposing forces joined their hands together to make him lose elections again and again. Ironically, he only won one election and had to suffer continuous political failures for standing by his ideals. In that way another politician I have seen is the Chief Minister of Bihar Nitish Kumar who could not be manipulated by these allurements. As a close friend I have seen and experienced his simplicity many a times when he visited Tapoban or when I met and stayed with him at his residency in Patna. Sri Pradeep Giri is another Nepali politician that I know whom I have seen that despite of his great intelligence, caliber and recurring opportunities is never lured by power, position and money.

To be free from the temptation of money, power, sex and intoxicants requires a very disciplined, strong and exceptional mind which can see beyond the smoke of these poisons. Anyone running an ashram, or in any kind of leadership position, needs to bear in mind that these temptations can be the reason for somebody's fall, and they should create a management system which minimizes these temptations. There was a great chance that I could have given into my greed, and be lured into embezzlement.

This would have tainted my soul forever, and my whole spiritual life would have gone down the drain.

Today I am grateful to Bhagwan for taking special care to make my life difficult and physically hard. If it wasn't for him rowing my boat, I don't know what shore it would have landed on. Rumi says, "If you are irritated by every rub, how will your mirror be polished." It is only because of Osho's rubs that I am still on the path. Oh Master, thy grace is infinite.

What Next?

The quiet city of Pune had been taken by storm. Living aloof and detached from it all in his Lao Tzu House surrounded by tall bamboo groves at Koregaon Park was the eye of this storm, Bhagwan Shree Rajneesh. A huge spiritual magnet, Bhagwan was pulling every spiritually inclined soul towards him from all around the world. His rebellious and soul provoking ideas stirred the inner depths of young seekers around the world, and all rushed to be at the feet of this charismatic mystic to hear what he had to say. His outrageous discourses ringing with naked truth, half-baked but juicy stories of what went inside his modern ashram, and the unconventional lifestyle of this new godman had caught the attention of the global media, and everyone took notice. By 1979, Bhagwan had become the new fuel for headline stories of all daily newspapers worldwide. You could love him, you could hate him, but you could not ignore him.

Unlike nature's storms which devastates, Bhagwan's storm had the opposite effect - it transformed the city of Pune. With thousands of foreigners coming to the city every day, and staying for long periods, Pune's economy boomed, providing work for everyone. New hotels opened, new restaurants and businesses sprang up, new shops and vendors sprouted forth, and new rickshaws were constantly filling the streets. People could earn money even by renting their tiny bamboo huts to the hippie *sannyasins* of Rajneesh. With Bhagwan's presence, the economy of the city thrived, so much so that the ashram came to be awarded by the Indian government for its contribution to the tourism industry. The Ashram was also recognized by the government of India for its outstanding publications winning the best publication award for three years in a row. Sometime later, the Shree Rajneesh Ashram was earning more foreign currency and bringing more tourists than the Taj Mahal itself.

The ashram flourished. New properties were purchased, new facilities were added and new groups and therapies were introduced. It was a haven as a spiritual growth centre, and Pune was the place to be. However, Bhagwan's storm also had its destructive effects. It destroyed our conditionings, our egos and our expectations. He was operating on our age-old notions and carving his Homo Novus out of us; we were the guinea pigs for his New Man, and he left no stone unturned in the process.

It had been two months since I had been on Bhagwan's surgery table, and it was time I was shifted to a better position. On the last day of the month, I went to my coordinator to receive my new duties. Throughout the month, I had kept on reminding them that I was a qualified engineer so that upon the change of duty I would be given a job that suited my skills. If not the ashram engineer, my targets were at least the reception or the bookstore where the work was much easier. But all was in vain; I was shifted to the garbage department.

I tried my best to convince my coordinator, but instead, received a long lecture on surrender and how I was not total in my surrender towards the ashram. And so began my thirty-day adventure with the ashram garbage. I felt like the uncared, unloved and unwanted disciple, just like the unwanted dirt and filth I had to handle. I had come to be with my master, but it seemed he couldn't care less about what I wanted.

My work was to collect all the ashram garbage from the containers, and then transfer it to the municipality truck which came to collect it. The great disadvantage of being a garbage man was that I had to be with the garbage all day. I had to wear orange shorts and t-shirt, and would be smeared all over with garbage. The dirtiest and worst garbage was from the hospital, and consisted of used sanitary napkins, phlegm, blood, pus and what not.

My Indian and Nepalese friends who used to visit the ashram those days had been used to seeing me in my former role as a centre leader, conducting meditation camps, initiating people into *sannyas*, and giving lectures, they were shocked to see me in Pune as a garbage man in half dirty pants and tshirts. They thought great misfortune had befallen me, and some of them literally cried at my pitiable situation. When Swami Anand Ramesh, who is the president of Tapoban's trust today, saw me running around in my shorts he burst into tears, questioned Bhagwan's reason for doing this, and asked me to return to Nepal.

When my close friends visited Pune, they would buy me dinner, and at least for a few days I would have the regal treat of a Gujarati *thali* at the Dream Land hotel. A Gujarati *thali* is an assortment of dishes arranged as a platter for lunch or dinner in restaurants and homes, and originating in Gujarat. Every state of India has its own cuisine and the name of the state in which each style originated is placed before the word "*thali*", which literally means platter.

I have a deep association with Gujarati food and I can never forget the treats at Dream Land. My mouth waters even today when I think of the variety of delicious food we ate there. As the restaurant was always crowded, we would have to wait in line for an available table. While we waited in the lobby, the hotel would serve us *chaach* (salted buttermilk) or water.

When we were finally ushered inside, the waiters would steadily bring out the various delicacies and place them on our plates while I would be eagerly devouring them. The Gujarati *thali* started with a tasty snack such as *pakodas*, *samosas* or *kachoris*. This was followed by the main course which consisted of *puris*, sweet and sour lentils, plain chapatis with ghee, *missi roti*, steamed basmati rice, half a dozen curries and vegetables cooked in Gujarati style, cucumber salad with various chutneys, Gujarati *pakodas*, roasted *papad* or the Indian style nachos made with ground lentil seeds with pepper, *dahibada* and then *chaach* and a sweet dish to finish. I will always remain a big admirer of the Gujarati gastronomy, and above are only some of the items from the long list of mouth-watering Gujarati delicacies.

Becoming the garbage man also came with its own privileges. Firstly, my duty hours decreased. I had to work from 10:00am to 6:00pm, which meant I could now listen to Bhagwan's discourses every morning and join the evening celebrations. Many people could not go out to eat after morning discourse as their duty started immediately and they had to go for work empty stomach. Seeing this time constraint Bhagwan ordered Laxmi to at least give free breakfast to all the staffs as the ashram was now economically getting stronger. So the new privilege that I experienced as a garbage man was that I got breakfast free at the ashram. It was limited to one piece of bread, one banana and cup of tea but still it was a great blessing in my situation. Working inside confined rooms for two months from morning tonight, I had totally forgotten what the evening looked like. For the first time in two months I was able to experience this long-missed beauty. I still remember how happy I felt looking at the fluid crimson light spreading across the Pune sky just before the sun bid farewell to Earth. With so much free time I was also able to take part in the evening dance celebrations at the ashram.

The other privilege I received being a garbage man was the luxury of a hot shower. When my duty hours were over at 6:00pm, I could bathe in the ashram bathroom using free soap provided by the ashram. On my first day, I was so disgusted that I finished a whole bar of soap. The bathroom with the hot water and soap felt like the biggest privileges in my life at that time. When one is going through hardships, one learns to value even the smallest of things.

What I remember even today is that great feeling I would get after having a shower and putting on a clean robe. I really felt like an emperor. Although the master looked like he was being harsh upon me, he was nourishing me inside with his energy. I felt such an upsurge of his energy in me, that despite being a garbage man, I felt no less than a king every evening - every morning I was a garbage man, and every evening I would become an emperor. Even today, I am ready to give up everything I have if I could relive that wonderful feeling I used to have almost every evening. This was the time when Bhagwan was working upon me and changing my chemistry, preparing me for my future.

Come the third month, I had very little money left. I had borrowed from all who could give me a little money, so then I started selling my belongings. I sold my sleeping bag, pen, shoes - I sold everything that was possible to sell. After the first month, I hadn't had to pay for my entry pass, which was a great relief to me, but I still needed to manage my own food and pay for my accommodation which was 6 rupees per night. I still remember how the free entry pass had looked to me, like a pass to heaven.

My lunch hour was between 1:00 and 2:00pm, but I never ate lunch. I used to feel so disgusted with all that garbage that I couldn't even imagine eating anything. During that month, I ate the free breakfast each morning at the ashram, and that would see me through until dinner in the evening. Sometimes I would have dinner at Premji Restaurant near the ashram. The owner had become my friend, and would give me a discount there, and sometimes when he felt great compassion for me, I was offered a free mango *lassi*.

I was a beggar, collecting garbage, and feeling like a king. What greater an adventure could one ask for. Yet just when I thought I had figured out where I was standing, a secret was revealed to me that stole the earth from under my feet, and wiped away the sky from over my head.

I Remember
My Past Life

In October 1969, I attended my first meditation camp with Bhagwan, called *Main Mrityu Sikhata Hun* in Hindi. During that camp, he spoke in depth about the mysteries of death, what happens after death and before birth. As you must know by now, I always had a deep interest in the esoteric and mysticism. From my very childhood, I had a burning quest about everything in life, and more so about death. I had questions that needed answers. I had puzzles that needed to be solved. So when Bhagwan spoke about the most mysterious subject that haunts every man, it only instigated my quest. I was also curious to know about my past life.

When I invited Bhagwan to Patna in January 1970, I got the chance to talk with him in detail. He had mentioned, in his discourses at *Main Mrityu Sikhata Hun*, past life experiences, or *jatiyasmriti*. Buddha and Mahavira recommended this technique for their disciples for a deeper understanding and detachment. I asked Bhagwan to help me remember my past life by teaching me the techniques of *jatiyasmriti*. He looked at me for a while and said, "All will happen naturally in its good time. Don't worry about it. Keep on meditating and it will happen by itself."

Like all disciples, I also lacked patience. I was very impatient and curious to know about my past life. But nothing was happening. No matter how much I meditated or tried, the magical revelation was not taking place at all. Life has its own rules and its own ways. Regardless of how much we try to bend things according to our wishes, existence always functions in due course, and nothing ever happens before that.

When I took *sannyas* with Bhagwan in 1974, I had two questions: one was about the mystics that I had met and how they were connected with their masters who were not in the body but were still guiding them. I had seen this miracle with my own eyes. One of my friends was being guided by his master from the astral plane. So in my second meeting, I said to my guru, "Bhagwan, I want to connect with you astrally." He chuckled and said, "It will happen."

My other question was about my own past life. At a glance, Bhagwan could see the past, future and present of a person. I wanted him to at least say something, even a hint would have been extremely helpful. Bhagwan had replied, "Too much eagerness about this is not good. When you are ready it will happen on its own."

I was a stubborn seeker, and in many of my personal meetings with him, I asked him mostly about this. I could see that he didn't really appreciate it. He told me, "If you have your

अभी जिस काम में लगे हैं, वह करें ।
और पहले के जन्म की फिक्र छोड़ें ।
सहज रूप से सब हो ही रहा है ।
बस बहते जायें ।

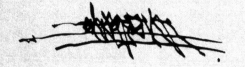

■ *English translation of Osho's letter in Hindi from page no. 260*

Continue the work that you are doing now.

And forget about past lives.

All is happening spontaneously.

Just flow with it.

past life experiences before your mind is ready for it, it might leave you permanently disturbed. And you might also misuse it. If it happens prematurely it will be dangerous. So keep meditating and forget it."

How could I forget it? It was not just esoteric curiosity why I constantly bothered my master, I had my own problem behind it. From my very childhood I used to see recurrent visions and dreams which were a great mystery. I could not make anything out of them and they only made me more confused. My visions used to be in fragments like a jigsaw puzzle without all the pieces. Even though I had the puzzle in my hand, I did not have enough pieces to come to a conclusion.

I pleaded with Bhagwan until 1977, and in the end when it was too much, he totally discouraged me.

Bhagwan had said that when a seeker matures in meditation, and if there is a necessary purpose behind it, existence reveals the memory of past lives to an individual. He also added that as long as one desires for it, it will not happen. In my futile effort to solve my puzzle, I did everything possible to remember my past life. Between 1974 and 1977, I tried all the techniques possible, including past life regression, but all in vain. My persistence and patience reached a saturation point, and in 1977 I totally gave up and closed the chapter from my side, then forgot all about it.

It was only after two years that things started unfolding by themselves. For three months I had been cooking and scrubbing and cleaning. Not only physically was I worn out, but internally old layers of my conditioning were falling off. Brick by brick, Bhagwan was bringing down the walls of my ego and prejudices. He was freeing me of borrowed knowledge and was giving me my own eyes, eyes that could see, and a heart that could understand.

I even felt as though something was crystallizing inside me. The great alchemist was at work.

During my garbage duties, my lunch time used to be between 1-2 pm. Everybody used to go to eat their lunch either at the ashram kitchen or at the nearby eateries. I used to be so much disgusted with my own body smeared with filth that I couldn't even think of eating. On the wide verandah of the hospital there was an old sofa, which is where I rested during my lunch hour. Sometimes I would take a quick nap or just read the old magazines or newspapers that were kept there for waiting visitors.

I still remember that fateful day – I had laid down on the sofa as usual for my afternoon rest, when a magazine caught my eye from amidst the piles of newspapers and magazines. It was the prestigious English monthly magazine, *The Society*, published from Bombay. I flipped it open and found an article written by the world famous Maharani Gayatri Devi of Jaipur, who was also an ex-member of the Indian Parliament. It was an article about the old royals and their palaces. As soon as I opened the magazine, I saw some pictures which were the same images that I used to have in my visions. Immediately a link was created, and slowly the puzzle began to fall into place; the connection between my fragmented visions and a bigger picture had begun to grow.

The content of that article written by the Maharani formed the missing link that I had been looking for all those years. Immediately I wanted to write down everything and show it to Bhagwan to get his confirmation. In a state of great exhaustion and let-go, my mind had fallen away, lifting the cloud over my consciousness. In that state of great relaxation, when I was neither expecting nor making any effort, the great mystery that had haunted me for many years was slowly revealing.

That night I had a vision in which I saw some missing links which further confirmed my revelation of the afternoon. The next morning, I wrote a long letter in Hindi for Bhagwan and gave it to Ma Laxmi. In the letter, I explained everything that had happened to me in the afternoon, and asked him for a meditation technique so I could further explore my past life. The following morning, I received a very small note in Hindi, which was the Zen stick of my master. The letter is attached here in the book.

It was short and harsh.

"Your excessive interest in your past life shows that you are not total in your present work. Put your total energy into the work that the ashram has given you." My heart sank with these harsh words from the master, but what saved me was the last line. In answer to my asking for a technique, he had replied, "When things are happening naturally and spontaneously, why do you need a technique?"

This line saved me. It confirmed that my experience was authentic.

After this revelation, I became very excited and wanted to know more and more about it. I started to do more research on it. I started visiting bookshops looking for books that could tell me more about my past life. On the MG Road in Pune, there was a famous bookshop called Manney's which was the largest bookshop in Pune those days. As I had a day off on every Wednesday and also I was free after 6:00pm, I would go there in pursuit of any book that could tell more about my past life. I found a book that was written by a famous royal that was related with my past life. This was a precious find and I wanted to buy it, but it cost two hundred rupees, and at that time I simply couldn't afford it. It was a huge amount for a book and it was impossible for me to buy it.

I used to go to the bookshop whenever I had time after my work and as I did not have money to purchase the book I would sit there and read a few pages everyday and then again put it back to read it next day.

Existence unfolds in the strangest of ways. In these forty-seven years of my association with Bhagwan in this life, thousands of miracles have occurred in my life for which I could find no rationale, no explanation. There are so many incidents, which I have not been able to understand even today. Bhagwan never claimed any miracles, and always urged us to live a simple life. But this didn't mean that the inconceivable never happened around him, in fact life was never straight around him, and I can only be grateful to my master for all the pits and valleys he brought into my life, for making life so colourful. He would take us on great flights into the world of the unknown, but he also made sure that our feet were firmly grounded on the earth.

Just after a few days, to my utter surprise, I received a money order of exactly two hundred rupees from one of my close friends and a very senior and loving *sannyasin*, Swami Ram Chaitanya *jee* of Bihar. This was an unexpected gift from a friend with whom I had no financial relationship or expectation with. He had no idea about my financial crisis in Pune. How could he send the exact sum that I needed for the book? He himself was a village school teacher and not a very well-off man. This amount could have been a great relief to my ongoing financial hardship and could have fed me for many days and could have bought many of my essentials. But the book was far more precious to me, and I could not resist the temptation.

I went straight to Manney's and bought the book. It was published by an English publishing house, so it was very expensive.

After many months, I met Swami Ram Chaitanya and asked him why he sent me the money that I had never asked for. He told me that during his meditation one day he felt a great urge that I am in need of two hundred rupees. This idea came to him repeatedly during his meditation. He arranged the 200 rupees and sent it to me through a money order in care of Ma Yoga Laxmi.

That book is still with me and it revealed to me the missing links to the stories of my past life. Later on during my *darshan* with Bhagwan he was happy with my remembrance and also answered some of my queries regarding my past life. Life is full of mysteries, and can never be totally rationalized.

The Story of
the Lost Watch

After three months in Pune I had finished almost all the money that I had brought from Nepal. It was enough to give me a comfortable life for my ten days stay which I had planned earlier. But private plans never work around the master; he always has a better plan for us. Who knew that I would be staying for so long leaving everything behind, not caring for my work, my family and all that needed my attention and concern back home.

Amidst all the struggle and complaints, I have to admit, something was crystallizing in me. The backdrop of my outer chaos only created the contrast for me to see the inner calmness and joy that was taking birth inside. Only a person who has stayed in a buddhafield, and has been on the surgery table of the master can understand this feeling. Of course there was great physical suffering and my ego was hurt every moment but at the same time I was being nourished by a divine drunkenness of his energy. It only grew as days went by.

People say that *sannyasins* sacrifice a good life in the world by leaving behind everything and choosing to stay at the ashram. This is not true. In fact I think it needs a great sense of wisdom, aesthetics and sensitivity to see that there are much better things to pursue in this world that give a greater sense of contentment and bliss than futile and frivolous joys of the mundane.

Many incidents took place in my life when I was living and working in the ashram that baffled me and pushed me to the edge of losing the soundness of my mental state of being. I will never be able to draw a conclusion as to why they happened with me. This was the life around Bhagwan, the unpredictable and unexpected always waiting to pounce upon you just around the next corner. Today when I reminisce, it has all become a sweet memory.

Most of those who came to Bhagwan overstayed and ran over their budgets, it was a common practice in Pune to buy and sell used goods amongst the *sannyasins*. I had sold all my belongings that could be sold. What was still left with me was a treasured original Swiss watch that a relative had got for me as a gift from Switzerland. I liked it very much and during my working hours I used to properly place it in a pouch along with my keys and the little money I had left with me.

The cook at the Indian restaurant, who was not a *sannyasin* but a paid worker, loved my watch and would appreciate its beauty every time he got a glimpse of it. He was the one who had taught me how to cook and was my 'guru *jee*' by all means. I treated him with a great deal of respect. So before putting my beloved timepiece up for sale amidst the *sannyasin* buyers, I felt the responsibility to first ask its long-term admirer, the cook, whether he wanted to buy it.

It happened so that the cook needed a good watch to wear on his wedding day as he was soon going to get married. He happily agreed to buy it and asked for the price. I asked him to offer the price and he happily agreed to pay 300. Although the watch was much more expensive, 300 was still a large amount for me and it could have provided me with 60 lavish meals at the Premji restaurant. I agreed to sell it to him. He took the watch and told me that he would bring the money to pay me the next day.

There was another Punjabi *sannyasin*, Swami Satish, in my department who knew about my watch and was himself looking for prospective clients for it. When I told him that I had sold it to the cook for three hundred rupees, he cringed at the whole deal.

"I can easily get a higher price for such a beautiful Swiss watch. You made a huge loss. Did you take the money?" He asked.

"No, he'll give it tomorrow."

He stared at my face with great displeasure, as if I was a fool, and said "What? You gave him the watch without taking the money. How could you trust him? He won't give you any money. Anyhow ask for the watch and tell him that you can only give it when he brings the money."

Satish had easily maneuvered me and had planted seeds of doubt in my mind, he clouded my mind. One of greed and another of suspicion. He put me in a great predicament. I badly needed the money and that watch was my last belonging left. What if Satish was right and the cook wouldn't give me the money, which was not entirely impossible. I was not in a position to take such a big risk but how could I ask it back as I had already handed it over to him.

With great difficulty I went to the cook and said, "Can I wear the watch for one more day, my relative brought it for me from Switzerland and I really love it. You can take it tomorrow."

He understood my intention and said, "So you don't trust me?"

He gave the watch to me saying, "All right, give me the watch tomorrow when I bring the money."

With a bit of shame I took back the watch. A great burden was lifted from my heart and I happily put the watch in the pouch along with the little money and my keys. The whole day I scurried around the ashram collecting the garbage bins and then unloading them into the trucks. In the evening tired after finishing my work and feeling content that my cherished treasure was still with me I put my hand on the pouch to feel the watch. To my utmost shock the pouch was empty. I had left the chain open and everything inside had fallen off. The watch, my money and my suitcase keys, everything was gone. You can imagine how I felt. My heart was in my mouth and breath left my body for a few seconds. Even if I lost three million rupees today, I wouldn't feel the same amount of shock I felt at that time.

I searched the whole ashram and flipped every stone. I tossed the kitchen garbage and explored every bush. I couldn't sleep the whole night and kept on searching for the watch. The next morning, the cook came with the money. When I told him that I had lost the watch, he couldn't believe it. He said, "Now that you have found someone who will pay more than three hundred, you are going against your word. Here take three hundred," he said and threw three hundred rupees cash on the floor. He even added a further fifty rupees, saying "I really like that watch and I am going to wear it for my wedding."

This was one of the most shameful moments of my life,

I kept telling him that I had lost it but he wouldn't believe me. This event brought a great rift in our friendship, but that was not the end of my sorrow. I had not only lost my watch but also the key to my suitcase and the little money I had left with me. There was a guy in the dormitory who could open locks but I couldn't afford him as he asked for 5 rupees. He told me that if I brought the suitcase to his shop in the city it would cost me just 1 rupee. I burrowed some rupees from Satish and walked 4kms carrying the suitcase on my head all the way to MG road like a coolie just to save 4 rupees. I had to again carry back the open suitcase back to the ashram.

Next morning when the garbage truck came, I told the garbage men who had become my close friends about my story. The poor simple men who are usually from the lowest caste in India were sympathetic folks. They decided to unload the entire garbage from the truck and helped me to go through the heaps of garbage thoroughly. We tossed the mountain of filth and went through every piece of garbage but all in vain. It was a very draining work to unload and reload the garbage but we couldn't find anything.

When the children at the ashram saw me looking for something they came to me and asked, "What are you looking for?"

"I am looking for my watch, has anyone of you seen it?

"Oh yes I know who has it." Said one of them excitedly.

"Tell me who?"

"I will tell you but first you will have to buy us ice-cream."

So I bought them the ice-cream and they happily devoured on it. I again asked them, "So who has the watch? Now tell me."

"Oh! it was not me who knows where it is. But I think Govinda knows it. He was talking about it." Said the child.

I was so angry at the kid but I controlled my anger and asked him, "So where is Govinda?"

He pointed towards another kid at a distance and said, "He knows where your watch is."

I rushed to the other kid and asked him, "Govinda do you know where my watch is?"

The kid replied, "Oh yes I know where it is."

"Please tell me then." I was getting frantic.

"First buy me an ice-cream and then only I will tell you." he demanded.

I had no other option but to buy another ice-cream. I had nothing but this meager hope that this kid would help me find it so I took the chance.

Govinda slowly finished the ice-cream as he looked at me with his big eyes.

"Now tell me where it is. Where is the watch Govinda?" I asked.

He scratched his head for some time, pretended to think with a confused look and replied, "Oh! It was not a watch, it was something else. Now I remember." And ran into the crowd of sanyasins and disappeared. I was already going through immense torment and the kids added to it by making a fool out of me, they also made me spend the little money that I had left with me in buying the ice-cream.

The pangs of attachment haunted me for many days and everyday during my break from 1 to 2pm I used to go around the ashram where I was working, searching for the watch. It was as if

I had gone mad. I turned every stone in the ashram and searched every corner and bush where I was working. I asked every person several times if they had seen my valuable watch. I couldn't stop thinking and searching for it. It was my last treasure. And I couldn't understand whether the sky had swallowed it or the earth had sucked it.

After three weeks of my desperate but fruitless inquiry and search, one night when I was sleeping, Osho appeared in my dream. He was beaming mischievously at me holding the watch in his hand and said, "Don't waste your time looking for the watch and put your total energy into work, your watch is with me."

Attachment Brings Misery

The distance between Somji Estate dormitory and my working place, *His Place* was about 1 km and I had to walk to and fro several times which consumed my time and energy. Many of my *sannyasin* friends had purchased a bicycle. Those who could afford had a motorbike and others had a bicycle. I also wished to have a bicycle so that I could save my time and energy. But I could not afford to buy a new one. When the *sannyasins* left Pune, especially those from the West, they used to sell their belongings to other *sannyasins* at the ashram at a cheaper price. One of my dormitory mate had finished his visa and money and was going back to the West. He had purchased an old second hand bicycle and wanted to dispose it before leaving. He wanted forty rupees for his already very old rickety bicycle. This was the cheapest cycle available and a perfect fit for someone like me. I purchased it and it gave me one of the greatest pleasure of my life. Even the expensive automobiles that I owned in the later phase of my life could not match with this joy.

It was the best buy of my life. I could cover the distance between my workplace and the dormitory in no time. With this means of transport I could even frequent the railway station for my cheap food. I was immensely happy as I had a space to sleep in the dormitory, I was allowed to work in the ashram and I was even attending Osho lectures and evening music group. My energy was very high and I used to joke with my friends that my enlightenment was not that far, the only thing that I needed now was free foodpass. That would have been the ultimate luxury in my life. My colleagues who had free food pass were free from the worries of the most important necessity of feeding themselves. The free food pass was my ultimate dream in those days.

I rode my bicycle for about six weeks and then again as fate would have it, hell broke loose upon me. My beloved cycle got stolen from the ashram's parking area. I knew how usual it was to lose things in India so I was very particular and was using a five rupees lock for the forty rupees cycle. It was a great calamity for me. It was my cherished treasure and had given me great comfort. It broke my heart when it was lost. I searched for the cycle everywhere in Koregaon Park and its surroundings but all in vain. The thief was much smarter than me and I could not get any trace of it. My last luxury was also stolen from me.

Again I had to face the inconvenience of walking on foot and it gave me even more pain than before because I had now tasted the pleasure of having a bicycle. I still remember the pinch of it.

In the November of 1985 when Osho returned back to India after Rajneeshpuram, I was staying with him in Manali for a few weeks at the Span Resort. I had seen Osho's fleet of Rolls Royces and his luxury in Rajneeshpuram. In Manali he was living in a small cottage of fourteen by eleven ft. The electricity supply used to be cut as the voltage was very low and the geysers and heaters were not working properly. For his bath the hot water used to be brought in a bucket from the kitchen. He came to the resort from the airport in an old and dirty ambassador taxi. There were no vehicles available for his local transportation. Just few days ago, he was an emperor in Rajneeshpuram and now here he was with the most minimal amenities. Just a week before, he had a fleet of ninety six Rolls Royces and probably one of the best bathrooms with all the modern amenities including a Jacuzzi, sauna and a steam bath. Now he didn't even have a bicycle.

Osho used to go for morning and afternoon walk on the bank of the Vyas River and used to sit silently on a wooden bench facing the river. Usually he used to sit alone in silence but on some mornings he used to call his disciples for necessary information and instruction. On the very first day I arrived in Manali, Bhagwan called me for a personal *darshan* on the bank of Vyas River.

Later I was summoned many times to this *darshan*. It was one of the best times of my life. To sit at the feet of my master on the bank of a beautiful mountain river surrounded by dense Himalayan forest. On clear days we could even see the snow capped mountains. Sitting alone with the master in that surrounding was a rare opportunity and the vivid memory of those golden moments is treasured very carefully in my heart. I would soar high to the peaks of consciousness in his drowning presence intoxicated by his energy and grace. It was a precious moment

of my life. The disciple was sitting at the feet of the master in the company of the mighty Himalayas. Nothing could be more perfect for me. Few words were spoken and most of the time what needed to be conveyed was conveyed in silent communion.

Osho used to sit on a wooden bench and I used to sit at his feet on the sand of the river bank. For most of us Rajneeshpuram was our dream city, our home, and we all had the pain of losing it. We were all very sad after the destruction of Rajneeshpuram and were all missing it tremendously. Amidst all this the only person who was not sad and was calm and composed was Osho. There was no sign of any gloom on his face, he didn't miss anything. He was enjoying his long cherished dream to live in the solitude of the Himalayas.

"I love the Himalayas...

Switzerland is beautiful but nothing compared to the Himalayas. It is convenient to be in Switzerland with all its modern facilities. It is very inconvenient in the Himalayas. It is still without any technology at all — no roads, no electricity, no airplanes, no railroads, nothing at all. But then comes the innocence. One is transported to another time, to another being, to another space.

The Himalayas have attracted for centuries and centuries the mystical people. There is some quality of mystic atmosphere in the Himalayas. No other mountains in the world have that quality – the height, the eternal snow that has never melted, the silence that has never been broken, paths that have never been trodden. There are some similarities between the Himalayan peaks and the inner consciousness." - Osho

The mystic had arrived in the laps of the ageless Himalayas and had become a part of the grandeur that it was.

Osho was fully content and there seemed to be no trace of worry or stress on his face. He was at home and at peace. He would show me the billowing clouds and the transparent waters and ask me, "Do you have such beautiful rivers in Nepal?" To which I would immediately reply, "Bhagwan there are even more beautiful Himalayan rivers in Nepal. Nepali Himalaya is more virgin, wild and beautiful than the Indian Himalayas."

One day during the *darshan* I could no more contain myself and asked Osho, "Bhagwaan don't you miss anything? Your comfortable Lao Tzu House, your luxurious gardens and bathroom and the fleet of your Rolls Royces? Don't you miss our dream city Rajneehpuram. Here you live in a small room which does not even have an AC."

As he was free and I could say anything to him, I told him about my bicycle which I had lost in Pune many years ago. I told him that the memory of it haunted me even today. The pain of losing that rickety third hand bicycle was still alive in my heart like a pinch.

I asked him, "You have lost 96 Rolls Royces. Don't you remember them? Don't you miss the luxury of Rajneeshpuram? Should I go to Chandirgarh and buy a generator for your electric supply or go to Delhi to ask my friends for a car for you?"

Bhagwan said, "Don't do that. I don't miss anything. I am immensely happy to be back in India especially in the Himalayas. How beautiful is this river and these mountains. Himalaya is the best place to live and die. I am in the Himalayas, Why should I miss anything?"

I was surprised by his answer and then Bhagwan gave me one of the greatest teachings of my life. He said, "I fully enjoyed Rajneeshpuram while I was there but I don't miss it now because

I was never attached with it. You miss things because you thought it was yours, you are miserable now because you were attached with them. I lived in Rajneeshpuram in totality so I don't miss it. It is a general habit of people that they don't enjoy things when it is available and they miss it immensely when it is lost. I enjoy my life and everything moment to moment. It is not the lost things that give you misery but the attachment that you have for it. You still feel the pain because you thought it was your bicycle and it should not have been lost. Try to understand, it is not the bicycle that gives you the pain but the attachment of it. If it was somebody else's bicycle it would have made no difference to you. I am not attached with anything or any person. I enjoy each moment and accept life as it comes to me."

Even today those words are afresh in my memory and are written on my heart in golden letters. Every time I face troubles in life, each time I have a crisis or I lose something or someone that is dear to me, I remember these words of Bhagwan and this helps me to come out of my sorrow.

The Laundry Man &
the Gift of Gurupurnima

It had only been ninety days in Pune, but with so many events happening every day, it felt like a lifetime had passed. I had cooked, cleaned, scrubbed, starved, remembered my past life and had lost my precious watch. These few months had been more eventful than my whole life. After the third month ended, I felt that maybe the good days were ahead. I was fully assured that the reason of all this torture by my master had fructified so I had finally had the visions of my past life and all these torture was being done to nullify the bad karmas of my past life.

Here I want to remind the readers that on a spiritual path a seeker may experience all sorts of otherworldly experiences that cannot be rationalized through logic and reason. One may also experience different kinds of powers and *siddhis* and I have

seen that many seekers have gone astray from their paths because of this. There will always be a tendency to exhibit these powers and talk about one's experiences but there is no value of it on the path of true seeking rather they only help in glorifying one's ego and can be a great hindrance to one's spiritual growth. The powers, the *siddhis* and the experiences come and go, of course they make the journey very colorful but they are not our ultimate destination, it is unwise to be attached to them or boast about them.

My master always prevented me from spending too much time in esoteric gossip and discouraged me from delving too much into it. Little stories and experiences I share in this book have also been written after the permission of my master and with the sole intention that it will in some way inspire and help seekers on the path who are going through similar experiences, that it will help them to get an understanding and insight into their own situation.

Although it was immensely painful and at times I wanted to run away from my master, today I can understand why my master was so hard upon me and always hammered my ego pursuits. I am immensely grateful to him that he was always there to ground me and bring me back every time I went astray which he is doing even today.

When I remembered my past life I thought I had made a great achievement and my master would be very happy with me. Bhagwan responded very indifferently and told me to focus on my work instead. Although he confirmed my experience, he didn't leave this opportunity to hammer my ego. I could not afford to dwell too much in the fantasy of my past life and had to come back to my real world where I was an ashram garbage man waiting for his next job change. Nevertheless I had a great hope that I would now be shifted to a comfortable and a better job. Many junior *sannyasins* from Nepal and India whom I had introduced to Bhagwan and some had even taken initiation from me where doing better jobs than me and in a much comfortable positions in the ashram with foodpass and accommodation so now I was hopeful that this time I would also be shifted to a much better work setting. To my utmost shock, after the completion of the third month I was told that now I had become the ashram's *dhobi* - the washer man.

This meant washing countless numbers of bed sheets and table clothes and towels in a day and there was no washing machine at that time in the ashram and everything had to be washed in a very crude way.

I had to burn the giant kerosene stove and boil water in the huge pots with washing soda. Just recently I watched a very interesting Bollywood film called Masaan which revolves around the lives of the undertakers on the Hindu ghats of Benaras. A scene in the film reminds me of my own life as the *dhobi*. Just like how the undertakers stir and turn the bodies being cremated on the pyre. I had to stir and turn the dirty clothes there using a big bamboo stick.

There was a quota that I had to wash around 100 bed sheets, 100 towels and some table cloths every day. Boiling them in hot water in soda was not difficult. The difficult part was rinsing them with fresh water after they were boiled. The most difficult thing was drying them by twisting the cloths and getting the water out of it. As there was no drier it had to be hung on the roofs on drying lines. After drying the clothes everything had to be collected and given to ironing room.

The only luxury in my life was the open air on the terrace when I used to go to hang the cloths and again go back to take them when they had dried. In order to elongate my only leisure time I used to come down very slowly taking long and slow paces. If my coordinator saw me coming down he would shout at me and say, "Can't you walk a little faster? Why do you always walk like a lethargic man with no energy?" I also used to get agitated and answer him, "There is already a quota of how many cloths I am supposed to wash every day, what is your problem in how I walk if I am fulfilling your quota?" The German coordinators used to be toughest of them all, they were the best hard task masters you could get. " He would reply, " You lazy Indian, you are never going to change."

Somehow I managed the two weeks as the laundryman. It was the month of July and the whole ashram was being readied for the celebration of Gurupurnima or the Master's day. Until Osho was in his body, the celebration days used to be celebrated with great gusto and fanfare and thousands of *sannyasins* from all over the world came to the ashram to be in the presence of the master and rejoice in his energy. Osho's Birthday, Osho's Enlightenment day and The Master's day held a great significance and was celebrated with live *kirtans*, music, meditation and great feasts were arranged for free and even those without food passes could join in and eat.

After Osho left his body Osho's Mahaparinirvana day and the above celebration days used to be celebrated at his ashram in Pune until the year 2000 AD. Osho has specifically spoken in his discourses about the significance of these celebration days and how it is easier to connect with the master's energy on these days. Videos of these celebration days from Pune I, Rajneeshpuram and

Pune II in which Osho used to sit with thousands of his disciples who had gathered to celebrate these days and meditate in his energy are still available. However after the year 2000 the Pune management imposed its fabricated verdicts and has banned the celebration of these days at Osho's ashram in Pune.

As it used to be in those days, the whole ashram prepared for the Gurupurnima and one could feel a sense of great excitement and joy everywhere. Sannyasins had already started pouring in from all over the world and the ashram became more crowded as the dates neared the full moon. There was more work in every department and the numbers of my laundry also increased proportionally. The hard work required by the laundry department gave me no time to join in the excitement, my laundry work kept me well engaged and occupied.

My body was in great discomfort because I had to remain whole day in the wet room with the smell of soda and bleach. It was a very unhealthy work situation. The most difficult part was to rinse and twist the cloths with my bare hands. My arms used to ache in the night and I used to feel excruciating pain. It was becoming too much for me. As there was no provision to say no to the work and ask for a change I decided that I should return back to Nepal where relatively a comfortable life awaited me where I was a center leader and respected amongst the *sannyasins*. I was praying to Bhagwan asking him to give me an easier work otherwise I had to go back which I did not want.

My prayers got answered and all of a sudden one morning I was summoned to the office. During the Gurupurnima large number of Indian *sannyasins* from all over India used to come to Pune and since they had very limited money the ashram was very considerate for them and used to arrange new affordable dormitories for them. The office thought that since I could communicate well with people I was made the coordinator of the new dormitory. The main dormitory was still coordinated by Mahesh. I was his assistant and had to look after the new dormitory which was a rented place for ten days. This looked to me like I had gotten a gift from my master on the occasion of the coming Gurupurnima. It was like I had won a lottery ticket.

This sudden change in my department unburdened me of all my woes. Compared to my previous work that demanded so much of my physical energy it was as if like I had nothing to do. As a dormitory coordinator all that I needed to do was collect 10 Rupees per night for accommodation and food from those who wanted to sleep in the dormitory and make their beds.

Life as a dormitory coordinator had its own perks. I could sleep the whole day in the dormitory bed as I waited for the *sannyasins*. There were *sannyasins* from all over India and all of them brought food with them from different places. I used to have a good time chatting with them and sharing their food. All I had to do was to make sure that the water faucets, the bathroom and the lights were in order and for a person who was toiling all day for months, this was the ultimate luxury. I had ample amount of free time and I could also go to Bhagwan's discourses in the morning. It seemed like my fate had finally changed.

I was only nurturing an illusion.

The Bandits
of Chambal

While I was working as a dormitory in charge during Guru Purnima celebration I came across a group of visitors from Madhyapradesh. They were all well built and gleamed with the robust radiance of an athlete. Amongst them there was one who seemed like their leader, who was well respected by the entire group. They used to massage him, follow his lead to meditation hall or kitchen and were always seen around him. They were very lively and often their uproarious laughter filled the dormitory. As I became friendlier with them, the jigsaw came together and the truth was revealed to me that they were former bandits of the notorious Chambal valley.

Sometime ago they had randomly stumbled upon one of Osho's books in Hindi, and the group leader, who had a remarkably

288

charismatic personality, took an immediate liking to Osho. Since they lived in wilderness and had plenty of leisure at their hands they all started to read Osho. They also learned the technique of Dynamic meditation and acquired a tape from somewhere. So every day they did Dynamic meditation. They found the meditation so addictive that they started doing it twice daily, once in the morning and once in the evening. By the time they arrived at the ashram, most of them had already reached a certain state of meditativeness.

The leader had fallen in deep love with Osho. Gradually, those who were not interested in Osho and meditation left the gang and joined the different group of bandits. Only those who were interested in meditation and spirituality remained with the leader. As they were very innocent of heart, they started having beautiful experiences in meditation.

But the one incident that particularly stunned me was the one when the leader was suddenly possessed by Osho and started giving the sermon to his group in Osho's voice. In between 1977 to 1981, during the Pune I days, Osho suddenly used to go into silence. During such times, Osho wouldn't appear for morning lecture or evening *darshan*. We were told that Osho was in seclusion because of his poor health but later on I realized that whenever he had to do some deeper and esoteric work on his disciples spread across the world, he used to go into seclusion and silence. So, the period of silence was not only because of his health but had an inexplicable esoteric purpose.

During one of the full moon nights of such ten days silent seclusion, the bandits had gathered to listen to Osho discourse at Chambal valley. As the night deepened, the moon cast mysterious trance and everyone felt a presence that had permeated the place. Suddenly the leader was possessed by Osho, and went into a trance-like state and started speaking in Osho's voice. The voice told them to abandon their dangerous profession and to do something simpler to earn their livelihood. It also directed them to come to Pune ashram.

The strangest of it all was the fact that we at Nepal had experienced something similar on the very night, too. The same night a bunch of us had been meditating at Asheesh, when suddenly all at once, we all decided to go to Nagarkot, a resort town in high mountains of Nepal It was a winter night and definitely not the most appropriate of the weathers to go to a hill-station. But we were as though pulled by some mysterious vortex of energy. We couldn't reason out the temptation and eventually drove up to the station. On reaching there, just as the bandits of Chambal had reported, one of us got possessed and the person started speaking in the voice of Osho, too. We received a short message, which turned out to be an important and inspirational message for all of us there that night.

It was uncanny that the exact same incident happened to people as far apart as Chambal and Kathmandu on the same night. But later I heard from many friends that the similar event had happened across the world on the same night. Not just this instance but every time Osho went into silence, he manifested into myriad different forms to guide and inspire his disciples.

Just as the incident marked a deep impression on me, the incident also changed the whole lives of the bandits. The gang had arrived with the leader to be initiated into Neo-Sanyas. They left their notorious and dangerous profession and started living simply as farmers, rejoicing every little gift life had to offer with their unquenchable appetite for life.

The Zorba from Akola

I have met many remarkable men and women who came into my life and left profound impacts upon my psyche. Life never remained the same after meeting them. In my book 'Lone Seeker Many Masters' I have written about thirty two such individuals who form the constellation of my inner cosmos. However many stories still remain untold, the saga would be incomplete without the mention of a few such people who added to this experience called life.

If someone asked me what I was missing the most during my stay in Pune those days, my answer would be a good meal. I was eating off street vendors and cheap *thalis* in Pune and this had already taken its toll on my health. And apart from that I was starving for a proper meal.

On a fine day a very loving *sannyasin* suddenly arrived in

my life and we became good friends. He was in his early thirties. Although I don't remember his name but what I remember is that he was from Akola in Maharashtra. He was a jovial and warm person.

The arrival of this new stranger solved my food crisis for many days. He had come to Pune for a short visit and during his visit he used to invite me to have lunch with him at the Gujarati restaurant and he used to feed me with the delicious Gujarati *thali*.

As I was going through great ordeals of my life bestowed upon me by my master, meeting him was a blessing to me. I can't forget the care and the warmth of his heart. He used to take me to public swimming pools and treat me at good juice bars and eateries. We became very good friends during his two week stay in Pune.

Slowly I came to know about him and that he was from a village near Akola in Maharastra and that he belonged to a lower middle class family. There was a rich man in his village, the *zamindar*, who was very cruel and used to exploit and torture the innocent villagers. He had a very atrocious nature. He used to beat the poor villagers and sexually abuse their women to whom he had lent money and could not pay him back in time. The whole village was angry with him but nobody had the courage to oppose him. My friend could not tolerate this injustice. One day when the landlord was beating a villager he just jumped into the brawl and beat the rich man. He was a well built strong man and he gave a good beating to the landlord and broke his hand. The rich man was very influential in the village so Akola Swami had to escape from there to save his life or from being imprisoned. As the landlord wanted to take revenge he filed several forged cases against him and the police was searching for him to arrest him. He was an absconded criminal.

Akola Swami used to go to his house every night to get some supplies and money. He was a *sannyasin* and he told me that he felt a great pull to come to Osho but he didn't have the travelling expense. The upper floor of his house was made of steel truss and galvanized iron sheets. To meet with his travelling expense he sold the roof of his house. In Pune looking at his extravagant life and the way he was spending, no one could tell about his background. When I came to know his whole story, I had great difficulty eating the expensive Gujarati *thali* he was feeding me at Hotel Dreamland when I remembered that this money had come from selling the roof of the first floor of his house. He told me that any day he could be arrested and he would have to stay for a long time in Indian prison. So he was hiding and not staying in his village. He was a very joyful and happy person and was least bothered about his future. He was a real Zorba of Osho.

Our friendship grew very deep with time and I became very fond of him. I invited him to Nepal and that he could come to Kathmandu when I was back. I promised to arrange for a job and shelter for him. He was immensely happy and he told me that he would come as soon as I was back in Nepal. I finished my Pune episode and when I was back in Nepal I wrote him a letter to inform him that I was back and that he could come help me to run the center and that I could arrange for his food and shelter. I thought I would be able to arrange a job for him so that he could maintain himself.

He wrote back to me that he was going to come and even mentioned the date of his arrival. But strangely he did not come to Kathmandu and never wrote me back. After few months when I again went to Pune, I tried to trace him down and find about him. I was worried that he could have been

293

arrested. It took me some time to find a common friend who knew both of us. He told me that the Swami from Akola was coming to Nagpur on a motorbike when he was hit by a truck and met with an accident. Sadly he couldn't survive the accident and died at the spot. I was moved to tears and could not stop crying when my friend told me that when he died there was a plane ticket in his pocket for Kathmandu via Delhi.

The Swami from Akola was an emperor in true sense. He was a real Zorba and he didn't like to travel like me in second class sleeper trains. I don't know from where he had arranged the money but with whatever he had he was planning to come to Kathmandu via air like a Maharaja that he was. In those days travelling in a plane was a big luxury for me, I could not imagine how a poor man like him could dare to come in a plane when cheap alternatives were available.

His life had gotten very complicated and there was no end to his problems in his village. I feel that existence wanted that he should be free from all those legal hassles and complicated problems and should be given a new beginning in a new body. I have trust that he must have been born somewhere and must be a joyous *sannyasin* enjoying life to the fullest and must be sharing with his friends whatever little he has with the same enormous generosity of his heart.

My friend from Akola was a real Zorba. He lived like a prince and died like a King.

The Twists and Turns, and Finally the Departure

After ten days it was Gurupurnima and as soon as the celebrations finished, the dormitory was closed and I was asked to go back to the laundry department. I was shocked and I thought maybe they didn't know that I had already completed a month and it was time that I was moved to the next department. I explained the administrators about my predicament and told them that I had already finished a month in the laundry. To my utmost surprise they told me that since I had not completed my full month of work, I had to work as a laundry man for a whole month.

Of all my duties at the ashram this was the hardest one and now I had to work an additional month. I may never be able to express it in words the displeasure I felt at that time. With a very heavy heart and tears in my eyes, I started the work again. A part of me was saying that this was too much for me and that I should return home, but another was saying that this was a test of my surrender and I should not give up. In one of the discourses of Osho I attended, he said,

"A Guru will take such harsh tests on you and he will keep on testing you until you totally break down. Your mind will want to say no, but if you keep saying yes to your master then you will win."

So with a strong determination to gain victory over my own mind I said yes! I surrendered and decided to do what I was given instead of putting my mind into it. After working in the laundry for just a few days a new twist came in my story.

I have always been a people's person and it takes no time for me to make friends wherever I go. Even today this trait helps me immensely when I travel around the world to do my master's work and spread his message. Within a period of conversation I have made great friends who have lasted for a lifetime and I truly cherish them all. I am only a messenger of Osho and I enjoy being with people, talking with them and sharing my love for my master with them. I still remember what Osho had said to me when I had shown resistance in doing his work. In my early days I had faced great opposition and reluctance from people when I tried to spread Osho in Nepal. After being disheartened by these experiences I had told my master that I was not capable of working for him and spreading his message. In response to my predicament Osho had answered, "You don't need to do anything. There is not much work to do. Whoever you meet, just give them love and nothing else. Rest I will do."

From that day all I have been doing is nothing else but giving love to whomsoever I have met on the path and today a large caravanserai of beautiful inspired individuals who love Osho and are living his vision has formed. All of this had happened with the seed of love that Osho planted in me.

After spending so much time in the ashram the management had come to know by then that my public relations was very good. They needed a new public relation officer who could counsel and convince and market the therapy groups in the ashram and that is when I came into the picture. I was made the new public relations officer for the various therapy groups. I had to assist the therapists and talk to the people about the various therapies.

I could sit all day in the balcony and watch the view. Another luxury was that there was free tea in the therapy room and I could drink tea all day. It was good tea made in the ashram. Even little things were so precious for me. Those were my best days. The therapists also liked me very much. When the management wanted to transfer me, the therapists went to Laxmi and said "He is the best PRO we have had till date. Indians are very rough and they don't know how to handle guests, he is the best Indian you have sent."

I thoroughly enjoyed my time being as the PR for the therapists meeting and talking with all kinds of people that came for the groups. In this way I spent the next 20 days in great luxury and joy. It was to be my best month in Pune that year. Soon a letter arrived from Kathmandu calling me back. My friends had written that the center in Kathmandu was about to be closed and had requested Bhagwan to send me back to Nepal.

I only met Osho twice in the whole time. First when I arrived and the next was when I was leaving. This was in 1979. He only talked in the discourses and gave *shaktipat* during the *darshan*. In the beginning years he talked with all those who came for *darshan*, later as the number of *sannyasins* increased, he only talked with those who were taking *sannyas*. Osho only gave energy *darshan* and that was very valuable. Later after 10th March 1981 he stopped giving *sannyas* and *darshan* as well. Bhagwan instructed Swami Teertha to give *sannyas* to foreigners and Ma Yoga Laxmi to give *sannyas* to Indians. However, as Ma Yoga Laxmi refused it as she had too many responsibilities and she didn't want to become a *sannyas* facilitator, this responsibility was passed on to Swami Satya Vedant.

I finally got a message from Laxmi. "Bhagwan took a very difficult test of you and he is very happy with your work." She said. "He wanted you to say no at least once. He wanted you to say that I cannot do this work but you passed the test and he is very happy with your work." She said that nobody wanted me to leave as all the group leaders had liked my work as the PRO. "I also don't want to send you at all but without you the center is suffering in Nepal and you also have to complete your incomplete engineering projects as your clients are also calling you, so you have to go back."

This way I was sent back in five months and my heavenly romance with Bhagwan in Pune that was full of all kinds of twists and turns finally came to an end as I returned back to Nepal.

My Conversation with the Departed King

The unknown and the esoteric have always fascinated me. As a young spiritual seeker, I used to be elated just by the thought of the mystical dimensions of life. There used to be a great longing in me to immerse into these areas and explore the wombs of the esoteric, to understand the mysteries of life, of death and the thin line that separates the two. I had a great curiosity to know what was on the other shore. Because of this very longing one would find me often at the doorsteps of *babas*, *sadhus*, mystics, occultists, psychics and seers. The Indian sub-continent caters as a rich plate of delight for one with such appetite. One finds myriads of techniques available here and thousands who claim to be adepts in this science, but of course the garb of a seer serves as the best hide for the frauds and most of the times it is easy to find great thugs and charlatans there than it is to come across a genuine mystic.

When I was young I was very much thrilled by the very thought of conversing with departed souls. And that is how I discovered the planchette, the method of conversing with departed souls through automatic writing and table turning which kept me indulged for many years. I had a friend who had great skill in it. In fact he had a *siddhi*. I couldn't call the souls all by myself and needed his help. It was very easy for him. He could call anyone within a minute including enlightened souls. And our guests included the likes of Shree Aurobindo, Mahatma Gandhi, King Mahendra and many other well-known people. It is a crude method and generally does not help in one's spiritual growth. In 1974 at the time of *sannyas* when I told Osho about it he didn't like it but seeing my great interest and curiosity, he allowed me in the beginning and didn't stop me but advised me not to misuse the technique. I had great interest towards the esoteric and at times my master used to censure me of my inclination. In the beginning Osho allowed me to use this technique and said that I could use it use it only for the growth of spiritual work. After some years he asked me to totally stop contacts with disembodied souls and asked me to work on getting directly connected with Osho himself.

The planchette can be a good medium to learn about unknown secrets. I am reminded of the time when we invited the soul of the Late King Mahendra of Nepal and the things he revealed to me. Everything that he predicted to us came true in the future. The King also revealed to us many other secrets which are not known publicly so I am not allowed to mention it here. When one has access to information that is not known to everyone, it is possible to misuse it and that is why my master warned me against it.

One evening in 1975, I asked him about my past life. At that time I had no idea about it and it was King Mahendra's soul that revealed to me for the first time of my royal connections in my previous life. He told me that I belonged to the same group as he was from. He was indicating towards my life born in a Royal family in one of the famous kingdoms in India which was later revealed to me in Pune.

There were many things that the king's soul revealed to me which astounded me more in the future than at that time as all of it got fulfilled later.

I asked the King's soul, "Have you heard of Bhagwan Rajneesh?

"This name is getting popular in our world also and many are talking about him." He replied.

"Are you interested in him?" I asked

"No, I am not interested in him." The Late King clearly stated.

"Where do you live nowadays, Your Majesty?" I asked

"I live behind the Pashupatinath temple in the Mrigas*thali* forest." The soul replied.

"Are you happy there?" I enquired.

"I am very happy and content here," was the reply of the soul.

It is not a mere coincidence that some people in this world are born with more privileges than others. Everything is a consequence of the karmic game. Today when I look at it, I can totally understand why one person is born as a King while another is born as a beggar. King Mahendra is a *sannyasin* from past life and has a virtuous past. He is a highly elevated soul and it is not surprising that he had more privileges at his immediate service which were bestowed to him right at his birth. When I did more research on this I found out that all Maharajas and rich, famous and charismatic personalities have a virtuous and spiritual past.

I have to admit that the King's soul helped me many times and was very generous towards me. At that time, I was working as an engineer for the Nepal government. I was transferred to the Soaltee Oberoi hotel to supervise the constructions there. I was not happy with my senior and I wanted to change my job. I was under a great predicament so I decided to go to my royal advisor. The King's soul gave a very strange answer; he asked me not to leave my job and said that my boss would have to leave instead. I couldn't believe what the King had said but unwillingly I listened to him and stayed back. To my utter surprise my senior had to soon leave the job and I was promoted to his position. Thanks to the science of occultism, I was conversing with the former King of my country and I could ask him anything, a privilege that involved utter complexity and least probability in real life. The source to reveal the unknown was at my fingertips. How could I miss this opportunity to ask the question that could accelerate and help the work that I was doing.

"Is there anyone at the palace who would be interested in Osho?" I asked.

"Birendra has a potential." replied the departed King. I already knew that the King had a spiritual potential but never in my wildest dream had I imagined that the soul of his father would take his name, and that the present King of my country had the potential to become an Osho disciple. This was in 1975. When I told this story to my master, he approved of Birendra's inclination towards spirituality and said that there was great possibility of him walking on a spiritual path.

King Birendra was a very gentle man and was popular with his people and was referred as the People's King. His leniency and willingness to change according to time and people's interest proved him as a democratic ruler and everybody loved him. His spiritual traits were evident in his humble and gentle persona. It was not a surprise that Mahendra's soul had taken his name.

"How can I introduce Birendra to Osho as I know no one in the palace?" I asked

The soul immediately replied through automatic writing, "Ranjan Raj Khanal."

At that time I had never heard of this name and didn't know who he was. It was only after a year when this high ranking government officer came to our center Osho Asheesh in Tahachal that I first met Sri Ranjan Raj Khanal who was then the principal private secretary to King Birendra and a spiritual seeker himself. He was brought to Asheesh by Prof Renu Lal Singh. To my utmost surprise, all of King Mahendra's predictions came true by word and it was indeed Ranjan Raj and Prof. Renu Lal who were both his personal secretaries, who first introduced Osho to King Birendra. I sent many of Osho's books to the King through Ranjan Raj *jee* and Renu Lal *jee* and this is how the King developed his interest in Bhagwan which only grew with time.

It was because of Ranjan Raj Khanal that Osho could come

and stay in Nepal in 1986 after being deported from America in spite of the resistance by a religious fanatic group. That time the American administration did not have a good relation with the Osho movement but Birendra's government provided us the security and the permission to invite him here. The government provided us all the facilities and told us that Osho could stay here as long as he wanted. But unfortunately in spite of Birendra's interest in Osho and Bhagwan's constantly pointing towards Birendra's potential of becoming his disciple it could not happen. The King had also sent a message that as Osho had just been deported from America it was not the right time for the King to meet him. He had said, "Keep Osho in here and he can build his new commune in western Nepal. After the media hype cools down I will come to meet him."

King Birendra could not become an Osho disciple and I partially consider it as my mistake as well. I could not come in contact with him personally and I didn't make the enough effort for it either. Maybe it was not the existential wish.

In later years also I used to send Osho's videos to the King through my respected friend Krishna Prasad Bhattarai, when he was the Prime Minister of Nepal. Every Wednesday the Prime Minister used to have a private meeting with the King and before he went to the palace I used to meet him and send Osho's books, cassette tapes and videos with his discourses as gifts for the King. I still remember a similar Wednesday when I had once sent two videos of Osho to the King. I waited for Bharrarai at the Prime Minister's residence in Baluwatar until he returned back from the palace.

After he returned from the meeting to his residence, he said to me, "Our meeting lasted for an hour and we spent 45 minutes just talking about you and Osho. We could only spend 15 minutes on our agenda."

Osho greeting sanyasins and other visitors during his stay in Nepal in 1986.

Evening darshan at Soaltee Oberoi, Kathmandu, 1986

*Swami Anand Arun asking questions to Osho during evening discourse at
Soaltee Oberoi, Kathmandu, 1986*

Osho giving evening discourse at Soaltee Oberoi, Kathmandu, 1986

*Swami Anand Arun greeting Osho during Osho's walk at Soaltee Oberoi,
Kathmandu, 1986*

Osho greeting sannyasins during his walk at Soaltee Oberoi, Kathmandu, 1986

Osho answering questions of Swami Anand Arun during his stay in Manali, India, 1985

Osho greeting sannyasins during his walk at Soaltee Oberoi, Kathmandu, 1986

*Morning view of the Osho Tapoban Meditation Hall
with the Nagarjun Hills in the background.*

Sannyasins during a meditation camp at Osho Tapoban

Sannyasins during White Robe celebrations at Osho Tapoban

The Osho Samadhi at Osho Tapoban

The Mystic Shivapuri Baba temple at Osho Tapoban

Guest rooms and therapy rooms of Osho Tapoban

OSHO COMMUNES & MEDITATION CENTRES IN NEPAL

Sannyasins after sannyas celebration at a meditation camp, Moscow, Russia

Prayer Meditation, Russia

Sannyas Celebration, Russia

Sannyasins of Osho Nirvana Ashram, San Deigo, California, USA

Meditation Camp, USA

Meditation Camp, Australia

Meditation Camp, Australia

The Magic of Osho

In October 1977, a group of ten Nepalese decided to travel with me to Pune. The group consisted of my parents and seven other eminent figures including the former Minster and member of parliament, Bharatmani Sharma and his wife; Govinda Pradhan, the general manager of the only national daily Gorkhapatra; Mukti Man Rajbhandari, the general manager of the government shoe factory and his wife; Professor Umanath Sharma of Tribhuvan University and Krishna Prasad Gyawali who was the Joint Secretary in the Ministry of Agriculture. My father was a high ranking administrator of Nepal during the monarchy and also the private secretary of B P Koirala, Prime Minister of Nepal. Afterwards, he also became the private secretary to other Prime Ministers of Nepal including Matrika Prasad Koirala, Tanka Prasad Acharya and K I Singh. My mother was among the first women parliamentarians of Nepal and the first woman from Nepal to have gone on a political delegation to Soviet Russia in 1953.

They told me that they were just going to Pune out of curiosity to see what is happening there and they were not ready to take *sannyas*.

While travelling in the train from Patna to Pune, I overheard them discussing Osho while I was sleeping on my berth. They would say, "Osho has a very hypnotic presence and Arun will insist us to become a *sannyasin*. We have our own faith and we should stick to our glorious traditions. We should be rigid in our decisions and not give in."

Throughout the journey the wives kept on reminding their husbands about Osho's hypnotic presence and Arun's strong insistence and not to be carried away.

Bharatmani's wife would say to him, "You are very emotional and you melt very easily. I am scared that you will be mesmerized by Osho."

Bharatmani *jee* proudly boasted about his Hindu roots and the deities he worshipped and said that it was impossible for him to take Osho's *sannyas*.

Similarly Mukti Man's wife would keep on warning him, "Be careful not to be hypnotized by Osho."

My *sannyasin* friend who was also travelling from Patna to Pune in the same train told me, "Why have you come with such a negative group. They keep on talking so much nonsense about Osho every time you are not there."

I was so happy and overwhelmed that such highly regarded and renowned figures of Nepal were going to Osho that every time the train stopped I used to bring them different local delicacies

that were available at the train stations we stopped at. Seeing my enthusiasm and care, my friend told me, "Remember my words, no matter how much you try to impress them not even one of them is going to take *sannyas*."

When we arrived at the ashram the first lecture that our group attended was in Hindi on Meera Bai, the female enlightened devotee of Lord Krishna. Except for me, everybody else was a non *sannyasin* so we were not allowed to sit in the front and we had to sit in the back. As Osho arrived in the Chuangtzu auditorium he gracefully climbed the dais whereupon he greeted everyone with his namaste. In his crisp white gown with full sleeves and his flowing beard, Osho looked impeccable in his style as he took the seat and crossed his legs over the other leaving one of his velvet slippers on the floor while the other remained on his foot. I was always moved by the physical grace of Osho and the enormity of his personality. As we sat there I was overwhelmed by joy and was trying to figure out what impact was he having on my group.

The lecture started with Ma Taru singing a few Meera *bhajans*. As Bhagwan closed his eyes listening to her, the whole auditorium ringed with the sweet songs of Meera in the Rajasthani dialect flavored with her eternal longing for Krishna. A milieu of love and devotion filled the whole auditorium. Osho started the lecture by narrating the life story of Meera. Osho is a great storyteller and in his soothing voice Osho was pulling the strings of our hearts as he beautifully brought to life the life-incidents of the great devotee.

Every time I visited Pune, during the first few lectures I used to be so overwhelmed by emotion that I used to cry looking at Bhagwan throughout the lecture which would subside after two three days of my stay. On that day also as soon as Osho started to speak I started to cry. But I was surprised to hear sobbing sounds coming from our group and when I looked up I found that all the women in our group had been touched by Osho's magnetic presence and were crying. Nepalese are simple, heart oriented people and it does not take too long to bring them to the heart-space. As the lecture progressed I noticed tears were floating from the eyes of the male members as well. Except for my father and another gentleman each one of us had tears in our eyes.

The lecture finished and Bhagwan left, along with him he took away all the doubts and prejudices that my group of proud individuals so dearly held against Osho just before we entered into the ashram. The whole group had fallen in love with Bhagwan and if that was not enough my mother had already decided to take *sannyas*. All the women voiced out their decision that they also wanted to take *sannyas*.

Muktiman *jee*'s wife who was continuously warning him in the train exclaimed in joy to her husband, "I don't care what you do. I am going to take *sannyas*. This is such a precious moment, how can I miss it? I am not going to lose such a great opportunity."

"I have also already decided to take *sannyas* and I was only scared of you," shouted the overjoyed Muktiman.

Except for three members of the group, my father, the former minister and the professor, everybody else decided to become Osho's disciple. My father said that he would think about it later, precisely because he thought he would be defeated in front of his son whose *sannyas* he had always criticized. Bharatmani Sharma was worried about his high political career and thought that he would not be able to walk in the parliament with the *mala*. Umanath Sharma was a devout Hindu and had a reservation against Osho because he had criticized his favorite Hindu saint Tulsi Das.

In my heart I knew that the master was at work and all the members of my group had headlong fallen in love with Osho. I was fully assured that the idea of taking *sannyas* had already been sowed into the hearts of the other three as well and it was only a matter of time before they expressed it. I only had to wait and see how long they could resist the magic of Osho.

Heart Attack,
Rejection & Sannyas

Ma Yoga Laxmi was immensely happy when we went to her office and asked her for an appointment for *sannyas*. She was happy that the *sangha* was expanding in Nepal and was kind enough to arrange the *darshan* for the same evening.

If I was happy you should have seen my group members. They were over joyous and could not stop talking about Bhagwan. These were the same people who were skeptical about Osho all the way on our journey from Patna to Pune. After the discourse nobody returned as the same person, an alchemical change had taken place in each one of them and the critics had returned as lovers. They had allowed Osho to enter into their hearts.

After their first Bhagwan experience the group was so exhilarated that even after we returned back to the hotel they were still talking about their morning adventure. My mother was a chronic heart patient and the level of the excitement was so high for her weak heart to bear. She had a heart attack. This diluted the joy of the group and we were very much concerned for my mother. She was laid down on the bed and a medical help was sought. As her whole body was shivering after the attack we rubbed the ointment Vicks Vapourub which had a very strong smell of menthol all over her body and we gave her emergency medicines. She was advised to take a complete bed rest.

In that eventful day, this was the most unexpected turn of events. As the evening approached for the *darshan* my mother started to weep and cry as she would miss the *sannyas* that evening. I tried to console her and told her that as we were going to stay for a longer period she could take *sannyas* any day but nothing could console her. She didn't stop crying and said, "I was the one who decided to take *sannyas* first and now I am going to miss it."

In the evening when others were getting ready for *darshan* my mother also stood up and said that she was also going to go. We were very much concerned about her health so I tried everything to console her to stay back but she would not listen. I told her it was compulsory to take shower before meeting Osho, with odorless shampoo and soap as he was allergic to smell. My mother's whole body emitted a strong smell of menthol because of the ointment and she could not take a shower as the doctor had advised her to keep her body warm and not to expose it to water. We tried to convince her that before *sannyas* it was compulsory to take shower. There were sniffers at the Lao Tzu gate and I told my mother that they would not let her go inside.

My mother was emotionally driven and nobody could stop

her. After few minutes she was standing in the queue outside the Lao Tzu house. We were very much concerned about her health and now I was scared that after being rejected entry because of the smell of the menthol on her body she could have another heart attack. Even the other *sannyasins* who were standing in the queue were objecting why we had brought her along with us. They were scared that their body might catch her smell and they would also be rejected. The sniffers at the Lao Tzu gate were very strict and if they smelt even a light fragrance they would reject the person and nothing could be done. The whole time I stood there in the queue with closed eyes praying to Bhagwan for help. When I opened my eyes it was a heart attack situation for me instead. My mother had already entered the gate and the whole group was accepted. To my utmost surprise, the only person who was rejected was me.

My mother who was embalmed in the smell of menthol glided in without an objection while I who was very particular about these things and had taken a fresh shower with the ashram-made odorless soap was rejected. My mind was baffled and I could not understand what was happening. I insisted that I wanted to go with the group but the sniffers were very adamant. I challenged them that I knew the discipline and I had never been rejected but to no avail. So I had to stand outside the Lao tzu gate when the whole group went in for the *darshan*.

Later on I realized that this whole sniffing business was a device of Bhagwan of only allowing people that he wanted in the *darshan*. Maneesha, Shunyo and Radha are some of the names I remember from the group of sniffers who used to take turns in the sniffing duty. They were totally tuned with Bhagwan and I am sure that he was using them to filter out those who he did not want in the *darshan*.

That evening my parents were called first and Bhagwan gave them special attention and maximum time. If the *darshan* happened for an hour my parents took half of the time. Bhagwan asked them to freely talk about their life's problems and their questions. Later on I realized that it was a good thing that I was rejected because in my presence they would not have been able to open up and talk about the private side of their lives. Even Ma Laxmi and the whole group of those sitting for *darshan* were surprised why Bhagwan gave so much attention and time to a Nepali couple.

My mother was a determined lady, she surpassed all her ordeals and took *sannyas* that evening and became Ma Sumitra Bharati. The other five including Muktiman and his wife, Bharatmani's wife, Govinda Pradhan and Krishna Gyawali also took *sannyas* along with my mother that evening.

During the meeting with Bhagwan, my parents freely expressed their unhappiness and complained to Bhagwan that I didn't listen to them and did everything according to my own will. To which Bhagwan told, "Don't worry, he is at least totally listening to me and I am taking care of him."

My mother complained about my failed marriage and that she wanted to get me married again to which Bhagwan immediately replied, "Haven't you already given him enough trouble by forcing him for marriage? Don't torture him anymore."

My mother was silenced by Bhagwan and she had nothing to say.

In their very first meeting Bhagwan invited my parents to stay in Pune which was a surprise to everyone.

He said to my father, "You have already been in high

government posts and seen the ways of the world. It is high time that you now devoted your time for your spiritual growth. Why don't you take *sannyas* and stay here in Pune?"

"I have many responsibilities back home and I need some time to think about taking *sannyas*. Apart from that we are old now and we can't work like other *sannyasins* here in the ashram. "My father replied.

"Who is asking you to work here? Leave your house in Kathmandu to Arun to run the centre, the ashram will give you a room here and whenever you feel like you can contribute few hours at the book stall." Bhagwan pointed out that his parents were also old and lived in the ashram.

Bhagwan went out of his way in showing his kindness to my parents. My parents didn't understand the weight of it and probably they were not ready for such a blessing. They were not fortunate enough to accept this divine invitation. My father made different excuses about his responsibilities back home and denied his offer.

Bhagwan was still kind enough to tell them that when the new commune would be built in Kutch, he would keep a place for them and that they should come and live with him in the new commune.

Bhagwan usually never requested anybody to take *sannyas* but that evening he asked two people for *sannyas*. One was my father and the other was the former minister Bharatmani Sharma. He told to the former minister, "You have already become a minister and have had an active political life. There is nothing more for you to see. Why don't you take *sannyas*?"

"Bhagwan when I became a minister I was only 25 years old and my term was very short. I still have a very strong desire to become a minister again. I will take *sannyas* after my desires are fulfilled." Bharatmani replied.

"Why do you think that *sannyas* will hinder you from becoming a minister? In fact it will help you." Bhagwan answered.

But Bharatmani also could not decide on time and left the *darshan* without taking *sannyas*.

When we came back the whole group was rejoicing in Bhagwan's energy. Everyone was happy. They had been immensely touched by his energy and their joy knew no bounds. Now there were seven *sannyasins* in the group including me. Those who remained were my father, the former minister and the professor.

The Saga
of Bharatmani

The next day all of us went for the morning discourse. Bharatmani *jee* was a sensitive man with a soft heart. As Bhagwan continued with his discourse series and spoke on the songs of Meera, I saw all his resistances of the previous night fall off as his eyes expressed it in the form of tears that didn't stop until the lecture ended. Bhagwan was a great orator and I have not come across a man with such expressive skills. His discourses were a sheer delight and were a combination of poetry, wisdom, philosophy, logic, fables and jokes. His messages intertwined with these ingredients, always made his discourses very interesting and insightful. Never in history a spiritual sermon has been so juicy and colorful and at the same so scientific and factual. They ringed with naked truth and were potent with his vision so powerful that if followed carefully could transform the whole of humanity. Bhagwan was not an old wine in a new bottle, not a continuation of an old tradition. He was the beginning of a new era and what he was saying was the road-map towards the new man which he called the Homo Novus.

Osho's sharp eloquence was always complemented by his crisp soothing voice. His voice has a special quality to it and has a great hypnotic power. Even today listening to his recorded discourses, his voice carries a fragment of his being and energy in them. It is a meditation in itself to listen to Osho. Osho used to speak in Hindi and English in every alternate month. Many foreigners who didn't understand Hindi would also come and listen to his discourses in Pune. They would say that his voice was so beautiful and hypnotic that just to sit there and listen to his words and the pauses between them would take them on trips to no-mind. Osho was not speaking to our minds, he was not trying to convince us or convert us. Through the path of our hearts he wanted to reach our being and ignite the potential that we all had in us. He was the finger pointing towards the moon.

After the discourse ended that morning Bharatmani *jee* came to me and said, "I can't hold it anymore. I want to take *sannyas*, please arrange for my interview with Bhagwan."

I immediately went to Ma Laxmi and asked her for an appointment. It was the beginning of Bharatmani's ordeal. Laxmi looked into the appointments and said that *darshan* for the next two days were fully packed and that he could only take *sannyas* after two days. I asked her to fix the appointment and went to tell Bharatmani. As soon as he heard that he had to wait for two days. Bharatmani started crying saying that since he had not listened to Bhagwan before, he was being rejected for *sannyas*. I consoled Bharatmani and told him that he could take *sannyas* after two days and it was only a matter of a short time. For the next two days Bharatmani wouldn't stop crying wherever we were and it became a matter of great embarrassment and torture for all of us. The more he listened to Bhagwan in the morning discourses, it only made him regret more of what he missed and would continuously curse his mind and ego for not listening to him. Although he was a politician his heart was like that of an innocent child.

When finally the fateful day came for the appointment, Bharatmani's excitement knew no bounds and the whole afternoon he readied himself for *sannyas*. As the evening approached he carefully took shower with an odorless soap purchased from the ashram and in no time he was standing in the queue outside the Lao Tzu house spick and span and ready for *sannyas*. We went to drop him at the gate and waited till he was ushered in.

As we stood there looking at him, we couldn't believe our eyes. When it was Bharatmani *jee*'s turn to get in, he was sniffed and then rejected entry. Bharatmani stood right there outside the Lao Tzu gate and started crying bitterly like a baby. "I know because I said no to Bhagwan in the interview, now he is torturing me." He kept on crying and we had to console him and I promised him that I would get an appointment for him for the next evening. I went to Ma Laxmi and fixed his *sannyas* for the next day. It was a surprise why the sniffers had rejected him as he had spent so long cleaning himself and we could not smell any odor coming from his body.

Bharatmani was heartbroken by the rejection. The next afternoon he spent the whole day scrubbing and bathing to get rid of the smell that only the noses of the sniffers caught. He even used caustic soda to wash himself to get rid of the smell.

As the evening approached Bharatmani started getting

nervous and was very conscious about being odorless. We again repeated the same ritual of dropping him at the Lao Tzu gate and kept our fingers crossed hoping that he would be taken in. The queue slowly moved as people entered the gate or got rejected. Bharatmani's nervousness could be seen on his face. The proud and boastful minister now looked like a coy, obedient and well behaved schoolboy. The sniffer came close to him and took a deep inhalation. Lo and behold! He got rejected for the second time. The sniffer just shook his head and asked Bharatmani to step aside.

This was too much for Bharatmani. He did what none of us had expected or dreamt of in our wildest dreams. The six feet tall, well built Bharatmani laid down flat right there on the ground outside the Lao Tzu House and started howling and beating his chest. He threw his hands and legs in the air and started crying bitterly. "I am going to commit suicide if you don't let me in. I am not going anywhere. I know Bhagwan is torturing me because I said no to him but I am not going away without *sannyas*." Bharatmani had a very peculiar way of crying, he would scream and howl like a child in his grown up voice. By now everybody knew that Bharatmani had come in my group and he was from Nepal. A big scene was created outside the Lao Tzu house and I felt extremely embarrassed. Somehow we managed to pull him back to his feet and took him back to the hotel but he didn't stop crying throughout the way back.

He didn't stop crying even in the hotel. All of us sat in his room trying to console him down. Finally when he fell asleep we went to our rooms to get some sleep. And suddenly there it was again, the sound of Bharatmani bellowing. We rushed into his room to find him banging the bed with his closed wrists and legs like a stubborn child while he howled and cried. The Parsi

337

lady who was the owner of the hotel came to me and whispered in my ears in her peculiar Parsi tone. "Does he have epilepsy? I have an herbal medicine from my local doctor. Why don't you give it to him?" Our whole group had to face the embarrassment of Bharatmani's abrupt outbursts wherever we went.

The next evening I dropped Bharatmani at the Lao Tzu gate and rushed to the Francis house where Bhagwan's parents stayed. I was extremely embarrassed and didn't know in what new ways would Bharatmani embarrass us so I just wanted to be away from the scene. I was talking with Bhagwan's father when a western *sannyasin* came running to the Francis house calling my name. As soon as he saw me he told me, "Arun, a fat Nepali is lying on the floor outside the bathroom and crying like a crazy man. He has blocked the doors and no one can go to the bathroom." I immediately knew what had happened and rushed to the event-scene. Bharatmani had been rejected again and he was again crying at his misfortune. I called all our group members as I had no courage to collect him alone. When we went there Bharatmani was lying outside the bathroom, his huge body spread across the floor while he screamed and howled. We somehow collected him and with great difficulty took him back to the hotel.

I had now figured that Bhagwan was playing a game with Bharatmani. When he had asked him for *sannyas* the former minister had rejected it. Now Bhagwan was making him crave for it so much that it became impossible for him to live without *sannyas*. It was not the fault of the sniffers; It was all Bhagwan's doing. As I said before the sniffers were only his mediums in tune with him. Even though it was not their fault, I had to do something. I went to Ma Laxmi and complained to her that the sniffers had rejected Bharatmani three times and it was ridiculous. She called the sniffers and scolded them and asked them how it was possible that the same person could be rejected three consecutive days when he has taken all the care. She fixed the appointment for him and asked them to let him in the next day.

Poor Bharatmani had become like a mouse drenched in rain. As he stood outside the Lao Tzu house in the queue next day with his head held low and half of his hair fallen off due to the caustic soda, he was a sight of dejection. He was extremely nervous and was sweating. He had no hopes that he would be allowed inside. I was fully assured that if he got rejected again we would have to call an ambulance that day. Finally the sniffer smelt him and said that he could go. He just stood there with his head held down. The sniffer nudged him and said that he could go. Bharatmani couldn't believe his ears. Suddenly he sprung back to life, his shoulders widened and his chest swelled up. He walked in like he was a proud army general who had just won the war. That evening Bharatmani took *sannyas* from Osho and became Swami Bharat Yogi.

When we came back to Nepal, Bharatmani's *sannyas* became a matter of great talk in the Nepalese political circle as he was a very influential and renowned politician. The whole Kathmandu knew about it and in a way it became a good advertisement for our meditation center.

The Last Wicket Falls

T he next day I requested a *darshan* interview with
Bhagwan. Since it was not so crowded those days
it was easier to get appointments. Ma Laxmi put
my name in the evening *darshan* list and I prepared myself for
the *darshan*.

That evening as I approached Bhagwan for *darshan*, he
chuckled at me and said, "8 wickets are down Arun." I laughed
back and replied, "Bhagwan but one still remains." I was referring
to my father. Bharatmani and Professor Umanath had now taken
sannyas and the only person remaining was my father. Bhagwan
looked at me and said, "Don't say anything to him. He is ready and
willing but he is not taking *sannyas* because of you."

My father had always criticized my *sannyas* and was not
happy with me. No father wants to be defeated by his son and my

Ma Sumitra Bharti and Swami Kedar Bharti during darshan with Osho.

father felt that if he took *sannyas* it would be his psychological defeat in front of me. This had put my father into a great predicament, he had long fallen in love with Bhagwan and wanted to take *sannyas* but at the same time the ego of a father did not want to be defeated in front of me.

The father and son relation is very complex and no father wants to look small in front of his son. Except for Bhagwan's father, Swami Dev Teertha Bharati, in history no other father of an enlightened mastered has accepted his son as his master. No father wants to bow down in front of his son. Bhagwan's father was a very simple man and must have immense humility in him to not only accept his son as his master but to also bow down and touch his feet in reverence. Eventually with Bhagwan's love and guidance and his own constant meditation and practice, Swami Devteertha Bharati attained enlightened before his death and left his body as a fully liberated soul.

Ma Sumitra Bharti taking sannyas from Osho.

Swami Kedar Bharti taking sannyas from Osho.

I strongly wished for my father to take *sannyas* but as Bhagwan had asked me not to say anything to him I didn't utter a word about it until the last day of his stay. I could however see that my father was in turmoil and was struggling between his desire to take *sannyas* and the reluctance to give in to his son's path.

It was the last day of the Nepali group's stay in Pune so we were given an appointment for the leaving *darshan* with Bhagwan. As the evening approached we were surprised to see my father dressed in orange. He had gone to the market on MG Road and had bought orange clothes himself without telling anyone of us. He had decided to take *sannyas*. Everybody in the group had asked me to arrange the appointments with Bhagwan but my father chose to go and talk to Laxmi himself and had already arranged for his *sannyas* appointment.

As the *darshan* started my father's name was called out and he was called the first. As usual Bhagwan again gave him much love and attention and listened to what he had to say. Bhagwan gracefully touched his third eye and put a *mala* on him. Mr. Kedar Singh, the reluctant highbrow officer from Nepal became Swami Kedar Bharati. I noticed a very interesting thing about Bhagwan. Just until before the Sannyas, Bhagwan was referring to my father as 'Kedar *jee*' which in India and Nepal is a way of calling people with respect especially for those who are elder to you. As soon as Bhagwan gave *sannyas* to my father immediately the *jee* dropped and he referred to my father just by his first name. Bhagwan was immensely kind to my father and he again invited him to come and stay in the ashram.

He said, "After you are done with your responsibilities in Nepal, handover the house to Arun and you and Sumitra can come and stay here in the ashram. We will probably have moved to the new commune in Kutch by then and you can stay there. "

When my father asked Bhagwan what meditation he should do, Bhagwan suggested him to do Nadabrahma meditation. My father had never done it before so he persisted on Bhagwan to explain the meditation to him.

"You can learn it tomorrow afternoon when the meditation happens." Replied Bhagwan who had many other people waiting in queue to talk to him.

"But we are leaving tomorrow morning Bhagwan." My father persisted.

"You go to Laxmi's office and learn it from her tomorrow morning." Replied Bhagwan.

"But we leave early in the morning." My father stubbornly wanted Bhagwan to teach him the meditation.

"Ok, then you can learn it from Arun at Asheesh. He will teach you."

My father did not want to learn anything from me that's why he had emphasized so much in learning it from Bhagwan. At the *darshan* Bhagwan advised the whole group of Nepalese to support me and help me in spreading his vision in Nepal. Bhagwan blessed the whole group and we returned back to the hotel in much joy. That night we made a grand celebration as the last and the most senior member of our group had taken *sannyas*.

The next day when I went to see off the group, the same people who had so much against Bhagwan now had tears of gratitude in their eyes for me for bringing him into their lives. The whole purpose of my parent's visit to Pune was to complain about me and persuade Bhagwan to convince me to do things that they wanted for me. A great alchemy had happened and as the train left the platform that day, it carried away transformed individuals who had washed away their prejudices and notions against Bhagwan by coming into his presence and knowing the real man. Even my parents had sincere tears of gratitude in their eyes.

Vimal & the Extra Bed

D uring the Pune visit episode a strange incident happened with us that needs to be mentioned which proved to me that everything is taken care of once we learn to surrender. I witnessed this time and again in my own life and in the lives of people around Osho.

When I arrived in Pune with nine other members including my parents, the first thing was to look for a hotel. As most of the people in my group were well off, they wanted to stay in a good hotel with proper amenities. We needed five double bedded rooms and we searched for it everywhere in the list of hotels that matched our budget. Strangely nowhere could we find a single hotel with our requirements. It was always that there was an extra bed combination while we only needed ten beds.

October being the tourist season it was usually crowded but

346

not so much that we couldn't find one hotel of our requirement. Pune was a thriving city and had many hotels but strangely on that day it seemed like all hotels had run out of five double bedded rooms. We were bemused by this unexpected experience of hotel searching in Pune. The heat and pollution of Pune and the never ending search of hotels was too much for my caravan consisting mostly of high-browed individuals living a comfortable life back home. So finally we decided to take the three double bedded rooms for the couples and one five-bedded room for the four single men. We had to unnecessarily pay for one extra bed in our room.

After the group settled down, I decided to go out to get some essentials. When I arrived at the train station I saw the tall lanky figure of Vimal standing at the station with a small bag hanging from his shoulder. Vimal was a young *sannyasin* of late twenties who used to visit Asheesh and meditate with us back in Kathmandu. He was a student.

I was surprised to see his face amidst the railway station crowd and asked him, "What in the world are you doing here Vimal?"

"When I reached Asheesh and heard that you guys had left for Pune to see Bhagwan I couldn't stop myself and left for Pune immediately from Asheesh and took the train to Pune ." he replied.

This was the way of Vimal. He was a man of abrupt decisions and he didn't think too much and once he took a decision he never looked back. This I came to know of from my association with him in the days to come. He had arrived in Pune straight from Asheesh without any luggage or money.

I asked him, "Where will you stay?"

"I don't know. I don't have any money on me and of the little that I had I bought my ticket to Pune." He replied.

I suddenly knew why we were not able to find 5 double bedded rooms and were forced to stay in a five bedded room with one extra bed that we didn't need. It was for Vimal. It seemed as if existence had planned everything ahead and had kept a bed for this young man who had come from so far away to see Osho without any financial arrangement and only on trust.

I told Vimal, "So it was because of you that we had to take so much trouble. A bed is already waiting for you at our hotel." And I took him to the hotel.

When I took him to the hotel, the group had mixed reactions about this new member. As Vimal had no money I decided and declared to the group that we would all contribute fifty rupees each to Vimal. I saw how easy it was for me and Professor Umanath to give the money although comparatively we had less money than the other members of the group. Everybody else was not happy with this decision but reluctantly all of them contributed, so we gave Vimal five hundred rupees so that he could buy himself gowns and entry passes for the ashram and sustain himself with the remaining money. We used to contribute for his food and didn't let him pay at restaurants because we knew that he didn't have much money. I overheard one of the well-off members of our group say "Why has Arun *jee* brought this man with him, we are ourselves in a foreign land and now we have to take care of this beggar." This is when I realized that the more people have on the outside they become poorer on the inside and it is rare to find someone who is rich both in heart and pocket.

Vimal stayed in Pune for 6 month after we left. He had a heart of a warrior and was always ready to take the jump whenever needed. He was a real *sannyasin*. When he came back to Kathmandu I asked him how he survived in Pune and just like my former experiences he told me, "As soon as I ran out of money there was always somebody who would invite me over to their house for a lunch or a dinner. Some people also gave me money so I had a very comfortable stay." I saw that he had actually gained weight since the time we had left him.

Later Vimal stayed with me at Asheesh and helped me immensely in running the center. He was always ready to do anything and had immense amount of energy. He had a wife and two children. Vimal was like an ancient hermit and sometimes when he was in deep contemplation he used to tell me, "One day I will go far away and disappear from this world and nobody will be able to find me." I always saw that Vimal had a deep sense of detachment in him and he never clung to anything.

One fine afternoon just like he had predicted, Vimal took a few thousand rupees from the Welcome Center at Asheesh and left. He only took what was necessary for his journey and left the rest of the money. He left everything behind including his children and his wife. As Vimal was working for me at the center, I thought it was my responsibility to take care of his wife and children and offered to do so but the family didn't agree with it and took them back to the village. It has been 30 years today but he never returned back. There was no trace of him, I searched him in his favorite places in Gosainkunda and Rishikesh but all in vain. When I heard that he was seen in Gosainkunda, I even made a trip there expecting to find him but I couldn't find him there. I always expected that one day he would show his face just like how he had appeared at the train station but that day has still not come.

Later I had a dream of my master in which I asked him about Vimal. Osho told me not to worry about him. He said, "Don't disturb him. He is meditating somewhere in solitude in the Himalayas and is growing well spiritually and I am taking care of him. You don't worry about him."

Bhagwan's Little Monsters

Today the management at the Osho ashram in Pune has imposed strict rules against the entry of children. Children below 12 years of age can only enter the ashram during lunch times only for an hour that also after going through an HIV test at the arrival. This is one of the many ridiculous rules that have been created to indirectly discourage people from visiting the ashram. This is what happens when an ashram turns into a corporate house and goes into the hands of businessmen.

When Osho was alive, Osho gave special care to the children at the ashram and made sure that they were respected and given absolute freedom so that they can grow up to be free and responsible individuals. Osho was very outspoken about his views regarding the growing population of the world. He advocated

that a strict one-child policy was needed for 20 years to balance the adversities created by the overgrowth of population in poor countries. So in the whole history of Osho communes whether it was in Pune or America no *sannyasin* couple living in the ashram gave birth to children but when *sannyasins* brought their children to live with them, Osho welcomed them and made sure that the right ambiance was created for them so that they could grow up as free individuals without being polluted by any kind of conditionings.

"Always remember: children are not adults; you should not expect adult things from children. They are children! They have a totally different vision, a different perspective. You should not start forcing your adult's attitudes upon them. Allow them to remain children, because they will never be again; and once lost, everybody feels nostalgia for childhood, everybody feels those days were days of paradise. Don't disturb them. Children bring freshness into the world. Children are new editions of consciousness. Children are fresh entries of divinity into life. Be respectful, be understanding."

At Osho Tapoban, we have tried to create a similar space for children. Many children come here and live with their parents, some of them are here since they were infants and have today grown to be mature adults. Even during retreats parents bring their children. While the parents are meditating some follow them and meditate while others choose to stay outside and play. Compared to adults it is easier for a child's innocent and less conditioned mind to go deep into meditation and they can progress really fast. They are more close to meditation than adults and they always bring a beautiful lighthearted playfulness to the retreats. In-fact I have not seen better meditators than children and I think they should also be given the equal opportunity to embark on this beautiful journey.

No child should be forced to follow the faith of their parents. It should always remain a matter of personal choice and freedom. At Tapoban, we do not impose meditation or *sannyas* upon the children. It does not only apply for children, to force meditation or *sannyas* upon any person is violence. But sometimes when children decide to take *sannyas* and request for it, this desire should also be respected. We cannot see what spiritual legacy a child carries within him, sometimes a very old soul could be living inside a young child without which it is not possible for anyone to show interest in meditation and *sannyas*. It is totally up to their personal choice and freedom whether they want to continue with *sannyas* or not when they turn into adults, and that decision should also be respected.

Our education system is designed in such a way that it corrupts the innocence with which children are born. It does nothing but serves to the objective of our social structure to produce complying money making machines that follow the mass trodden path towards society's futile ambitions and dreams. Osho was totally against this. He wanted to entirely revolutionize the education system and create a new one that nurtures individuality, where creativity and originality remain the core of the learning process. Osho was for an education system that respects and nurtures the individuality of a child. He called the school in his commune the No-School where children were allowed absolute freedom to choose and study what they wanted to study and when they wanted to study. A teacher could only teach a child when the child was ready for it. His vision for this neo-education system is compiled in his book '*Siksha Mai Kranti*' which has been translated into 'Revolution in Education'.

Today when I see the kids at Tapoban, I am reminded of the children that used to live in Pune I. Osho always respected their opinion, their freedom to say and be who they really were and treated them with the same acknowledgment and respect as mature adults. This is the reason why the children living in the ashram were so rebellious, so original and fresh. There was always a sense of command and authority around them, their sharp intelligence and presence of mind would sometimes leave us speechless. Sometimes it was a hard time for us with our conditioning to be around these little rebels of Bhagwan.

I remember a funny incident with one such kid in the commune. In those days the little *sannyasins* used to get lots of pampering and love. A child in a commune cannot remain attached only to his biological parent as there are hundreds of aunts and uncles who are pouring their love upon him. I also had a little friend and I loved him a lot. Every time we met he would ask me to buy him ice-cream or candies and I would get him what he wanted. I am sure I was not the only one.

In those days I barely had enough money to sustain my stay in Pune and was living on the minimal resources. One day I met the little *sannyasin* as I was passing by and he asked me to buy him an ice-cream. I had no money with me so out of frustration I took out both my pockets and showed it to him that it was empty. He stared at my pocket and left me just as he had appeared without saying anything.

After some time his face gleamed back from the crowd and he was coming towards me. He walked to me and asked me to put forward my hand. I thought he was again up to some new trick he had learnt. Amused and surprised by his reappearance, I complied with his request. He put his hand in his pocket and took out a Ten rupee note.

He gave that money to me and said, "Here, you take it and in the future if you ever run short of money just let me know."

I was awestruck by the gesture of this little *sannyasin*. It was very funny and surprising at the same time and I was left speechless. Even today when I remember this incident it makes me laugh a lot. That was my little *sannyasin* friend and these were the children around Bhagwan, his little monsters.

Miracles
Around Osho

I t was Gurupurnima of 1976. Asheesh Rajneesh Meditation Centre was gaining momentum and a few interested friends, who had been connected through the Peepalbot stall, started visiting the Centre. We had started regular morning and evening meditation. But the Saturday afternoon *satsang* became really popular among the visitors and a good number of people started attending the weekly meeting. All the programs were free of cost and moreover, we used to serve delicious snacks after *satsang*, which became an added attraction. Our tea soon became renowned as one of the best in town. I used to inspire all the visitors to go visit Bhagwan at Pune. So, for that particular Gurupurnima celebration, about ten people became ready to visit Pune and a few wanted to take *sannyas*.

Since all of them were travelling to Pune for the first time, they wanted me to go along with them. We decided to travel up to Patna on bus and board a train from there. Naturally, they were very excited to meet Bhagwan. I was also happy because I would have a few more fellow sanyasins in Nepal and since some of them were high government officials, they would also be a great support for me to run the Centre.

Unfortunately, my manager, who had grown tired of my regular leave-requests, refused to grant me the leave at the last moment. He said that since a very important construction work was going on, he couldn't spare me a holiday. The group had already booked the itinerary and I couldn't ditch the plan. But the more I requested my manager the more stubborn he grew. I only had two alternatives – either resign from the job and join the group anyway, as I had done several times earlier, and which had already earned a bad reputation for me so the next employment would have been difficult if not entirely impossible. Or I should persuade the group to travel on their own. It was very difficult to choose because I could no longer afford to lose my job and at the same time I very much wanted to meet Bhagwan.

Eventually, I confided my situation with the group and told them to travel on their own. They wanted to cancel the trip because they were apprehensive about travelling to the ashram all by themselves. But I wrote a letter to Laxmi and assured them that they would be taken care of at the ashram.

They reached Pune. Laxmi took good care of them as I had requested and they were granted a *darshan* with Bhagwan. All of them got initiated into *sannyas* that very evening. During *darshan* Bhagwan asked them why I hadn't joined them. They told Bhagwan how my boss had refused to grant me the leave at the last moment and that I didn't have an option except quit my job if I wanted to join them. As my friends later recounted to me, Bhagwan became silent for a moment and said, "Tell him not to resign because he doesn't have any other source of income."

They also informed Bhagwan that I had been transferred outside Kathmandu valley in a much better post and a position of financial gain but I had refused to go there because of the Meditation Centre. The declination had further enraged my boss. This was also why my leave request wasn't granted.

Bhagwan listened everything patiently and he said, "It is good that he didn't leave Kathmandu for the sake of the ashram because without him the center will simply wither away."

This conversation happened in the evening *darshan*. The next morning I reached the construction site at eight. The chairman of Royal Drugs appeared at the construction site out of the blue. Although we had been working for the Royal Drugs Company for a while, I had only met the chairman a few times. It was also unusual because his work hour was from ten to five. He came to me and asked if I had constructed a drug house before. The Royal Drugs Company was the first pharmaceutical company in Nepal so there was no way I could have a prior experience. I replied to him that I was learning by my own experiences and through the little literature that was available.

"If you have some time to spare, I would like to send you for a training to Bombay to get practical insight into the specific details of a pharmaceutical company because Bombay has all the important drug manufacturing companies of India," he told me. Some of his classmates and friends were the CEOs and Managing Directors at some of the reputed pharmaceutical company. He said it was important to visit those industries to study the special finishing and the technical details, which are vital in maintaining the hygienic condition of a pharmaceutical factory.

I was overjoyed because this would give me an opportunity to have a short visit to the Pune Ashram as well. He asked me how soon I could leave. I told him I could leave as soon as possible but I had to get the permission from my boss for that. I happened to tell him about my recent tiff with the boss and how they were not very pleased with me. I was afraid they wouldn't grant me travel permit, let alone provide any financial support.

The chairman told me not to worry about the financial aspect, as his company would bear all the financial cost of my visit and my training. And since he was one of our major clients, he could easily persuade my General Manager to grant me the permission to visit industries at Bombay. He asked me again when I could leave at the earliest. I replied I could leave any day. Then he asked further, if I could leave for Bombay that very day. I replied I definitely could. He asked me to sit in his car, took me to his office, arranged my air-tickets and released a handsome sum as an advance for my Bombay trip.

He called my General Manager and informed that he wished to send me to Bomaby for on-spot training in some of the major pharmaceutical factories at Bombay. He also informed that Royal Drugs would cover all my expenses. Much to my surprise, my boss replied that it was a wonderful idea except that the National Construction Company Nepal (NCCN), where I was employed, wanted to bear the expenses. The Chairman insisted on paying for all my expenditure. Weirdly enough the two men broke into an argument as who was to bear my expenses.

The Chairman looked at me and said, "You just go to your home and prepare for the departure. We will settle down the financial issue you just try to fly this very evening." I couldn't believe my ears.

I reached my office. I had already received my tickets and advance for the travel. My General Manager called me to his office and handed me a good amount for my travel expenses. I was confused as whose advance I must accept. At the end, I left for Bombay with both the sums. The Chairman of Royal Drugs had left his car at my disposal. The driver drove me to the airport. Soon, I was flying to Bombay on an Air India plane, something I hadn't really done before as my finance never allowed me such a luxury. Previously, I had always been a faithful sleeper-coach passenger on a train.

I got my trainings at some of India's best pharmaceutical companies such as Relaxo, Indi Pharma, Sandos, etc. I tried to finish my training as soon as possible because I wanted to go to Pune and meet Bhagwan. So, after a few days of training, I took leave and went straight to Pune. This time I had enough money and didn't have to stay at Mobokos. I stayed in a comfortable hotel at Pune, which was again a luxury I hadn't indulged in before. I got a *darshan* with Bhagwan the very evening I reached Pune.

My Nepalese friends were still at Pune. All of them had taken *sannyas* and they were greatly surprised to find me there so soon and also in a good shape, clad on unusually good outfit and with a heavy purse. I invited all of them to my hotel for dinner.

During the evening *darshan*, I touched my master's feet and told him the whole story in brief. I told him it was a surprise, and a pure grace for me to have arrived at Pune. Only a few days ago it had seemed impossible for me to come and that too, to travel via air and to end up at one of the posh hotels of Pune. Osho smiled and said whenever you will have a genuine and deep longing to come close to me, existence will intervene and always grant the wish, even if it might look impossible at times.

The most telling example of this is the story of Krishna Narayan Bharati or Gajar Baba. Gajar Baba was the only Indian sanyasin to have attended all five World Celebrations at Rajneeshpuram. Considering how even the most affluent Indian *sannyasins* could only manage to attend one or two of the World Celebrations, it is still a great mystery to me how Gajar Baba, who used to be a relatively unknown kitchen staff in the Pune Ashram Kitchen and used to sleep in the Burning Ghats, managed to be there at each celebration.

Gajar Baba lived his whole life in such silent obscurity that many people didn't even know his name and simply referred to him as Gajar Baba or the Baba who chopped carrots. I came to know him more intimately in 1983, when we were both travelling on the same plane to Rajneeshpuram. As I was walking through the aisle, I saw a vaguely familiar figure approaching me. On closer inspection I realized it was none other than Gajar Baba. But awkwardly enough, he was walking on the aisle barefoot with a small *jhola* (cotton bag), in his hand which I realized was his only luggage. When he came close enough, the first thing I asked him was about his slippers. He said with unfeigned innocence, "I was wearing an old pair of slippers. Before boarding, one of the slippers ripped apart so I just disposed them."

It still surprises me how he managed to get the visa for all celebrations, as the American authorities were specifically strict towards Osho *sannyasins* and it was very difficult for Indian *sannyasins* to get American visa those days. Gajar Baba used to be a primary level school teacher at some village in Bihar. He could neither read nor write in English. And moreover, Gajar Baba lived under a very trying financial situation. He used to get food pass at the ashram but the ashram didn't provide accommodation, so the whole day he used to work at the ashram and in the evening he used to go to the Burning Ghats, the closest cremation site from the ashram, where he slept with beggars and a few other *sannyasins*, who couldn't afford to pay for accommodation as well. Gajar Baba seems to be one of those mythical tantrikas of whom we read in books. He used to sleep on a worn out rug with the dog, which was known as Bhairav.

Gajar Baba suddenly came into limelight when Osho declared some of his disciples as Sambuddhas, Mahasattvas and Bodhisattvas in 1984. And to everyone's utter astonishment Krishna Narayan Bharati was one of the few Indian *sannyasins* who had made it to the list. Many of *sannyasins* only came to know of him after this incident. But even then he continued living his simple life. I think he even left his body at the Burning Ghats so that even after his death, he wasn't much of a trouble for people. But amidst all hardship, Gajar Baba not only managed to have an unflinching devotion towards his master but also broke free of the wheel of life and death.

The Forgotten Promise!

My mother had an ailing body with many health issues. She had already gone through a few heart attacks and had also gone through an operation for breast cancer. My mother was an active politician and she had a very active social life. My father had also served some high administrative positions in the government and was dear to many powerful men that ruled the country. Due to my parent's political connections our house used to be a political hub of Kathmandu and used to be frequented by all the who's who of Kathmandu from Ministers, politicians, businessmen to artists and writers. Even today many of these people remember my parents and when I meet them at some public event they share with me their memories with them, especially of the delicious meals that my mother used to cook for her guests.

Although my mother was unhappy of my becoming a *sannyasin* in the early days, I saw her love grow for Osho with every passing year after she took *sannyas* herself. Unlike for my father it was easier for her feminine heart to surrender to Osho and accept her son's master as her own.

Osho always gave special care and attention to my parents. I don't know if he did this on purpose because they were my parents but he was always very kind to them but he was very different towards me. Most of the times he was hard upon me and treated me harshly. Bhagwan knew that my parents were not very happy with me for opening the center at home so I think he also did this to ease the situation for me back home. Whatever the reason was, my parents were lucky to always get special attention and time from Bhagwan whenever they visited him.

The memory of that evening is still vivid to me. My parents were already *sannyassins* and were visiting the master in Pune. It was my parent's visiting *darshan* and they were talking to Osho. Usually Osho did not talk much long with Indians and Nepalese as they had less complex issues compared to the western *sannyasins*, so a short conversation and a blessing was enough. But as always that day also Osho intently listened to my parents as he looked at them with his large eyes. My mother was complaining of her ailing body and her health problems while the master attentively listened to her. The doctors had told her that with her failing health she would only survive for a very short time and my mother was very sad about it.

With a heavy heart and great sadness she told Osho, "Bhagwan the doctors are saying that I will only survive for a short time."

Bhagwan looked at her for some time with his piercing eyes and asked her, "Forget all that the doctor has said, you tell me Sumitra how long do you want to live."

My mother was caught unguarded and she couldn't say anything to this unexpected question from the master.

Bhagwan asked her again, "Tell me how long do *you* want to live?"

Again after not getting any reply from my surprised mother, Bhagwan chuckled and said, "Don't worry you will live as long as you want and will only die when you wish to die."

The *darshan* was over and soon we forgot what Bhagwan had said.

It was seven years after the *darshan*. My mother had surpassed all the predictions made by the doctors. She had become healthier and her overall quality of life had also improved after *sannyas*. Of course being an operated cancer patient and being a chronic heart patient she had a fragile health but still she lived as if it was by her own strong will to live. That year my mother's health conditions deteriorated and she had to be admitted to the hospital. It had already been a few days and I used to spend my evening with her after my office. It was Saturday and I was planning to meet her after the weekend satsang was over at Asheesh. On that Saturday my mother was to be discharged from the hospital as the doctors said that she was well enough to go home.

I was at Asheesh and was preparing for the afternoon satsang when suddenly I felt a strong urge to go see my mother. The satsang was scheduled in the afternoon and many *sannyasins* had already started to come. I couldn't understand why I felt such a strong desire to go to the hospital. My mind kept on saying that

I was going to see her in the evening as she was already going to be discharged. Even the *sannyasins* who had gathered at Asheesh requested me to go after the satsang and that they would also accompany me to the hospital.

I couldn't control my feelings and finally decided to go see my mother with one of my friends, Swami Ravi Bharati. She looked more radiant and jovial than before. It was a light atmosphere and we were all in a good mood. The Doctor had already discharged her and he told me that I could take her home now.

We were packing her belongings just as we were talking to each other my mother looked at me and said, "This body has become useless and I can't use it anymore. I can't work or meditate with it, why don't you ask your guru to free me off this body.. I don't want to live anymore."

I was in a very light mood so I replied to her, "There is no medium between a master and disciple, it is an individual relationship. He is also your guru so if you want, you request him personally." She said, "You are senior disciple than me and you are working for him so you are closer to him and your prayer will be more effective than mine."

I jokingly replied, "Everybody is equally intimate and dear to Osho and how can I being a son ask for my mother's death? How can you expect me to be so heartless?"

We were all joking and everything was happening in a very jovial mood. My father was also laughing along with us.

My mother was sitting on her bed and I was sitting beside her and suddenly she joined her hands and prayed to Osho, "Oh Bhagwan! This body has become useless and it is no use to me anymore. I don't want to live in this body. I can't work or meditate through this body. Please take me and give me a healthy body."

Surprisingly something we had never expected happened right in-front of our eyes. My mother immediately rolled her eyes and without a delay of a second, life left her body in an instance. A person who was just about to be discharged from the hospital and was joking and laughing with us just few seconds ago was no more there. The very moment she decided that it was enough and it was time to leave, she left her body.

It was a Saturday and in no time all the *sannyasins* that had come to Asheesh for the satsang gathered for my mother's send off. The word spread very fast and when we reached the Pashupatinath burning ghats for her cremation, hundreds of *sannyasins* were waiting at the cremation grounds for her death celebration. People have always been scared of death and it is one of the biggest taboo that mankind holds today. Osho changed this perception forever, at least for his *sannyasins*. Osho looked at death not as an end but as the ultimate culmination of life and asked his *sannyasins* to celebrate death.

"The greatest mystery in life is not life itself, but death. Death is the culmination of life, the ultimate blossoming of life. In death the whole life is summed up, in death you arrive. Life is a pilgrimage towards death. From the very beginning, death is coming. From the moment of birth, death has started coming towards you, you have started moving towards death.

Laughter. Yes, laughter is the Zen attitude towards death and towards life too, because life and death are not separate. Whatsoever is your attitude towards life will be your attitude towards death, because death comes as the ultimate flowering of life. Life exists for death. Life exists through death. Without death there will be no life at all. Death is not the end but the culmination, the crescendo. Death is not the enemy it is the friend. It makes life possible.

My sannyasins celebrate death too, because to me death is not the end of life but the very crescendo of life, the very climax. It is the ultimate of life. If you have lived rightly, if you have lived moment to moment totally, if you have squeezed out the whole juice of life, your death will be the ultimate orgasm."

The burning ghats of Pashupatinath overflowed with hundreds of orange clad *sannyasins* dancing and singing around my mother's funeral pyre and they kept on pouring in from all over Kathmandu. It was a curious sight for the Kathmanduites and the tourists who had come to visit the Pasupatinath temple and soon thousands of people had gathered to witness this sight. Many newspapers covered the story in the papers next day. My mother was very fortunate to have such a grand farewell with so many *sannyasins* celebrating her departure. As I stood there looking at the dancing flames swallow my mother's body, I suddenly remembered what Bhagwan had said to my mother years ago, "Don't worry you will live as long as you want and will only die when you wish to die."

Osho had fulfilled his promise to his disciple and Ma Sumitra silently departed from this planet.

When an enlightened master says something the whole existence speaks through him and fulfills it in due time. My whole life is a testimony to this truth. Osho promised many things to me and all those things which looked far fetched and impossible to my mind at that time have all manifested today. I have realized that not even a word uttered by an enlightened consciousness can go wasted in this existence. I have seen great mysteries unfold around Osho and great miracles take place like it was an everyday mundane affair.

Osho once said, "Be realistic; Plan for a miracle."

With Osho, everyday is unpredictable and full of miracles. And this was just the beginning! Much more was to unfold very soon.

About Osho

December 11, 1931: Osho is born in Kuchwada, a small village in the state of Madhya Pradesh, central India.

March 21, 1953: He becomes enlightened at the age of twenty-one, while majoring in philosophy at D.N. Jain college in Jabalpur.

1956: Osho receives His M.A. from the University of Sagar with First Class Honors in Philosophy.

1957-1966: University Professor and Public Speaker.

1966: After nine years of teaching, he leaves the university to devote himself entirely to raise human consciousness. He starts being known as Acharya Rajneesh.

1970-1974: He lives at the Woodland Appartment, Mumbai. At this time he is called Bhagwan Shree Rajneesh and he begins to initiate seekers into Neo-Sannyas or discipleship.

1974–1981: Moves to the ashram in Pune. During these seven years he gives a 90 minutes discourse nearly every morning, alternating every month between Hindi and English.

1981–1985: Moves to the US. A model agricultural commune Rajneeshpuram rises from the ruins of the central Oregonian high desert.

In January 1986 he travels to Kathmandu, Nepal and speaks twice daily for the next two months. He leaves Nepal and embarks on a world tour.

1987–1989: Moves back to the commune in Pune, India.

19 January, 1990: Osho leaves his body. Written on his Epitaph over his *samadhi* in Kathmandu, Nepal and Pune, India are his own words:

Osho
Never Born, Never Died
Only Visited This
Planet Earth Between
Dec 11 1931 - Jan 19 1990

OSHO TAPOBAN

Location: Easily accessible from the city of Kathmandu, Osho Tapoban is located 12 kilometers west of the Tribhuvan International Airport in Kathmandu. Situated in thousand acres of beautiful, lush forest at the dramatic foothills of Nagarjuna Hills, Osho Tapoban is home to abundant wildlife and is a delight for nature lovers. The commune is a perfect destination for a relaxed spiritual retreat away from the fast-paced city life.

Uniqueness: The commune is a strong Buddhafield inspired by the vision of Enlightened Master Osho and welcomes thousands of seekers from more than 80 countries. Tapoban provides an opportunity for a new way of living -with more awareness, sensitivity, relaxation, celebration and creativity. Many options for self exploration are available throughout the year in the form of meditation camps and therapies.

Meditation Programs: Year-round, Osho Tapoban offers a daily schedule of six meditation sessions (one hour each), morning yoga and evening *arati* in the Rajneesh Dhyan Mandir. Meditations include both active and passive Osho meditation techniques.

Osho Tapoban Transformation Intensive: From 1-21 of every month indulge yourself in an intensive holistic package at Tapoban for inner growth as well as physical and mental wellbeing. This uniquely designed package at Tapoban caters to the need of your body , mind and soul. It will not only help you explore the inner depths of your being but also help you cleanse your body and integrate and lighten the mind.

1st week : Shuddhi- 7 days of *Osho No Mind* along with *Panchakarma* detoxification at Osho Arogya Mandir and Spa.

2nd Week: Sadhana: Sadhana- 7 days of Intensive Tranformation Meditation Retreat includes more than 8 hours of intensive practise of Osho Meditation techniques per day.

3rd Week: Samadhi- 7 days of Osho-Neo Vipassana includes Vipassana practise with Osho intensive techniques that complement and help seekers in their silence and awareness practise. (It is also possible for you to join any of the single week packages)

Group Therapies: Includes Osho No-Mind Therapy, Osho 21- day Mystic Rose Therapy, Breath - Bridge to existence group, 3-day Intensive Enlightenment and other therapies.

Osho Sannyas Celebration: Every Saturday and during every meditation camp, an unforgettable *sannyas* celebration is held when new friends are initiated into Osho neo-sannyas.

Spa Center-Osho Arogya Mandir: Osho Arogya Mandir is a fully equipped Spa with facilities for Ayurvedic and Naturopathic detoxification through *Panchakarma*, *Shirodhara*, and modern day spa treatments of sauna, steam bath, massage, and other body therapies. The packagaes offered include Rejuvenation, Detoxification, Weight Loss, Relaxation and *Kaya Kalpa* packages.

Osho Samadhi: The open air Osho Samadhi is a unique marble structure that encloses Enlightened Mystic Osho's sacred ashes. The samadhi is built around a beautiful tree under which the Buddhist mystic Nagarjuna attained enlightenment.

Shivapuri Baba Silent Temple: Adorned with traditional Malla styled bricks, this silent temple is dedicated to the enlightened mystic Shivapuri Baba. Open for silent sitting and meditation.

Cuisine: Osho Tapoban features three dining options for our guests.

The Sujata Kitchen: Our main dining hall serves three delicious meals a day, offering Indian and Asian vegetarian meals, featuring simple, fresh food, beautifully prepared.

Mariam: Fully equipped with modern amenities, this small kitchen is for our International friends who want to cook their own food according to their taste and preference.

Zorba the Buddha Restaurant: You can also enjoy continental and Western-stlye food, snacks, and beverages at our Zorba the Buddha Restaurant open from dawn till dusk, seven days a week.

Osho Welcome Lounge: Visitors can uncoil themselves in the relaxing ambience of the Osho Welcome Lounge at our entrance. You can purchase all your basic personal care needs and toiletries along with a large variety of meditation products, Osho books and CDs on site at the Nagarjuna Gift Shop at the welcome lounge.

Shuttle Service: The Commune also provides a paid shuttle service for airport pickup and drop-off or for sightseeing around the ancient cities of Kathmandu Valley.

Internet and Library: Osho Tapoban has a Wi-Fi facility, available inside the commune premises for internet access. You may also use the cyber connection at the welcome lounge. The Osho Library and Study Center has a large collection of Osho books along with audio and visual Osho discourses which are freely available to visitors and guests.

Accommodations: You have a choice of staying in our beautiful and fully equipped modern rooms or our more rustic cottages, both with attached bathrooms, situated in separate residential blocks spread across the beautiful commune campus. As we say here: "You can come and stay with us for a night or for the rest of your life!"
Email: tapoban@wlink.com.np
web: www.tapoban.com

OSHO BOOKS

Total set of 119 books in Hindi & English published by
Osho Tapoban is available at cost price at Osho Tapoban
Total Set of Hindi and English Books

₹ 10,200 /- (or NRs 16,200/-)

BOOKS IN ENGLISH

1. Meditation: the First & Last Freedom
2. In Search of the Miraculous
3. Meditation the Art of Ecstasy
4. Tantra the Supreme Understanding
5. I am the Gate
6. The Silent Explosion
7. Books I Have Loved
8. The Psychology of Esoteric
9. From Sex to Superconsciousness
10. My Way the Way of the White Cloud
11. The Dhammapada-Vol-1
12. Come Follow Me-Vol-1
13. Communism-Zen Fire Zen Wind
14. Why I am Not Against Sex
15. The New Man-The Only Hope for the Future
16. A New Vision of Women's Liberation
17. The Golden Future
18. Seriousness is a Disease
19. Life, Love, Laughter
20. Love Makes You Real
21. Money Can't Buy Love
22. Silence is the Only Answer
23. Sex Money & Power
24. Priest & Politicians: Mafia of the Soul
25. I Teach Religiousness Not Religion
26. Tantra Spirituality & Sex
27. The Tantra Experience
28. Gratitude
29. Mysteries Behind Sannyas & Mala (New Compilation)
30. Vigyan Bhairav Tantra (The Book Of The Secrets) Vol-1
31. Vigyan Bhairav Tantra (The Book of the Secrets) Vol-2
32. Vigyan Bhairav Tantra (The Book of the Secrets) Vol-3
33. Vigyan Bhairav Tantra (The Book of the Secrets) Vol-4
34. Vigyan Bhairav Tantra (The Book of the Secrets) Vol-5

ओशो पुस्तकें

ओशो तपोवन द्वारा प्रकाशित हिन्दी और अंग्रेजी की 119 पुस्तकों का सम्पूर्ण सेट ओशो तपोवन में लागत मूल्य में उपलब्ध। सम्पूर्ण सेट मूल्य ₹ 10,200/- (or NRs 16,200/-)

हिन्दी में पुस्तकें

१. जिन खोजा तिन पाइयां
२. ध्यानयोग प्रथम और अंतिम मुक्ति
३. गीता दर्शन-भाग एक
४. एस धम्मो सनंतनो-भाग एक
५. शिव सूत्र
६. अष्टावक्र महागीता-भाग एक
७. शिक्षा में क्रांति
८. ध्यान विज्ञान
९. संभोग से समाधी की ओर
१०. समाजवाद से सावधान
११. गहरे पानी पैठ
१२. साधना पथ
१३. सर्वसार उपनिषद
१४. एक ओंकार सतनाम
१५. अंतर्यात्रा
१६. व्यस्त जीवन में ईश्वर की खोज
१७. ध्यान एक वैज्ञानिक दृष्टि
१८. ज्योतिष अद्वैत का विज्ञान
१९. नारी और क्रान्ति
२०. मैंने राम रतन धन पायो
२१. संन्यास और माला के रहस्य
२२. विज्ञान भैरव तंत्र
२३. स्वप्न का मनोविज्ञान
२४. नारद भक्ति सूत्र
२५. हंसना एक महा औषधी
२६. एक ही दुःसंग, मन का संग
२७. बुद्धत्व के सूत्र
२८. कठोपनिषद
२९. निर्वाण उपनिषद

LONE SEEKER
MANY MASTERS
BY SWAMI ANAND ARUN

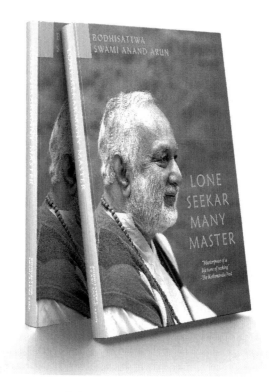

*"The masterpiece of
a life time of seeking"*
-The Kathmandu Post

A STORY OF A SEEKER AND
THE TREASURES HE FOUND
ALONG THE WAY

Also by Swami Anand Arun

In Nepali

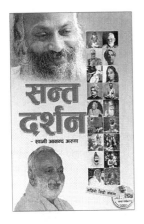  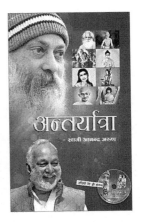

In Hindi

Upcoming books by Swami Anand Arun

The sequel of
IN WONDER WITH
OSHO

The second part
of LONE SEEKER
MANY MASTERS

For details:
Osho Tapoban
Nagarjuna Hills, Kathmandu, Nepal
P.O.Box 278, Ph: +977-1-5112012/13,
9841597788, 9841597788
Email: otpublication@gmail.com
www.tapoban.com